Stories of Therapy, Stories of Faith

Stories of Therapy, Stories of Faith

Edited by
LEX MCMILLAN,
SARAH PENWARDEN,
AND SIOBHAN HUNT

Foreword by
JACK BALSWICK
AND JUDY BALSWICK

WIPF & STOCK · Eugene, Oregon

STORIES OF THERAPY, STORIES OF FAITH

Copyright © 2017 Wipf and Stock Publishers. All rights reserved. Except for brief quotations in critical publications or reviews, no part of this book may be reproduced in any manner without prior written permission from the publisher. Write: Permissions, Wipf and Stock Publishers, 199 W. 8th Ave., Suite 3, Eugene, OR 97401.

Wipf & Stock
An Imprint of Wipf and Stock Publishers
199 W. 8th Ave., Suite 3
Eugene, OR 97401

www.wipfandstock.com

PAPERBACK ISBN: 978-1-4982-9173-6
HARDCOVER ISBN: 978-1-4982-9175-0
EBOOK ISBN: 978-1-4982-9174-3

Manufactured in the U.S.A.   MARCH 16, 2017

Contents

Contributors | vii
Foreword by Jack Balswick and Judy Balswick | ix
Introduction | xiii

Section One: A Larger Story

1. Social God, Relational Selves | 3
   Dr. Lex McMillan
2. Otherness in Relation: A Dialogic Perspective | 18
   Dr. David Crawley
3. Creating Space for Faith: Relationality and Dialogical, Incarnational Integrative Method | 39
   Siobhan Hunt

Section Two: Stories of Counseling Practice

4. Uniqueness and Belonging: Healing through Relationship | 61
   Jayme Koerselman
5. Designed for and by Love: Working with Families from an Attachment and Interpersonal Neurobiology Framework | 77
   Dr. Ruth McConnell
6. The Impact of the Concepts of *Perichoresis* and *Hesed* for Teaching and Family Relationships | 98
   Dr. Barbara Bulkeley
7. Christian Hope: Ethical Responses to Trauma | 114
   Lisa Spriggens
8. Boys in Trouble at School: "*I Am Becoming*" Stories to Live in | 129
   Dr. Donald McMenamin

9   The Undercover Anti-Bullying Team Approach: Using Relational Solutions to Address Relational Problems in the Classroom | 143
    Mike Williams with Lex McMillan

10 The *Tree of Life:* A Narrative Therapy Approach to Healing Identity in Response to Trauma among West African Children | 160
    Deborah Gill

Section Three: Stories of Counselor Education

11 Welcoming the Stranger: Teaching in a Context of Cultural Diversity | 177
    Watiri Maina

12 Doing Justice and Holding Care: Conceptualizing the Aims of Teacher-Student Engagement in Counselor Education | 194
    Sarah Penwarden

13 Psalm 23 as a Site of Integration: Telling a Story of Professional Counselor Identity Formation | 210
    Hannah Forde

Contributors

Dr. Lex McMillan, private counseling practitioner and senior lecturer in the School of Social Practice at Laidlaw College, Auckland, New Zealand.

Sarah Penwarden, counselor, supervisor, lecturer, and practicum manager in the School of Social Practice at Laidlaw College, Auckland, New Zealand.

Siobhan Hunt, research assistant in the School of Social Practice at Laidlaw College, Auckland, New Zealand.

Dr. David Crawley, spiritual director and senior lecturer in the School of Theology at Laidlaw College, Auckland, New Zealand.

Jayme Koerselman, psychology lecturer at Whitworth University and counselor in Spokane, Washington, USA.

Dr. Ruth A. McConnell, clinical counselor, and senior lecturer in the School of Social Practice at Laidlaw College, Auckland, New Zealand.

Dr. Barbara Bulkeley, senior educator and counseling programme coordinator at Bethlehem Tertiary Institute, Tauranga, New Zealand.

Lisa Spriggens, counselor, and co-head of the School of Social Practice at Laidlaw College, Auckland, New Zealand.

Dr. Donald McMenamin, counselor, supervisor and a lecturer in the School of Social Practice, Auckland, New Zealand.

Mike Williams, head of guidance and counseling at Edgewater College, Auckland, New Zealand.

Deborah Gill, counselor, group leader, and *Tree of Life* workshop facilitator in Auckland, New Zealand.

Watiri Maina, counselor, and lecturer in the School of Social Practice at Laidlaw College, Christchurch, New Zealand.

Hannah Forde, counselor and group facilitator in Auckland, New Zealand.

Foreword

BY JACK BALSWICK AND JUDY BALSWICK

We had the privilege of spending a sabbatical in 2012 at Laidlaw College in Auckland, New Zealand, where we became active participants of the counseling department. It soon become evident that something special was emerging among the brilliant and seasoned faculty members who combined a passion for biblical integration and counseling approaches. The publication of this book represents the validation of that unique combination. To put it simply, wedding an understanding of *human relationality* based on *social trinitarian theology* and *person-centered* and *narrative therapy*, this book provides a unifying and integrative model of Christian counseling.

To back up a bit, the invitation at Laidlaw came as a mutual desire for collaboration and dialogue about trinitarian theology as the basis of understanding God's intention for human relationships. Making social trinitarian theology a foundation for our own writings on relationships (marriage, parenting, friendship, sexuality, and human development) became part of our rich discussion with the Laidlaw faculty. We engaged in meaningful dialogue as we joined together to discuss theologically-informed understanding of the *goal* for all human relationships. God being understood both in terms of *particularity* (Father, Son, and Holy Spirit) and as *unity* (God is one) is a model for marriage in which two unique individuals become a "one flesh" unity. Spouses retain their individual differentiation and distinctiveness while forming an entity in which they speak as one voice. Parenting becomes a united focus of loving and disciplining children, while also respecting unique personality differences and listening to distinct perspectives. Human relationships in general are to be negotiated and developed along a dependency/independency continuum. At one extreme a person can be overly isolated/self-sufficient and virtually exclude others, and at the other extreme a person can be overly fused/connected and virtually engulf others in relationships. The relational goal is to find balance between connection and separateness in relationships (family and community) to thrive in life and in the world.

Parenthetically, it can be noted that Christianity is distinct from most other world religions in that salvation is described not as becoming one with God, but rather as being in right *relationship* with God. It is worth noting that in the book *The Trinity and the Entangled World: Relationality in Physics and Theology*, the eminent Oxford University physicist-theologian John Polkinghorne leads scholars in applying the concept of trinitarian *relationality* to understand the workings of the entire universe. Chapter one of the current volume elaborates very nicely on why social trinitarian theology is a perfect model that represents how God desires human beings to be in relationship. Dr. Lex McMillian surmises that social trinitarian theology indeed provides an understanding of the central role relations play in the formation of personhood, the quality or ethical shape of relating, and as an illustration of how human relationships are to be formed by "differentiated" persons.

Narrative therapy embeds the individual in the broader relational systems of community and culture. The narrative approach is based on listening to and understanding the *stories* of the person in context of his or her relationships. Just as the Bible presents the story of the Triune God seeking and relating to human beings, each person possesses a story of how she or he was formed and continues to be reformed by existing relationships and newly formed relationships. Dr. Donald McMenamin refers to this as "*I am becoming* stories." Drawing from narrative therapy pioneers, Epston and White, and their understanding of story as a series of events developed in a community context, McMenamin demonstrates how a community-based re-writing of troublesome identity stories brings new actions and possibilities. This is a practice that ultimately helps youth learn to enact a new vision of themselves as being made in the image of a relational God. This integrative model of Christian counseling is conceptualized as a relational process of not only understanding the other's story but in guiding that person to re-author their story as they seek to become more of whom God means for them to be.

Our longing to see the trinitarian model applied in an in-depth counseling approach has been accomplished by this faculty. We are indebted to them for a section entitled "Implications for Counseling Ministry" in the newly revised second edition of *The Reciprocating Self* book. Based on a social trinitarian theology, there are three major tenets of the "*reciprocating self*" model: 1) an individual's personal struggle and/or brokenness is not the result of one factor, but a multitude of interactive factors; 2) since the self develops as part of reciprocal relationships, a focus on a person's relationships should be primary; 3) a counselor should recognize that one's ability to deal with a person's presenting problem is not only based on counseling skills but on knowledge and understanding of an individual's development, relationship, and community.

The reader will find in this excellent book a sophisticated approach to integration that is well informed by theology, psychology, and family and narrative therapy. These scholars have provided a theologically sound theoretical and practical approach that makes a significant contribution to our field.

Introduction

In the vibrant South Pacific nation of New Zealand, lives are shaped by both the stories we tell, and our relationships with the land. Buffeted against the storms that circle the globe, and nourished by clear blue skies, our lives are etched and colored by experience and time. A particularly significant story is one about our nation's founding covenant in which indigenous *Māori* and European colonizers agreed to partnership in the 1840 CE Treaty of Waitangi. Now, many years later, as a group of counselors, we are participating in this tradition of partnership through weaving together stories of therapy and stories of faith. Our hope is that through dialogue with difference, our practices and relationships will continue to be shaped and developed.

While we have chosen to focus on our practices in dialogue with stories of Christian spirituality, our intention is to do so with humility. We recognize that at its heart spirituality is concerned with the ethical quality of relationships; with God, others, our embodiment, the land, and heritage. Our hope is that through telling stories, aspects of them will resonate with the stories that constitute our readers' hopes and values. Our interest is to consider our practices in terms of the intentions that often remain implicit within our practice actions. This is an interest that reverberates at the bicultural heart of our country: "Who are you connected to?" "How might we talk together in ways that develop mutual understanding?" and "What hopes do you have for our meeting?" We have not found the writing process easy, and we have been reminded that while we may speak with some measure of confidence about counselor theory, entering a process of archaeology of our theological and practice values on behalf of what we actually do is far more complex.

All of the authors in this collection are connected in some way to the counselor education program at Laidlaw College, Auckland, New Zealand.

We are a group of graduates, practitioners, clinical supervisors, and lecturers. A key ethos of our community is a commitment to dialogue between questions about human wellbeing that emerge in the work we do as counselors, and answers associated with Christian sources of understanding. We hold to the notion that because counseling is a value laden process, practitioners are obliged to reflect on underlying commitments, and the stories that give rise to these. Weaving is a key metaphor that illustrates something of the process we see ourselves engaged in. Stories of our lives and practices are woven together as unity in diversity. For us, weaving represents the reciprocity between unity and diversity—relation and otherness—that is associated with dialogue between stories of practice and stories of faith. It also represents dialogue between our lives as counselors and the lives of those who consult with us. For us, all of this finds meaning in the large Christian story of a God who is both one and many, and whose being consists in loving relationality.

As well as our endeavors being supported by the Laidlaw community, we are also appreciative of other voices that contribute to our ongoing formation. Particularly the scholars associated with the Waikato University counselor education program, Judy and Jack Balswick at Fuller Seminary in California, scholars at Regent College Vancouver, Jayme and Erinn Koerselman and Dan Allender of Seattle, Washington State, and the voices of many others resonate throughout our work.

Our vision for the collection is three-fold. First to provide a forum for our authors to write about their work with the idea in mind that conversation is constructive. Two, we hope to contribute to a community of support for others who are interested in integrative practice. And three, our hope in talking about faith related motivations for professional practice is that we might support the outworking of commitment to participating in God's shared life of love with a restoration *telos,* our vision of human wellbeing that we are oriented towards.

We asked our authors to select a cherished practice, to identify their ethical hopes for their work, and link these together with a theological concept or a piece of formal theological writing. Most of what followed involved collaborative conversation. We realized once the project got underway that there is a significant amount of vulnerability in articulating these matters. This vulnerability seems to connect with writing about very personal concerns in contexts where this is not usual. As such, we see here an articulation of the interweaving between the professional and highly personal—spiritual, theological, ethical—commitments that underpin our practices. Furthermore, while all of our authors claim Christian identity, only some have formally engaged in theological study. This has added further layers of vulnerability to the writing task. However, these challenges have been more than outweighed by the rich insights that have emerged, starting from where our practices are located, dialoguing with theological academic sources, and then moving back to more critically held practice. We hope that hearing this description of the writing process might sound a note of invitation for us all to put language to the ethical practices in which we are engaged.

Section One, *A Larger Story: Our Theoretical Standing Place*, includes three essays that set out central aspects of our theoretical positioning. Against the assumption that counseling is always a value laden process, Lex McMillan lays a foundation for the book by exploring how a social trinitarian theology offers a rich philosophical underpinning of relationality to counseling practitioners. David Crawley engages with Bakhtin and emphasizes the centrality of dialogic relating to trinitarian relations. Illustrating her discussion with her own experience, a recent graduate, Siobhan Hunt, discusses how the task of integrating Christian and counseling psychologies might be shaped by insight into trinitarian inspired ways of relating.

Section Two, *Stories of Counselling Practice*, is concerned with counseling practice and community work. Jayme Koerselman reflects on how his practice and thinking have being shaped by the analogy of the members of the Trinity relating with uniqueness and unified belonging. Ruth McConnell presents an overview of her parent consulting work. She incorporates research from attachment theory and interpersonal neurobiology by framing it within a trinitarian incarnational anthropology. Barbara Bulkeley, a therapist and educator, writes about how the biblical theology of *hesed* and *perichoresis* shapes both her teaching and family therapy practice. Then in the first of four examples of community interventions developed using narrative therapeutic insight, Lisa Spriggens argues for a therapeutic focus on responses when working with survivors of sexual trauma. She names an uncomfortable fact that the church has not always responded to victims of trauma well, and proposes instead what she refers to as a "theology of witness." Donald McMenamin writes about the ethical hopes of his work in re-storying and restoring young people's identities from problem-saturated identities as they step into "I am" stories. Next, Mike Williams discusses his innovative approach to bullying known as "undercover teams," and links his motivation for the work with his vision for justice. Deborah Gill traces her work with an approach known as "Tree of Life." She talks about her work assisting orphaned children to overcome effects of trauma, and reengage with cherished family and community stories.

Section Three, *Stories of Counselor Education*, is concerned with counselor education as an example of specialist practice. Watiri Maina considers her work as a counselor educator in settings that are increasingly characterized by difference. She reflects on her capacity to respectfully engage difference through positioning the work within the trinitarian invitation to offer hospitality. She also proposes setting aside usual emphases on cultural difference in favor of the insight that everyone can be appropriately viewed as "others" to be cherished. Sarah Penwarden offers Jesus' pattern of self-giving love and humility as a place to position counselor education practice so that students might be able to respond to invitations to enter dialogic relationships with educators, who at the same time hold responsibility for assessment and practice standards. Finally, another recent graduate, Hannah Forde, offers a powerful insight into the way her professional identity as a counselor has been storied within the overarching frame of the biblical narrative.

We hope that as you read you find yourself able to take the time to savor the words and the life stories that these represent. Furthermore, we anticipate that there will be some measure of resonance between the writers' and readers' lives and intentions. To this end, you may find three simple questions drawn from one of Michael White's[1] practice maps helpful:

- What strikes you in particular when reading these chapters?
- What does this impact say about what is important to you?
- How has witnessing others' articulation of their theologically-inspired practice moved you in your own hopes and values?

Siobhan, Sarah, and Lex

---

1. White, *Maps of Narrative Practice*.

References

White, Michael. *Maps of Narrative Practice*. New York: Norton Professional, 2007.

SECTION ONE

A Larger Story
Our Theoretical Standing Place

1

Social God, Relational Selves

Dr. Lex McMillan

As far back as I can remember I have been interested in understanding people and, in particular, what leads to experiences of flourishing. These inclinations may not be surprising given that I was raised in a community of Scottish Presbyterians surrounded by extended family, with a school teacher mother and an amateur philosopher father. This is to say that my childhood was punctuated with changing seasons, and cross-generational conversations about things as far ranging as animal husbandry, impacts of the Great Depression and world wars, care of the land, Celtic spirituality, and the writings of Christian thinkers including Lesley Weatherhead and C.S. Lewis.

I particularly remember experiencing joy as an eight-year-old discussing what may lie beyond the end of the universe, as we feasted on new raspberry jam and fresh bread. Given the prominence of these early experiences, when I began my formal counselor education I felt as if I was not entering something entirely new because its underlying emphasis on relating resonated with my experience. At another level, however, I have continued to be surprised by the exotic flavours the counseling enterprise has introduced me to. One particularly potent flavour involves the proposition that relationship forms the basis not only of human experience, but reality itself. Furthermore, I have been struck by the way this theme is also richly present in some streams of Christian theology.

I have two aims for this chapter. First, to argue for the value of pulling back the curtain on the large stories of wellbeing that underlie various counseling practices. Making these stories visible offers practitioners the possibility of choosing where to situate the work we do, rather than practicing without due regard for them. My second aim is to introduce social trinitarian thinking that is associated with the Jesus story. Social trinitarian thinking offers an analogy of God and humans as ontologically relational. This way of thinking about human wellbeing is particularly influential within my own practice and my academic community.

PULLING THE CURTAIN BACK: TOWARDS ANTHROPOLOGICAL VISIBILITY

A significant amount of scholarship has gone towards ensuring the professional counseling relationship is "safe," particularly with a view to protecting client self-determination.[1] While I value the guidance these perspectives provide me as a counselor, it also seems that there could be more discussion about the ethical assumptions that underlie the work we do. I say this because when counselors assume they share similar understandings, both with other practitioners and clients, important developmental goals may become obscured, and awareness of power may be diminished. Put differently, it is simply not possible to function as counselors without the influence of anthropological and ethical assumptions.[2] This recognition leads to the conclusion that all decisions about what needs to be talked about, and what is considered "normal" human functioning, raise significant ethical and political questions for counselors and their clients. By political I mean the power relations associated with who gets to speak, and who gets overlooked.[3] Put more simply, counseling is a value laden process.

Without this insight, counseling is surely prone to uncritically serve dominant cultural stories.[4] As an example, I refer to the western cultural emphasis on scientific epistemology that has tended to support individualized understandings of people. This way of knowing is evident, for example, in the discipline of psychology's particular concern with cognitive functioning. In relation to this phenomena, social psychologist Edward Sampson argues that modern psychology actually perpetuates the belief that individualised conceptions of persons are normal: "Without a field like psychology it would be difficult to sustain the belief that the self-contained individual

---

1. See, for example, Bond, *Standards and Ethics*; Corey et al., *Issues and Ethics*; Crocket et al., *Ethics in Practice*.

2. Browning, *Christian Ethics*.

3. Brugger, "Anthropological Foundations"; Brugger, "Psychology and Christian Anthropology."

4. See, for example, Bergin, "Psychotherapy and Religious Values"; Robinson, "Therapy as Theory."

holds the key to unlocking the major secrets of human nature."[5] I refer to this to illustrate my point that the human sciences, including psychology and counseling, are vulnerable to working as unrecognised instruments of societal power and control.[6]

When the potential for counseling to enact social control is considered from the perspective of the counselor's ethical commitment to work on behalf of human wellbeing, it follows that it is important for practitioners to seek, and to become aware of, underlying assumptions that influence the work. Put differently, there is value in deconstructing a counseling approach's view of "normal" wellbeing.[7] I say "value," because instead of serving hegemonic conceptions of well-being that are simply taken for granted and often unrecognised, counselors and their clients may benefit from being able to carefully choose therapeutic goals.

On first reading, my suggestion that counselors may benefit from choosing a philosophical and anthropological base for their counseling practice may seem straightforward, but it opens to the recognition that there is a general lack of agreement about how best to talk about what it means to be human and to experience wellbeing. For example, in spite of the church's and philosophy's long history of discussion, agreement on a consistent ontology of human personhood continues to be elusive.[8]

Aware of this, I wish to make a two-part suggestion. First, that we carefully select large cultural stories within which to locate counselor practices. I contend for this in order to address questions such as "How did we get here?" "How do we understand suffering?" "Which choices are more likely to lead to experiences of wellbeing?" and "How are we best to relate?" Furthermore, because wellbeing is an ultimate aim of counseling, I also suggest that as counselors we situate our practices within large stories that are more likely to be liberating than tyrannizing. This is one of the reasons I am proposing social trinitarian thinking that is associated with the Jesus story. It is my assessment that unlike some expressions of the Jesus story that are used to legitimise violence instead of wellbeing, social trinitarian thinking is more inclined towards a restorative social project that is ethically shaped by practices such as hospitality to others, offering forgiveness, and working for justice.

The second part of my suggestion is that a counselor's work may be supported by adopting social trinitarian understanding—and the love orientated way of relating this implies—as a *habitus* with which to construct

---

5. Sampson, *Celebrating the Other*, 42.
6. Foucault, "Subject and Power."
7. McMillan, "Troubling."
8. See, for example, Schwöbel, "Human Being"; Zizioulas, "Being a Person."

a personal and professional identity. I am using *habitus*—in a similar manner to French sociologist Pierre Bourdieu[9]—to refer to enduring patterns for living that are created through social processes. In this way I am joining with Stanley Grenz's suggestion that the Jesus story be used as a plot within which to retell one's own narrative, and hence make sense of one's own life.[10] When related to as a *habitus,* large stories—such as the Jesus one—are capable of providing answers to questions about life on the basis of meaningfulness, rather than on the basis of facts and truthfulness. In other words, narratives convince us of things because they locate specific experiences into webs of meaning that connect us to events.[11] Furthermore, adopting a narrative view of people supports my wish to avoid discussion in the context of counseling about the truthfulness, or otherwise, of the Jesus story. This is because I read the heart of the story to be an invitation to relate in a manner that leads to experiences of justice, freedom, and flourishing. I present, therefore, an aspect of the Jesus story that I wish to refer to as social trinitarian anthropology for consideration, not on the basis that it is true—although I believe this to be so—but because of its lifelikeness.

SOCIAL TRINITARIAN ANALOGY

The social trinitarian analogy of persons emerges from a reading of the Jesus story as God's self-disclosure to humanity. This analogy is derived from a conception of God who is both one and three; the otherness-in-relation of the Father, Son, and Holy Spirit.[12] A central feature of this analogy of persons is that it equally weights both otherness and relation. Rather than viewing people as complete in and of their individual selves, or merely as social constructions, this *relational* view of persons understands people to constitute each other through the quality of the relations they share. Furthermore, these ethically shaped relations involve both one another and God. It is thought that the Father, Son, and Spirit invite humans to participate in their shared life of love, as a social project with a restoration *telos*. I mean by *telos* a vision of wellbeing that human development is orientated towards.

    I want to emphasize two key contributions that I see social trinitarian thinking offering counselors who wish to thoughtfully engage practice in dialogue with Christian insight. First, its relational ontology opens well to conversations with postmodern perspectives on knowledge and

---

9. Bourdieu, *Logic of Practice.*
10. Grenz, *Social God.*
11. Bruner, *Actual Minds.*
12. Gunton, *One, Three, Many.*

identity—that we are shaped and known in and through relationship and social process.[13] Second, as a relational source of ethics, trinitarian thinking offers a comprehensive horizon for human development that involves embodied individuality, human relations, and an ethically shaped social context. Before going on to discuss this *telos* for development I will place the social trinitarian analogy in context.

SOCIAL TRINITY IN CONTEXT

Because a range of conclusions have resulted from seeking to understand God as Trinity, it is important that I place the approach that I am referring to as "social trinitarian" in historical and theological context. In straightforward terms, the history of understanding God as triune can be viewed as starting with the claim that Jesus Christ is one with God, and the challenge this brings to the Jewish view of God as One, for example, Deuteronomy 6:4 beseeches "hear, O Israel: The Lord our God, the Lord is one."[14]

Christian church history represents a range of responses to the challenge to remain faithful to the notion of God as One, while also taking seriously the implication associated with Jesus' life, death, and resurrection and the Holy Spirit's role in this; that God is also Three. The most rudimentary analysis of the range of church responses to this challenge identifies two streams of thinking. The first of these places primary emphasis on God's unity—or Oneness, and the second begins by emphasising God's relationality—or Threeness. Following developments of Karl Barth's (1886–1968) seminal work on the Trinity, a confluence between these two historical streams has developed.[15] This post-Barthian stream reengages with the Christian scriptures and the long-neglected patristic traditions,[16] and it calls theology to take seriously the central role of relations in human experiences of wellbeing. Taking relations seriously specifically involves valuing the role love may play in the shaping of individual and community wellbeing, *and the interdependence of the two*.[17] However, while it is now difficult for the western theological conversation to dispute this trinitarian understanding

---

13. See Gergen, *Relational Being*.
14. Deut 6:4, NIV.
15. Torrance, *Christian Doctrine*, 159–60.
16. Grenz, *Social God*.
17. See, for example, Torrance, *Christian Doctrine*; Gunton, *One, Three, Many*; LaCugna, *God for Us*; Volf, *After Our Likeness*.

of God, there is still work to be done translating these theological insights into understanding the lives of women and men.[18]

DIVINE PERSONS-IN-RELATION

My point is that through departing from the traditional western drive to develop plurality within the Trinity from the concept of God as one, an alternative—social—analogy of persons has become available. This social analogy of persons is one based on mutual acts of self-giving, rather than something that is intrinsic to an individual. Thus "*person* is a correlative term" in that it is through receiving and giving love that people are differentiated.[19]

This analogy offers three inter-related insights into the character of the divine that I take up below in terms of their implications for human personhood and counselor understanding. The first is the central role relations play in the formation of personhood, the second is the quality or ethical shape of relating, and the third is differentiated persons. I will introduce each of these characteristics in term.

One: God as Relational Unity

The relational dynamics of the Father, the Son, and the Holy Spirit's shared life are sometimes referred to in terms of *perichoresis*. Based on two Greek words *peri* (around), and *chorein* (to give way), *perichoresis* is helpful because it not only denotes personal co-indwelling, but also dance-like movement.[20] These *perichoretic* dynamics can be discerned in Jesus' prayer in John 17:1, "Father, the hour has come. Glorify your Son, that your Son may glorify you" and in John 16:14, where Jesus says the Spirit of truth "will glorify me." In passages like these, *perichoretic* movements of the Spirit glorifying the Son and the Father, the Son glorifying the Father, and the Father glorifying the Son, are apparent. In these examples, the Father, the Son, and the Spirit are represented as co-equals expressing intimacy and embracing in loving mutuality. The point I am making here is that the three divine persons "mutually inhere in one another, draw life from one another, 'are' what they are by relation to one another."[21] Trinitarian thinkers mean by this that the Father, the Son, and the Holy Spirit are three relations who *are* persons,

---

18. Grenz, *Social God*.
19. Ibid., 48.
20. Torrance, *Christian Doctrine*, 102.
21. LaCugna, *God for Us*, 270–71.

rather than three persons who *have* relations; in other words relation is the primary ontology.

Two: God as Loving Reciprocity

While it is clear that divine personhood is centred on relations, God would not be God if it were not for the ethical quality of love that shapes these relations. Pannenberg's theology helpfully develops an analogy of love through a correlation with Hegel's notion of self-differentiation. This view of love involves active concern for the welfare of the other. For example: "Jesus glorifies the Father and not himself, and precisely in doing so shows himself to be the Son of the Father." Furthermore, "the Spirit glorifies not himself but the Son, and in him the Father, precisely by not speaking of himself (John 16:13) but bearing witness to Jesus (15:26)."[22] The relevant point here is that diversity is able to be experienced within union when fellowship is shaped by love. This is to say that the Father, the Son, and the Holy Spirit exist in each other because their giving to each other opens space for *full* flourishing.

Three: God as Differentiated Persons

Based on human experience, we may assume that living lives that are radically open to others may well lead, not to experiences of flourishing, but to being diminished through conditional acceptance or even rejection.[23] Yet in the context of love, not only do the Father, the Son, and the Holy Spirit remain distinct, uniqueness is developed.[24] I mean by this that, far from being a threat, the mutuality of the triune life actually forms personal distinctiveness. One of the founding Christian statements of faith—The Nicene creed—confesses this analogy of the Father, Son, and Holy Spirit; one in which as differentiated persons they are without confusion and clear. This coherence of the uniqueness of the Father, Son, and Holy Spirit is at the heart of neo-orthodox theology. This is a form of unity that is orientated towards the affirmation and establishment of the particularity of the other, and not towards exclusion.[25] Now that I have highlighted relational unity, loving reciprocity, and personal differentiation as key aspects of a social trinitarian analogy of diving personhood, I move to consider human persons in the light of this.

22. Pannenberg, *Systematic Theology*, 315.
23. See, for example, Volf, *Exclusion and Embrace*.
24. Torrance, *Mediation of Christ*.
25. Gunton, *One, Three, Many*.

HUMAN PERSONS-IN-RELATION

The claim that we can learn about humans from a study of God may seem odd, however in Jesus we see the basis of trinitarian anthropology. This is the understanding that the human Jesus who stands as an embodied individual in relation to others also shares family relations with the Father and the Holy Spirit.[26] This is to say that God and humans are now ontologically linked because God entered human history at a specific time and place, and in doing so restored creation to participation in God through Jesus' own participation. Put yet another way, the Spirit-empowered life, death, and resurrection of Jesus—"the first-born of all creation"[27]—provides an *experiential* basis for knowing both God and humans as relational beings.

Limits to Analogising Between God and Humans

Questions remain about the extent to which it is appropriate to map God's social life onto human community. In response, I suggest plotting a path between the two extremes of, on one hand, dismissing the Trinity as a viable guide to human flourishing and, on the other hand, over-realising a correspondence between divine and human life.[28] This middle ground offers a means to establish principles, while avoiding the risk of collapsing distinctions between God and creation.

This relational view of unity between God and the natural world implies that, amidst the complexity of human community, God is always present, replete with desire. This is desire that strangers experience hospitality, prisoners liberation, the sick healing, and that people would respond to the invitation to partner in the creative formation of practical expressions of love. Furthermore, traces of divine love can always be found in experiences such as vulnerable caring, neighbourliness, seeking justice, and the offering of forgiveness. This trinitarian approach, one that follows the model of Jesus' teaching, invites counselors to question what, in every human situation, the signs of God's presence are, and how to respond, rather than questioning whether God is present or not.[29]

While these broad theological principles can be described with some confidence, it is important to engage in the application of them humbly, remembering that all attempts to speak of "a community of persons,"

---

26. Torrance, *Worship*.
27. Col 1:15, NIV.
28. Volf, "Social Program."
29. Bosch, *Transforming Mission*.

"*perichoresis*," or "relation," will never mirror God accurately. This is because even the best human attempts are limited by a combination of sinfulness—understood as the avoidance of relational encounter—and the finite nature of the human mind and language that account for our limited and partial grasp of the nature of God. These things imply both the need to be bold in imagining human communities shaped by love, and realistic enough to recognise that the gap between God and humans is so great that the traces of trinitarian life in human social engagement are necessarily faint.

I now move to ground the discussion more practically into three interrelated dimensions that constitute this dynamic conception of human personhood; embodied individuality, relational encounter, and social life.

One: Human Embodied Individuality

As I have said, trinitarian thinking affirms personal uniqueness in the context of loving relations, and community life. For humans, of course, this involves a reciprocity between embodiment that is shaped by significant relational experiences and other social forces, and in turn the influence of these embodied memories on subsequent relating. This implies that counselors must be willing to "listen" to people through the lenses of all three domains. For example, while embodiment is fundamental to personal and social life in that it is as embodied persons that the capacities of self-consciousness, presence, uniqueness, sexuality, community engagement, relationships, and agency all find expression, these things must not be considered apart from relational and social dimensions.[30]

McFadyen offers the concept of "sedimentation" to refer to the way in which the human body "holds" relational experience and social meaning. He speculates that these things become progressively layered into a person's embodied memory over time in a similar way that sand and other debris is layered into seaside cliffs. This notion of sedimentation implies that human action and subjectivity are not only shaped by present relational and social forces, but also previous experience.[31] Barth reasoned that "without ensouling the human person would be 'subject-less,' just as conversely a human being would be 'objectless' should the significance of the body be denied."[32] And so, the human body provides people with the potential for independent life and for subjectivity. These potentials are manifest in the unique mystery of perceiving, thinking and willing, desiring, and active existence. By virtue of

---

30. Balswick et al., *Reciprocating Self*.
31. McFadyen, *Call to Personhood*.
32. Barth, *Church Dogmatics*, 392.

these human capacities, a person is qualified to engage in partnership through hearing and responding to others, and to God who advocates for people to make decisions to live shared rather than isolated lives.

In spite of this trinitarian affirmation of the embodied dimension of human life, western religious anthropologies have tended to treat the body as something to be freed from, and failing this as something to be disciplined.[33] This dualism has also been expressed for centuries within the Church where, while on the one hand the human person has been considered "good," on the other hand the fleshly dimension of humankind has often been treated as "bad."[34] This stance can be contrasted with the affirmation that the human body is actually very good associated with the incarnation of the Son in the person of Jesus of Nazareth.

This emphasis placed on embodiment by trinitarian thinking suggests two things that I wish to emphasize. First, it invites us to "apprehend God bodily—not simply so we can make religious pronouncements about the bodily life, but so one's life may be redefined . . . mediating God's love for the world and his divine presence in the world."[35] The body, then, is the place within which relationships between God and humanity turn, as well as the hinge of relations between a person and her own self, family, community, and the world. Second, it is important to emphasize that wellbeing involves psychosomatic unity. Barth is careful to argue that the soul and body do not merely combine but, rather, that the person is "wholly and simultaneously both soul and body, always and in every relation soulful, and always and in every relation bodily . . . for the concrete reality of man consists in his being both, and only in both one."[36] More than this, unity or personal coherence ultimately develops as a gift of God's Spirit. I mean by this that the ongoing unifying action of the Spirit is needed if a person is to be more than a perplexing duality. This unifying action of the Spirit includes human individuals being addressed as beloved, receiving this address, and as a result coming to know oneself as loved. So while humans are called into existence as biological entities (objects) wellbeing involves becoming personal, thinking, moral agents open to being encountered by the call of love, and encountering others in the same way (subjects).[37] This all leads to the suggestion that from the trinitarian perspective human persons cannot

---

33. Hui, *Beginning of Life*.
34. See, for example, Fenton, *Theology*.
35. Hui, *Beginning of Life*, 83.
36. Barth, *Church Dogmatics*, 46.3.
37. Fee Nordling, "Embodied, Human, Sexual."

be understood exclusively as embodied entities, any more than they can as exclusively relational or social entities.

This claim has profound implications for the way the *telos* of human development is understood by people in the helping professions. For example, a counselor's field of enquiry needs to be broad and integrative enough to include questions such as, "What practices assist the development of self-awareness?" "What aspects of a person's body and soul unity need to be offered hospitality?" "How have significant formational relationships shaped the way my body responds to invitations to trust and move towards others?" "What wisdom might my body hold?" "How does my united self support and hinder loving encounter with others?" And, "Where is love at work in this person's life and relationships?"

Two: Human Relational Encounter

As I discussed above, humans have their being because they are freely loved by God and by others. This is to say that while humans exist bodily in space and time, they are created as male and female in and for relationship with divine and human others.[38] These relationships are intended to be experienced as joyous, sensual, and creative. It is in these face-to-face relationships that people make one another what and who they are. Just as the Father, Son, and Holy Spirit constitute the being of God, humans become authentically personal insofar as they engage in mutually constructive relations with one another.[39]

Trinitarian thinking suggests, then, that human wellbeing has something to do with participating in the same kind of ethical relations that shape the Father, the Son, and the Holy Spirit. These relations are subject-to-subject encounters through which we become more fully alive. Furthermore, these are not relational encounters that take place apart from the love of God, they are actually initiated by the Spirit and received by humanity. As such, it is appropriate to say that even personal identity is not a substantial part of an individual, but a product of participating in the triune life of love.

I wish to emphasise three implications of taking up this trinitarian understanding. First, the people who consult with counselors have come, and are coming, into being as persons. Therefore, the people we encounter as clients are persons-in-relationship who are being formed through experiences of love, and not-love, and how we relate to them—and them to others—is therefore critical. This infers that counselors might understand their work

---

38. Gunton, *One, Three, Many*, 222.
39. Gunton, *Triune Creator*.

in terms of participating with their clients and others in the co-creation of personhood, according to their clients' own aspirations, as they come to know themselves anew through the loving encounter of counseling. In this then we see the counselor participating in other-centred love through things such as vulnerable presence and work on behalf of liberation. And second, in counseling the person a client is—and is becoming—one that will grow and develop to the extent he or she is able to engage in the dance of love with God.

Three: Human Social Life

As well as social trinitarian thinking offering a means to bring together men and women's embodied individuality and relationality, it also provides a means to integrate sociality.[40] Social trinitarian thinking invites counselors to think of the ways our individual lives are constantly being shaped by the social processes associated with culture and language. I am making an ethical and political claim here, that as soon as it is acknowledged that humans are ontologically relational, we must immediately ask what *sort* of relating gives rise to experiences of wellbeing. I suggest, therefore, that counselors need to find ways to assist their clients to expose and engage the social stories that shape their "oughts" and "shoulds," and not only see these in terms of embodied relational experience. For example, a counseling conversation about a mother's struggle with despair needs to include enquiry about her communities' taken for granted assumptions about what success and failure looks like. Such an enquiry might reveal that her struggle is as much about inadequate income, a poorly insulated home leading to child sickness, and isolation associated with unsatisfactorily designed bus routes, as it is about problematic thinking or poor relational skills. Furthermore, social trinitarian thinking invites counselors to hold to a vision of life shaped by love. This is because, as Moltmann puts it:

> Nothing is as humanizing as love, and a conscious interest in the life of others, particularly in the life of the oppressed. For love leaves us open to wounding and disappointment. It makes us ready to suffer. It leads us out of isolation into a fellowship with others, with people different from ourselves, and this fellowship is always associated with suffering.[41]

---

40. Torrance, *Worship*, 38.
41. Moltmann, *Crucified God*, 62–63.

In conclusion, social trinitarian thinking invites counselors to commit themselves to integrate modalities in service of the large story of a world shaped by love, and to engage in this as a social project with a restoration *telos*. It seems to me that in practice this will involve engagement with some form of relational psychotherapy because it has the potential to work dynamically with both relational experience and embodiment.[42] It will also engage a hermeneutical or postmodern understanding of identity and power—such as narrative therapy[43]—in order to work with the complexity of social life and its impact of human experience. To this end I commend a careful consideration of narrative therapy because of its capacity to engage and identify shaping forces inherent in culture, language, and discourse.[44]

When the work is located within the social trinitarian story, I feel justified in advocating for drawing from these philosophically disparate therapies because this is a harmonising story. I mean by this that because it is ethically centred on cruciform love it offers an integrative way forward for counselors who find themselves caught up in the profession's history of sectarianism. A social trinitarian understanding offers a larger story within which to harmonise individual, relational, and social dimensions of human life. The result is the joining between the therapist's ethical intent for his/her work and his/her faith commitments, in dialogue.

42. Yalom, *Gift of Therapy*.
43. Freedman and Combs, *Narrative Therapy*.
44. Ibid.

References

Balswick, Jack, et al. *Reciprocating Self: Human Development in Theological Perspective*. Downers Grove: InterVarsity, 2005.
Barth, Karl. *Church Dogmatics the Doctrine of Creation, Volume 3, Part 2: The Doctrine of Creation*. London: T&T Clark International, 1960.
Bergin, Allen Eric. "Psychotherapy and Religious Values." *Journal of Consulting and Clinical Psychology* 48 no.1 (1980) 95–105.
Bond, Tim. *Standards and Ethics for Counseling in Action*. London: Sage, 2000.
Bosch, David. *Transforming Mission*. Maryknoll: Orbis, 1991.
Bourdieu, Pierre. *The Logic of Practice*. Translated by Richard Nice. 1990. Cambridge: Polity, 1980.
Browning, Don. *Christian Ethics and the Moral Psychologies*. Grand Rapids: Eerdmans, 2006.
Brugger, E. Christian. "Anthropological Foundations for Clinical Psychology: A Proposal." *Journal of Psychology and Theology* 36 no.1 (2008) 3–15.
———. "Psychology and Christian Anthropology." *Edification: Journal of the society for Christian psychology* 3 no.1 (2009) 5–18.
Bruner, Jerome. *Actual Minds: Possible Worlds*. Cambridge, MA: Harvard University Press, 1986.
Corey, Gerald, et al. (2010). *Issues and Ethics in the Helping Professions*. 8th ed. Belmont, CA: Brooks/Cole, 2010.
Crocket, Kathleen, et al. *Ethics in Practice: A Guide for Counselors*. Wellington: Dunmore, 2011.
Fee Nordling, Cherith. "Embodied, Human, Sexual: The Only Way to Be Christian." *Perspectives: A Journal of Reformed Thought* (November 2007). http://perspectivesjournal.org/blog/2007/11/15/embodied-human-sexual-the-only-way-to-be-christian/
Fenton, John Y., ed. *Theology and the Body*. Philadelphia: Westminster, 1974.
Foucault, Michel. "The Subject and Power." In *Michel Foucault: Beyond Structuralism and Hermeneutics*, edited by Hubert L. Dreyfus and Paul Rabinow. Chicago: University of Chicago Press, 1982.
Freedman, Jill, and Gene Combs. *Narrative Therapy: The Social Construction of Preferred Realities*. New York: Norton, 1996.
Gergen, Kenneth. *Relational Being: Beyond Self and Community*. New York: Oxford University Press, 2009.

Grenz, Stanley. J. *The Social God and the Relational Self: A Trinitarian Theology of the Imago Dei*. Louisville, Ky.: Westminster John Knox, 2001.

Gunton, Colin. *The One, the Three and the Many: God, Creation and the Culture of Modernity*. Cambridge: Cambridge University Press, 1993.

———. *The Triune Creator: A Historical and Systematic Study*. Grand Rapids, MI: Eerdmans, 1998.

Hui, Edwin C. *At the Beginning of Life: Dilemmas in Theological Bioethics*. Downers Grove, IL: InterVarsity, 2002.

LaCugna, Catherine M. *God for Us: The Trinity and the Christian Life*. San Francisco: HarperCollins, 1991.

McFadyen, Alistair. *The Call to Personhood: A Christian Theory of the Individual in Social Relationships*. Cambridge, England: Cambridge University Press, 1990.

McMillan, Lex. "Troubling the Idea of Normal: A Discussion about the Development of a Counseling Anthropology." Paper presented at the New Zealand Association of Counselors, Counselor Educator's Research Conference, Wellington, NZ, 2011.

Moltmann, Jürgen. *The Crucified God: The Cross of Christ as the Foundation and Criticism of Christian Theology*. Minneapolis: Fortress, 1993.

Pannenberg, Wolfhart. *Systematic Theology*. Translated by Geoffrey W. Bromiley. 1998. Grand Rapids, MI: Wm B. Eerdmans, 1998.

Robinson, Daniel N. "Therapy as Theory and as Civics." *Theory and Psychology* 7 no.5 (1997) 675–681.

Sampson, Edward. *Celebrating the Other: A Dialogic Account of Human Nature*. Chagrin Falls, Ohio: Taos Institute, 2008.

Schwöbel, Christoph. "Human Being as Relational Being: Twelve Theses for a Christian Anthropology." In *Persons, Divine, and Human: King's College Essays in Theological Anthropology*, edited by Christoph Schwöbel and Colin Gunton, 141–170. Edinburgh: T&T Clark, 1991.

Torrance, James. *Worship, Community and the Triune God of Grace*. Downers Grove, IL: Intervarsity, 1996.

Torrance, Thomas. *The Mediation of Christ*. Revised ed. Colorado Springs: Helmers & Howard, 1992.

Torrance, Thomas. *The Christian Doctrine of God, One Being Three Persons*. Edinburgh: T&T Clark, 1996.

Volf, Miroslav. *Exclusion and Embrace: A Theological Exploration of Identity, Otherness, and Reconciliation*. Nashville, TN: Abingdon, 1996.

———. *After Our Likeness: The Church as the Image of the Trinity*. Grand Rapids, MI: William B. Eerdmans, 1998.

———. "The Trinity is Our Social Program: The Doctrine of the Trinity and the Shape of Social Engagement." In *The Doctrine of God and Theological Ethics* edited by Michael Banner and Alan Torrance, 105–124. London: Continuum International, 2006.

Yalom, Irvin. *The Gift of Therapy: An Open Letter to a New Generation of Therapists and Their Patients*. New York: Harper Collins, 2002.

Zizioulas, John. "On Being a Person: Towards an Ontology of Personhood." In *Persons, Divine, and Human: King's College Essays in Theological Anthropology*, edited by Christoph Schwöbel and Colin Gunton, 33–47. Edinburgh: T & T Clark, 1991.

2

Otherness in Relation
A Dialogic Perspective

Dr. David Crawley

Rachel, primary narrator in the novel *The Girl on the Train*, muses on one of the many reasons her life is not flourishing:

> I am not a homeowner, not even a tenant—I am a lodger, occupant of the small second bedroom in Cathy's bland and inoffensive duplex, subject to her grace and favour . . . It's the loss of control. In Cathy's flat I always feel like a guest at the very outer limit of their welcome. I feel it in the kitchen, where we jostle for space when cooking our evening meals. I feel it when I sit beside her on the sofa, the remote control firmly within her grasp . . . I have lost control over everything, even the places in my head.[1]

On the face of it, Cathy has extended kindness and hospitality to a friend in need, but Rachel's lived experience is one of diminished space and power. The area to which her living has been confined physically is paralleled psychologically by a reduced sense of agency[2] in her relationship with her benefactor—a relationship conducted entirely on the latter's terms.

Reading these words recently evoked memories of stories I heard in the course of researching authoritative practices of religious leadership. Selina, one of the research participants, recalled the way her freedom to contribute to the life of her church was progressively restricted, to the point where she told a friend, "I feel like I've been presented with this very, very,

---

1. Hawkins, *The Girl*, 23–24.

2. Here I use the term "agency" in the sense of freedom to make one's own choices. I return to a more nuanced discussion of this notion later in the chapter.

very shallow coffin that I'm being asked to lie down in, and I don't think I can fit my body in there."[3] Her choice of metaphor spoke not only of the claustrophobic, shallow space left to her if she was to accept the new terms on which she would be able to participate in the life of the community, but also of a kind of death which such acquiescence represented for her.

Each strand of my present work—lecturer, spiritual director, pastoral counselor, church leader—positions me with power and influence in relation to others. Moreover, as an older, educated male of European descent, I am afforded privilege before I do anything. How I choose to negotiate these fields of power and influence, which exist between myself and the other in every relational encounter, has effects. In my practice, my intentions are, I trust, hospitable and benevolent. But what quality of space is experienced by the other in our interactions, whether in the classroom, direction room, or church setting? Is it expansive or constricting? Does it enhance life or diminish it? Do my ways of being with the other invite acquiescence or support agency?

The previous chapter offers an understanding of personhood in which individual, interpersonal, and social aspects are dynamically interrelated. Drawing on trinitarian theology, it offers a vision of human relationships in which the flourishing of self and other is bound up with participation in the divine relational project of social restoration. It is this ethical vision of human flourishing which informs the reflexive questions raised in the previous paragraph. The conviction at the heart of the present chapter is that the outworking of this vision within professional relationships is contingent not only on maintaining Rogers' "core conditions,"[4] but also on fostering a quality of conversational space which is best described as "dialogic."[5]

Dialogic approaches to therapeutic relating and other areas of professional practice are not new.[6] My intention in this chapter is to show how the dialogic literary theory of Mikhail Bakhtin (1895–1975) and certain Christian traditions may be brought into mutually beneficial conversation. Within Christian notions of hospitality, incarnation,[7] and trinitarian partic-

---

3. Crawley, "Questioning the Man of God."

4. Congruence, unconditional positive regard, and empathy. Rogers, "Necessary and Sufficient Conditions."

5. What I understand by the term "dialogic" will be made clear in the next main section of this chapter.

6. Anderson, *Conversation, Language, and Possibilities*; Gonçalves and Guilfoyle, "Dialogism and Psychotherapy"; Guilfoyle, "Using Power to Question"; Sampson, *Celebrating the Other*; Sullivan and McCarthy, "Dialogical Perspective on Agency."

7. "Incarnation" is a theological term which expresses the Christian belief that the divine nature is embodied in the person of Jesus Christ. In the prologue to the Gospel

ipation, for example, there are rich resources for elaborating an understanding of dialogue characterised by mutuality and self-giving love. In return, Bakhtin offers language and concepts which help me to reflect more sharply on how well my own practice embodies such love. In demonstration of this last point, the final section of this chapter considers three characteristics of dialogic conversations shaped by love.

CLARIFYING TERMS: DIALOGIC, MONOLOGIC, AND UNFINALIZABILITY

Dialogic: Multi-Voiced Encounter

Bakhtin argues that all words, texts, and language are *dialogic*, that is, double-voiced. The words I speak, write, or think are not original to me. Implicit in my usage of them is the presence of other voices and meanings. In conversation, a word or phrase carries certain meanings for each participant, and these meanings in turn are informed by other usages. Moreover, as post-structuralism contends, the significance of words is shaped not only by incidental utterances, but by the functions which they perform within influential wider narratives in the social context. For Bakhtin, then, as Vice observes, every utterance consists of the unique orchestration of well-worn words. As in everyday dialogue, all these languages "will interact with each other, jockey for position, compromise, effect a temporary stabilization, before moving on to the next construction of meaning."[8]

For example, when someone speaks to me in a spiritual direction or pastoral conversation of being troubled by "sin," a polyphony of voices enter our conversational space. The significance of this word for me is partly shaped by the mix of theological and therapeutic discourses to which I have been exposed in my training. Its meaning for both of us is also influenced by its cultural and theological usage within our contexts, as well as by our own personal family and church experiences. When all of these meanings "jockey for position," as Vice puts it, conversation and interpretation become issues of *power*. In other words, as the possible meanings (and implications) of "sin" are negotiated in my conversation with the other, whose voice will prevail?

Bakhtin contrasts what he refers to as *dialogized* and *authoritative* uses of language. A word or meaning is "dialogized" by an awareness that there

---

of John, for example, we read: "And the Word became flesh and lived among us" (John 1:14, NRSV).

8. Vice, *Introducing Bakhtin*, 46.

are other related voices and competing meanings which affect its usage.⁹ An "authoritative" use of language, on the other hand, is one which claims meaning in an uncontested way, as if no other voices need be considered. For example, I might (but wouldn't!) say to my troubled conversation partner, "What you call 'sin' is nothing but the working of an overdeveloped superego—you can ignore it." In terms of *The Girl on the Train* excerpt with which I began, I would then be holding the metaphorical remote control firmly in my grasp, and offering the other a position as a lodger within my semantic space.

Monologic: Single-Voiced Conformity

Bakhtin describes such authoritative uses of language as being *monologic*, given that they render dialogue, the "genuine interaction of consciousnesses," impossible.¹⁰ My research into people's stories of resistance to oppressive practices of religious authority, mentioned earlier, led me to conclude that monologic encounter is corrosive of human wellbeing and flourishing. As I listened to people describe the hopes they had held for their involvement in their various faith communities, no one described having wanted autonomy or control. Rather, all spoke of their expectations concerning the conduct of relationships (valuing of persons, acceptance of difference, respect, inclusivity, compassion, honesty) and of the ways they had hoped decision making and conflict resolution might have been handled (participation, collaboration, open communication, reconciliation, advocacy, the pursuit of justice). According to their own accounts, the contradiction between these hopes and intentions and the monologic practices of authority which they encountered in their communities affected their wellbeing—physically, socially, emotionally, and spiritually—and contributed to their eventual acts of resistance to such practices.¹¹

Unfinalizability: The Open-Endedness of Identity

Theologically, the destructive effects of monologic power relations may be explained with reference to the *imago Dei*¹² and God's liberating work in

    9. Bakhtin and Holquist, *The Dialogic Imagination*, 427.
    10. Bakhtin and Emerson, *Dostoevsky's Poetics*, 81.
    11. Crawley, "Stories of Resistance."
    12. This Latin phrase, meaning "image of God," refers to the Judaeo-Christian belief that human beings reflect the image and likeness of God: "God said, 'Let us make humankind in our image, according to our likeness'" (Gen 1:26, NSRV).

creation. Human beings are created in the likeness of a relational God, and the trinitarian analogy suggests that they will flourish within relationships characterised by a spacious reciprocity of love.[13] This assertion is further supported by the biblical theme of liberation from oppression. God's gift in Christ is freedom from domination, accompanied by a call to live within relationships of humility and love.[14]

It is interesting to place these theological perspectives alongside Bakhtin's view of the self, which he regards as having an open, never finally consummated quality. He uses the term *unfinalizability* to suggest a "capacity to outgrow . . . and to render *untrue* any externalizing and finalizing definition" of oneself.[15] Bakhtin declares, "I cannot, axiologically, fit my whole life into time—I cannot justify it and consummate it in full within the dimension of time."[16] There is a resonance here with a Christian understanding of human personhood as being continually in the process of being drawn into ever fuller "participation in the divine life ('theosis')."[17]

Unfinalizability does not imply a return to the self-emancipation narrative of humanism, which supports a quest for an individualistic "true self" and for autonomy. There may be a common emphasis on growing beyond limiting accounts of identity, but for Bakhtin it is the dialogic process of encounter, rather than an individualistic quest, which continually opens new horizons of identity. Indeed, the engaged presence and responses of a conversation partner have the character of gift, as they contribute creatively to the possibility of new meanings.[18] There is, for Bakhtin, an ethic of love which mandates this quality of engagement on behalf of the other.[19]

Bakhtin's notions of dialogic, monologic, and unfinalizability have sharpened my reflections on the dynamics of power within my own professional practice, and in the work of those who come to me for supervision. I have more to say about this in the final section of this chapter, but I want first to reflect on further resonances between Bakhtin's conception of loving, dialogic encounter and the ethic of love embedded in Christian traditions of hospitality, incarnation, and participation in the trinitarian project.

---

13. Grenz, *Social God*; Moltmann, *The Trinity*; Volf, *After Our Likeness*.
14. Gal 5:1, 13, NSRV.
15. Bakhtin and Emerson, *Dostoevsky's Poetics*, 59. Emphasis original.
16. Bakhtin, et al., *Art and Answerability*, 127.
17. Kelsey, "The Human Creature," 129.
18. Sullivan, "Self-Other Dialogue," 108.
19. Jacobs, "Hermeneutics of Love."

PRACTICES OF LOVE: HOSPITALITY, INCARNATION, AND PARTICIPATION

The imperative to *love* is inescapable in the Second Testament.[20] Love is the essence of the divine nature,[21] and of the two greatest commandments on which "hang all the law and the prophets."[22] For the apostle Paul, love is the greatest of the virtues (1 Corinthians 13:13). But how, in practice, is such love to inform the space between human beings in their encounters with one another?

Hospitality: Beyond Reciprocity

One significant way in which the Judaeo-Christian tradition has sought to answer this question is in terms of *hospitality*. In the original Greek texts of the Second Testament the word which English versions translate as "hospitality" is *philoxenia*, combining the words *philos*, "friend," and *xenos*, "stranger." Hospitality is about how one shows love and friendship to strangers. As is often pointed out, *philoxenia* stands in opposition to *xenophobia*, the fear/hatred of strangers.[23] Steeped in the Jewish tradition of unconditional kindness to strangers, the message of the Second Testament challenged contemporary Hellenistic practices within which hospitality was a strategy for gaining favour with those in a position to offer reciprocal benefits. Jesus, and later the early church, advocated hospitality toward the poor and vulnerable, that is, those unable to repay such kindness.[24] Pohl argues that this unconditional form of hospitality is subversive of social hierarchies:

> In contrast to a more tame hospitality that welcomes persons already well situated in a community, hospitality that welcomes "the least" and recognizes their equal value can be an act of resistance and defiance, a challenge to the values and expectations of the larger community . . . Many persons who are not valued by the larger community are essentially invisible to it. When people are socially invisible, their needs and concerns are not acknowledged and no one even notices the injustices they suffer. Hospitality can begin a journey toward visibility and respect.[25]

20. Jackson, *The Priority of Love*.
21. 1 John 4:8, 16, NSRV.
22. Matt 22:34–40, NSRV.
23. Russell, *Just Hospitality*, 66.
24. Luke 14:12–14, NSRV.
25. Pohl, *Making Room*, 62.

In the context of professional practice, this perspective challenges structures that limit access to those who share the social and economic privileges of the practitioners.

Yet even unconditional acceptance may result in patronising, monologic forms of hospitality, such as Rachel experienced in the home of Cathy, her supposed benefactor. The Christian tradition explicitly requires that we do better than this when it comes to creating hospitable space for the other. Here I note three perspectives on hospitality in support of this claim, each of which reinforces and enriches Bakhtin's ethic of dialogic encounter.

Welcoming Christ in the Other

Matthew's Gospel intensifies the Jewish call to unconditional kindness to strangers in its message that the vulnerable one who comes to us is Jesus himself ("I was a stranger and you welcomed me"[26]). As Pohl suggests, if we begin with the premise that Jesus meets us in the other, then we will be "more sensitive to what the guest is bringing to us, what God might be saying or doing through her or him."[27] Already in this one thought we are transported from condescension and control to a stance of respect, humility, and receptivity. This leads naturally to the second feature.

Willingness to Receive Through the Other

Pohl cites the advice of the early Christian preacher Chrysostom, who urged that hospitality be offered in ways that are sensitive to the dignity of the other, "to show by words and actions, that we do not think we are conferring a favor, but receiving one, that we are obliging less than we are obliged."[28] There is no pretence or false humility in this, because it is understood that in giving hospitality, hosts often find their own lives are enriched. In interviewing contemporary practitioners of hospitality, Pohl found the same perspective:

> Many practitioners commented on their joy and surprise in discovering how much they learned from the guests and how much the guests ministered to them . . . Experiences such as

---

26. Matt 25:35, NSRV.
27. Pohl, *Making Room*, 68.
28. Ibid., 69.

these reminded practitioners daily that the gifts of hospitality do not flow in one direction only; hospitality is a "two-way street."[29]

As I seek to create a hospitable, dialogic space in my classroom or office, I hope to serve the other without ulterior motive. At the same time, if in humility I am willing to acknowledge my own unfinalized personhood, and if I am receptive, then regularly my own horizon is enlarged through the encounter. Again this connects with the next point, which gets to the heart of what I want to say about hospitality and dialogic encounter.

Mutual Vulnerability with the Other

Welcoming and making space for the other's presence and voice, while valuing one's own, requires a particular kind of humility and vulnerability. Genuinely dialogic encounter, by definition, requires willing attentiveness to a voice which may speak in register alien to one's own, and this has the potential to alter one's own understandings, values, and sense of identity. In *Exclusion and Embrace*, Volf explains that the basic thought expressed in his metaphor of "embrace" is that "the will to give ourselves to others and 'welcome' them, to readjust our identities to make space for them, is prior to any judgment about others, except that of identifying them in their humanity."[30] This willingness "to readjust our identities" stands in contrast to the violence perpetrated when a nation colonizes and oppresses, destroys cultures, and imposes its religion, "all in the name of its identity with itself."[31] I suggest that what is said here of nations may be transposed to the realm of professional practice and interpersonal relating. To avoid simply colonizing or manipulating the other within a monologic form of relationship requires vulnerability and reflexivity on my part. How might my gender, my sexual orientation, my culture, my education, or my privilege, for example, be limiting my capacity to offer hospitable space for the other in which they are able to reveal difference without fear of being taken over or rejected?[32]

These invitations from the Christian tradition—welcoming Christ in the other, willingness to receive through the other, and mutual

29. Ibid., 72.

30. Volf, *Exclusion and Embrace*, 29. Original in italics.

31. Ibid., 16.

32. The assumption here has been that the practitioner is host. Béres points out that social workers and others are sometimes guests in the homes of others, and suggests that what they have learned from the discourses of hospitality will aid them in taking up this position in ways that are experienced as respectful and collaborative. Béres, *The Narrative Practitioner*, 128.

vulnerability—move us far beyond a hospitality intended to place the other under the obligation of reciprocity. They also transcend patronising, monologic expressions of so-called kindness which decide without consultation what it is that the other needs. Instead, they challenge us to offer a hospitable presence characterised by respect, attentive listening, dialogic conversation, humility, and—most challenging of all—vulnerability to shifts of self-understanding and identity, personally and professionally. These are daunting ideals. In the next section, therefore, I argue that our own efforts to be hospitable may helpfully be reframed as a participation in something beyond and prior to ourselves, namely the hospitality of God, revealed to us in Christ.

Incarnation and Participation in the Trinitarian Project of Love

In the Second Testament, Christ is not only the guest who comes to us in the vulnerable other, he is also the host who draws us into participation in his own hospitable mission. In John's account of the last supper, Jesus girds himself with a towel in order to wash his disciples' feet. He then calls on them to follow his example in the way they serve one another.[33] In Luke's account, Jesus offers bread and wine to his friends, representing the gift of his own life on their behalf. Again he invites them to reproduce his example "as one who serves."[34] As the apostle Paul encourages the Christians at Philippi to enter into relationships characterised by humility and attention to the interests of others, he points them away from the familiar logic of "selfish ambition" and "conceit," and invites them to participate instead in the paradoxical logic of the incarnation:

> Let the same mind be in you that was in Christ Jesus, who, though he was in the form of God, did not regard equality with God as something to be exploited, but emptied himself, taking the form of a slave, being born in human likeness.[35]

The incarnate Son of God eschewed the way of domination. Rather than seeing his divine status as something to be "exploited" (grasped after aggressively), Christ willingly assumed a self-emptying (*kenosis*) stance of other-centeredness.

There are echoes here of Volf's notion of willing readjustment of identity in order to make space for the other. In the case of the incarnate Christ;

33. John 13, NSRV.
34. Luke 22, NSRV.
35. Phil 2:5–7, NSRV.

however, Paul's words may point not so much to a *readjustment* of his divine status as to the humility and mutual deference which *belong* to the divine nature. The word "though" in the above translation ("though he was in the form of God") might suggest that Christ's *kenosis* was somehow in tension with his God-likeness. Yet there is no word corresponding to "though" in the Greek text. This passage is much debated by commentators, but I am persuaded by Gorman's extensive study, in which he summarizes Paul's paradoxical logic in this way: "to be truly human is to be Christlike, which is to be Godlike, which is to be kenotic and cruciform."[36] In other words, to enter into relationships with "the same mind" as Christ is to embrace the humble, self-giving love which is characteristic of the divine nature.

Transposing that perspective into the language of hospitality, I suggest that when we follow in the hospitable way of Christ, including its kenotic (self-emptying) and cruciform (self-giving) aspects, we participate in the larger project of divine hospitality. First Testament injunctions to hospitality are prefaced with reminders of the hospitality of God, "who executes justice for the orphan and the widow, and who loves the strangers, providing them food and clothing."[37] This is a powerful example of Bakhtin's dialogism: when God's people speak of hospitality, their meanings are drawn from ancient stories of God's unconditional kindness, and shaped by centuries of commentary. Therefore, as Pohl suggests, hospitality at its best always holds "some connection to the divine, to holy ground."[38] Beyond mere imitation, *participation* involves indwelling, and being formed by, the story of the one who most profoundly reveals the humble, self-giving nature of the godhead. For Paul's intention, as Gorman makes clear, is not so much to inform as to *form* the community, in its relationality, according to the narrative arc of Christ's self-giving love:

> A community that lives "in Christ" (Phil 2:1–5) will be shaped like the story of Christ narrated in Phil 2:6–8 as it experiences the present activity of Father, Son, and Spirit forming individuals

---

36. Gorman, *Cruciform God*, 162. I acknowledge the valid concern that for some people, a call to self-giving love may reinforce unhelpful gendered discourses of submission. Sarah Penwarden touches on this issue later in this volume, in her discussion of *kenosis*. Additionally, it is helpful to note that a trinitarian reading of the *kenosis* narrative makes clear that this is not a call to self-degradation. Within the relationality of the Trinity, mutual self-giving love does not diminish the dignity or the particularity of Father, Son, or Spirit.

37. Deut 10:18, NSRV.

38. Pohl, *Making Room*, 13.

and communities into the eternal, unchanging image of the eternal Son of God manifested in that story.[39]

In summary, the Christian tradition offers a rich context in which to set dialogic practice, namely participation in the hospitality and self-giving love of the Trinity, as revealed in the incarnation of Christ. Such participation is characterised by welcoming Christ in the other, willingness to receive from the other, and vulnerability to change through encountering the other. This vision of otherness in dialogic relation is challenging. It requires me to be transformed. Speaking personally, I hope for such transformation through contemplating Christ, indwelling the narrative of divine love and humility revealed in him, and trusting in the work of the Spirit.[40]

IMPLICATIONS FOR PRACTICE

The previous section outlines how I understand Bakhtin's notion of dialogic relational encounter to be supported and enriched by the Christian tradition. In responding to the invitations of that tradition, I find in Bakhtin's ideas a helpful lens through which to consider the quality of my interactions with others. The final section of this chapter therefore offers some thoughts of a "so what" kind in relation to professional practice, focusing on three features of conversation in particular.[41] In each case, I explore an aspect of process—what is happening in the conversation—alongside an associated aspect of what is happening for those participating. So dialogic engagement is connected with agency, appropriation of meaning is connected with internal persuasion, and space for play is connected with unfinalizability.

1. Dialogic Engagement and Participatory Agency

As a literary theorist, Bakhtin is interested in conversations between characters, and also in a character's dialogue with internalized others, and/or the self.[42] Drawing on Bakhtin's ideas, Sampson, a social psychologist, highlights the fact that an interaction may have the form of a dialogue—two people speaking—but in fact be monologic, because of the unequal terms on which the conversation takes place. He argues that "merely having a

---

39. Gorman, *Cruciform God*, 163.
40. 2 Cor 3:18, NSRV.
41. I have developed similar ideas in writing about issues of authority within spiritual direction conversations. See Crawley, "*Authority* in Spiritual Direction."
42. Bakhtin and Holquist, *The Dialogic Imagination*, 427.

voice is not sufficient if that voice must speak in a register that is alien to its own specificity, and in so doing lose its own desires and interests."[43] A genuinely dialogic engagement, he suggests, must involve "two separable presences, each coming from its own standpoint, expressing and enacting its own particular specificity."[44]

There is a tension to be maintained here, between individualistic and relational accounts of personhood. While it makes intuitive sense to speak of "two separable presences," as opposed to collapsing one person's subjectivity entirely into another's, Bakhtin's dialogism challenges the notion of entirely self-contained individual presences. The language through which a person makes meaning of their life "lies on the borderline between oneself and the other," and always "the word in language is half someone else's."[45] This means that any individualistic claim to authoritative meaning-making is ill-founded. As Sampson observes, it also implies a relational understanding of personhood (a perspective adopted by many of the authors in this volume):

> The dialogic position challenges the primary western understanding of ownership over one's own psychology, over one's mind, self and personality. Although, when I speak, it is my vocal chords that are vibrating, the voices which I use—the words, if you will—are never mine alone . . . Furthermore, we not only speak in many voices but participate in a process that is always jointly constructed and jointly sustained or transformed.[46]

Given this understanding of the joint construction of meaning, what place does dialogic engagement have for any notion of *personal agency*, in the sense of making choices in relation to one's own life? Some accounts of agency, including what Michael White refers to as the "emancipatory narrative" of liberal humanism,[47] have emphasised the freedom of individual persons to throw off repressive external constraints and become their "true selves." Positively, White acknowledges that this emancipatory narrative has often supported people in their efforts to resist "the various acts of domination they are being subject to," but he also critiques what he regards as its narcissistic tendencies.[48] An understanding of agency as personal autonomy may help people to name and challenge abusive circumstances, but it overlooks the ways in which a purely individualistic focus on the self contributes

43. Sampson, *Celebrating the Other*, 10–11.
44. Ibid., 15.
45. Bakhtin and Holquist, *The Dialogic Imagination*, 293.
46. Sampson, *Celebrating the Other*, 135.
47. White, *Narratives of Therapists' Lives*, 220.
48. Ibid., 234.

to structural inequalities and injustice. It also fails to recognise the authoring of life, identity, and meaning as relational achievements, rather than "self-celebratory monologues."[49]

Taking up the idea that "no single individual has complete control over the meanings that are conveyed by the language he or she uses," Drewery offers a relational take on agency. In place of autonomy, she views agency in terms of *participation*.[50] A relational understanding of personhood means that no one has complete autonomy or control, yet, within the dialogic process of negotiating meaning, each person may have *influence*. Juxtaposing metaphors, Drewery suggests that to act agentically is therefore less like being the cue that moves the first billiard ball, and more like throwing one's two cents worth into a conversation already taking place among several people.[51] To have agency, in this sense, is to have access to participation in the conversations that produce the meanings of one's life.[52] Personal agency is thus reframed as *participatory agency*. In Bakhtinian terms, I see this as having the opportunity to participate in genuinely dialogic conversation, particularly when that conversation has a bearing on the conditions in which I live my life. To return to the opening illustration from *The Girl on the Train*, it is the lack of such agency which leads to Rachel's sense of being reduced to the status of a lodger in a space owned by another, literally and psychologically.

Whether in spiritual direction, pastoral counseling, or in the classroom, I aspire to curate conversations which support participatory agency. If I am drawn into taking an authoritative position with regard to the construction of meaning, then the conversation becomes monologic—a pseudo-dialogue conducted on my terms. Dialogic and poststructuralist understandings of language show that this scenario cannot be avoided merely by trying to divest ourselves of power, or by making our own contributions sound tentative. The discourses of expertise (whether therapeutic, theological, or educational) which are prevalent in the wider social context inevitably position professionals and their words with influence.[53] Even in the most "person-centred" approaches, our responses—whether articulated by us or anticipated by the other—inevitably contribute to the dialogic process of

49. Sampson, *Celebrating the Other*, 15.
50. Drewery, "We Should Watch," 319.
51. Ibid., 316.
52. Ibid., 315.
53. Guilfoyle, "Dialogue and Power". The limited scope of this chapter does not allow for a detailed explanation of the notion of social/cultural discourse and its role in power relations and positioning. See other chapters in this book; Davies and Harré, "Positioning"; Winslade, "Utilising Discursive Positioning."

meaning-making in which the other is engaged. So rather than standing back from our own contributions, which will have effects whether we like it or not, I suggest that dialogic engagement and the agency of the other are better served when our part in the collaborative construction of meaning is transparent. Cooper and McLeod, for example, argue that a willingness to engage in such dialogue is key to building collaborative therapeutic relationships:

> It has become commonplace to talk about a 'two-person' relationship in therapy . . . where both client and therapist are actively present, in contrast to the 'one-person' relationship in which the client is present but the person of the therapist remains hidden.[54]

Furthermore, as noted earlier, for me to withhold my dialogized contribution to the other is, in Bakhtin's view, an ethical failure—a failure to love.[55] Without question, simply to listen well is in itself to offer a gift. But if my presence is entirely hidden behind a professional persona, or if I merely mirror the other's words, then creative possibilities for the opening of new horizons of meaning are diminished.[56]

The challenge here is to strike an appropriate balance between overbearing and absent forms of hospitality—avoiding authoritative positioning and monologic forms of conversation on the one hand, and, on the other, embracing the creative role we have in the co-production of new meaning. This is a hospitality which is both self-giving—offering warmth, food, and companionship—*and* self-restraining—allowing space for the other to move and to make their own choices as to what may be nourishing. It is important to acknowledge that in this dialogic process new meanings are also created for the one offering the hospitable space. As emphasised above, the host is vulnerable to having their own understanding and identity changed (and enriched) through encounter with the guest. When both parties are able to exercise participatory agency in the conversation, then understanding and response within dialogue may be "dialectically merged and mutually condition each other."[57]

---

54. Cooper and McLeod, *Pluralistic Counseling*, 38.
55. Jacobs, "Hermeneutics of Love," 37.
56. Bakhtin and Holquist, *The Dialogic Imagination*, 281.
57. Ibid., 282.

2. Appropriation of Meaning and Internal Persuasion

To address the next aspect of practice, an extra slice of Bakhtinian theory is needed. Dialogue occurs not only between persons, but within each person.[58] In considering the latter, Bakhtin distinguishes between "I-for-myself" and "I-for-others." I-for-myself is "the center from which my performed act and my self-activity of affirming and acknowledging any value come forth or issue."[59] This self comes to know itself through the responses of others, that is, through the "I-for-others." There is, therefore, a greater sense of centeredness and coherence in Bakhtin's view of the self than in the notion of a purely socially constructed, and therefore fragmented, self. I-for-myself represents an inner sense of self from which one judges, acts, and so on.[60] At the same time, the self for Bakhtin is malleable and open, as the I-for-others constantly develops through external relational encounters, and engages in internal dialogue with the I-for-myself.[61]

Bakhtin reflects on the formation of the I-for-myself and I-for-others in a child's experience, through "acts of recognition and love that come to him from outside—from his mother, from others who are close to him."[62] These are words "that *come to meet* his indistinct inner sensation of himself."[63] The words that shape our earliest sense of self are received as authoritative, absolute, but as the I-for-myself sense of self develops, so does the capacity for dialogic engagement with meanings offered as authoritative. "The ideological becoming of a human being, in this view, is the process of selectively assimilating the words of others."[64] Bakhtin uses the process of learning to retell things in our own words to illustrate this development, since it involves *appropriation*, and not simply rote transmission, of another's words. At this point, Bakhtin also introduces the notion of *internally persuasive discourse*. This is meaning that is received and eventually assimilated at the I-for-myself level. While in our earliest life the authoritative word is often also internally persuasive, it is the struggle between these two categories of discourse which over time shapes "the history

---

58. As strikingly represented in the novels of Dostoevsky. See Bakhtin and Emerson, *Dostoevsky's Poetics*.

59. Bakhtin et al., *Philosophy of the Act*, 60.

60. I-for-myself has some parallels to the notion sometimes used in counseling, of an internal locus of evaluation. I-for-others might be compared to an external locus of evaluation, although it is more an interface than something purely external.

61. Sullivan, "Self-Other Dialogue."

62. Bakhtin et al., *Philosophy of the Act*, 49.

63. Ibid. Emphasis original.

64. Bakhtin and Holquist, *The Dialogic Imagination*, 341.

of an individual consciousness."[65] In thinking about the appropriation of meaning, it is important to acknowledge that for Bakhtin even internally persuasive discourse is not static, but fluid. The internally persuasive word is creative and productive, jostling with other internally persuasive words and sparking fresh iterations of meaning.

Among the many words and ideas shared in professional conversations, some will be appropriated as internally persuasive, while others will not. For example, Guilfoyle observes that narrative therapy texts often depict clients as readily taking up the hopeful storylines which their therapists have skilfully detected within their problem-saturated accounts.[66] Yet in his own experience, this hasn't always been the case: "It is one thing for the therapist to listen for openings into agency-enabling stories. It is quite another for the client to step into them."[67] While narrative therapists "aim to follow trajectories suggested by the client's interests and preferences," their interest in transporting the client towards hope and agency may take them "ahead of, rather than alongside the client."[68] In his own practice, Guilfoyle has not abandoned the re-authoring strategy, but complements it by paying careful empathic attention to the subject position within which the client is constituted by the problem story. I see this as a more dialogic approach, in that it leaves room for creative contributions on the therapist's part, while helping to counteract a tendency for the conversation to tilt too quickly toward the therapist's own hope-inspired narrative, and away from what is internally persuasive for the client.

I have argued that developing dialogical working relationships invites practitioners to speak transparently, while privileging the other's ability to participate fully on their own terms. In Bakhtinian terms, this means that the word they offer will not (with some few exceptions) be an authoritative word. For Bakhtin, an authoritative word is one that "demands that we acknowledge it, that we make it our own . . . quite independently of any power it may have to persuade us internally."[69] The host provides generously, but then must step back to allow space within which the guest freely decides what—if anything—they find to be nourishing and needful for their journey. To that end, the host takes the time to listen carefully and humbly to the guest's own account of the journey, in order to better marry provision to need.

65. Ibid., 342.
66. Guilfoyle, "Listening in Narrative Therapy."
67. Ibid., 39.
68. Ibid., 40.
69. Bakhtin and Holquist, *The Dialogic Imagination*, 342.

Again there is need for nuance here. Where another's safety is at stake, for example, then an authoritative word may be appropriate. When the development of a person's I-for-myself sense of identity has been hindered by authoritarian relationships, or interrupted by trauma, then his or her capacity for agentic choices with regard to the meanings offered to him or her may be fragile and in need of nurture. In that instance, practitioners need to be especially cautious in offering contributions which may too readily be appropriated as authoritative. Part of their work will be to help the other to grow in his or her their confidence to engage in both outer and inner dialogue with regard to the meanings of his or her own life.

3. Space for Play and Unfinalizability

The final characteristic of dialogic conversations to be considered here is having *space for play*. Bakhtin emphasizes that the structure of meaning associated with an internally persuasive discourse "is *not finite*, it is *open*; in each of the new contexts that dialogize it, this discourse is able to reveal ever newer *ways to mean*."[70] In contrast, he argues, authoritative discourse "is by its very nature incapable of being double-voiced . . . there is no space around it to play in."[71] This suggests that openness and play will be hallmarks of richly dialogic engagements. Space for play within conversation suggests to me not only moments of lightness (to balance heaviness), but creativity, spontaneity, imagination, and freedom to try out new ideas. I think also of the freedom to play with—reconsider, deconstruct, and reconstruct—meanings and narratives that have claimed authoritative status, and which have had oppressive effects. Anderson describes the character of such a space (which she calls "dialogical space") within therapeutic conversation:

> Dialogical space refers to room in one's thoughts to entertain multiple ideas, beliefs, and opinions . . . Dialogical space or conversational context is critical to the development of a generative process that promotes fluid, shifting ideas and actions . . . Without dialogical space a familiar story cannot be narrated in a way that provides an opportunity for transformation in the narrating story and the self.[72]

---

70. Ibid., 346. Emphasis original.
71. Ibid., 344.
72. Anderson, *Conversation, Language, and Possibilities*, 112–13.

The idea of "playful approaches to serious problems" will be a familiar one to narrative therapists.[73] It may be less familiar to some of those who identify with the Christian tradition. Is God playful? The poets say yes! In Hopkins' poetic vision of a creation infused with divine presence, "Christ plays in ten thousand places . . . To the Father through the features of men's faces."[74] In discussing imagination in the work of Coleridge, Stockitt describes "the trinitarian God whose ways are not our ways and who constantly engages in the surprising, the dramatic, the unexpected, and the playful."[75] In light of the earlier description of our work as a participation in the divine project of love, a hallmark of such participation will be conversations which are similarly characterized by freedom of imagination, surprising turns, and playful exploration.

Bakhtin's emphasis on the open-ended, unfinalized character of meaning in language echoes his notion of the unfinalizability of persons, outlined earlier. The narrative therapy literature makes similar connections. Guilfoyle recalls White's use of the Foucauldian idea that "the person is never completely discursively tamed because other discourses and stories are always available."[76] Space for play implies freedom to try on such alternative meanings and narratives for size.

Guilfoyle further notes that some who study Foucault believe that he was influenced by the Nietzschean view that living beings are characterised by an "excess and overflow," which "power and discourse cannot completely contain."[77] He explicitly connects these ideas with Bakhtin's account of unfinalizability. He also observes the acute effects on people of finalizing modes of relationship. Resistance, he argues, "tends to arise spontaneously in the face of those definitions of identity which finalise—which prevent the person from becoming anything else."[78] This for me evokes the metaphor of the "shallow coffin," noted at the beginning, which Selina used to describe the felt effects of being given no room to play out her sense of call. These effects were pivotal in her narrative of resistance to authoritative practices of authority. The presence of resistance in conversation can be interpreted psychodynamically, but it also invites me to consider (first) whether my approach is being experienced in a cramping, finalizing way by the other.

73. See, for example, Freeman et al., *Playful Approaches*.
74. Hopkins, *Poems and Prose*, 51.
75. Stockitt, *Imagination and Playfulness*, 176.
76. Guilfoyle, "Listening in Narrative Therapy," 44.
77. Ibid., 45.
78. Ibid., 46.

Notions of play and unfinalizability therefore invite me to reflect critically on the ways I see and think about the people with whom I speak. Bakhtin's ethic of love, together with the example of Christ, calls me to view the other in ways that do not finalize, but which help to open up new and creative possibilities.[79] This is in tension with approaches which position the practitioner as expert, and which seek to diagnose the other in terms of prefabricated categories, or make finalizing assumptions based on gender, sexual orientation, race, or ability. Positively, it resonates with Michael White's consistent advocacy of the de-centred yet influential position for therapists.[80]

CONCLUDING THOUGHTS

My discussion of Christian ideas about hospitality focused on the host's, that is, the practitioner's, process. In the preceding reflections I attended more to the process of those whom we encounter in the course of practice conversations. Within a dialogic frame, however, these are overlapping perspectives. The call to welcome Christ in the other slows my inclination to assume an authoritative position in which I override the agency of the other, ignore the necessity of internal persuasion, or allow little space for play. A willingness to receive and learn through the other requires dialogic engagement on my part, attention to what *I* am experiencing as internally persuasive, and acceptance that my own horizons of meaning and identity must remain malleable and expandable. All of which invites me to experience mutual vulnerability with the other, and to trust that the ground between us is indeed made holy by the love that transcends both of us and draws us into participation in love.

Recalling Paul's words to the Philippian Christians, cited earlier, I find myself framing the invitation this way:

> Let the same mind be in you that was in Christ Jesus, so that even if your qualifications grant you the comfort of expertise, or your social context positions you with power, do not regard these privileges as something to be exploited, but instead focus on the priority of love. With the Spirit's help, encounter others as they are, not who you would prefer them to be, and risk vulnerability in offering yourselves to them as fellow humans, co-learners, and companions in the journey toward life.

---

79. Sullivan, "Self-Other Dialogue," 111.
80. White, *Therapists' Lives*, 109.

References

Anderson, Harlene. *Conversation, Language, and Possibilities: A Postmodern Approach to Therapy*. New York, NY: Basic, 1997.
Bakhtin, Mikhail M., and Caryl Emerson. *Problems of Dostoevsky's Poetics*. Minneapolis, MN: University of Minnesota Press, 1984.
Bakhtin, Mikhail M., and Michael Holquist. *The Dialogic Imagination: Four Essays*. Austin, TX: University of Texas Press, 1981.
Bakhtin, Mikhail M., et al. *Art and Answerability: Early Philosophical Essays*. Translated by Vadim Liapunov. Austin, TX: University of Texas Press, 1990.
Béres, Laura. *The Narrative Practitioner*. Baskingstoke, UK: Palgrave Macmillan, 2014.
Cooper, Mick, and John McLeod. *Pluralistic Counselling and Psychotherapy*. Los Angeles, CA: Sage, 2011.
Crawley, David R. "Authority in Spiritual Direction Conversations: Dialogic Perspectives." *Journal for the Study of Spirituality* 6, 1 (2016) 6–19.
———. "Questioning the Man of God: Selina's Story." *Australasian Pentecostal Studies* 18 (2016). http://aps-journal.com/aps/index.php/APS/article/view/9487
———. "Stories of Resistance to Religious Authority: A Discursive Analysis." PhD. diss., University of Waikato, 2014.
Davies, Bronwyn, and Rom Harré. "Positioning: The Discursive Production of Selves." *Journal for the Theory of Social Behaviour* 20 no. 1 (1990) 43–63.
Drewery, Wendy. "Why We Should Watch What We Say: Position Calls, Everyday Speech and the Production of Relational Subjectivity." *Theory & Psychology* 15 no. 3 (2005) 305–24.
Freeman, Jennifer C., et al. *Playful Approaches to Serious Problems: Narrative Therapy with Children and Their Families*. New York: W.W. Norton, 1997.
Gonçalves, Miguel M., and Michael Guilfoyle. "Dialogism and Psychotherapy: Therapists' and Clients' Beliefs Supporting Monologism." *Journal of Constructivist Psychology* 19 no. 3 (2006) 251–71.
Gorman, Michael J. *Inhabiting the Cruciform God: Kenosis, Justification, and Theosis in Paul's Narrative Soteriology*. Grand Rapids, MI: William B. Eerdmans, 2009.
Grenz, Stanley J. *The Social God and the Relational Self: A Trinitarian Theology of the Imago Dei*. Louisville, KY: Westminster John Knox, 2001.
Guilfoyle, Michael. "Dialogue and Power: A Critical Analysis of Power in Dialogical Therapy." *Family Process* 42 no. 3 (2003) 331–43.

———. "Listening in Narrative Therapy: Double Listening and Empathic Positioning." *South African Journal of Psychology* 45 no. 1 (2015) 36–49.

———. "Using Power to Question the Dialogical Self and Its Therapeutic Application." *Counseling Psychology Quarterly* 19 no. 1 (2006) 89–104.

Hawkins, Paula. *The Girl on the Train*. London, UK: Random House, 2015.

Hopkins, Gerard Manley. *Poems and Prose*. New York, N.Y.: Penguin Books, 1953.

Jackson, Timothy P. *The Priority of Love: Christian Charity and Social Justice*. Princeton, NJ: Princeton University Press, 2003.

Jacobs, Alan. "Bakhtin and the Hermeneutics of Love." In *Bakhtin and Religion: A Feeling for Faith*, edited by Susan M. Felch and Paul J. Contino, 25–45. Evanston, IL: Northwestern University Press, 2001.

Kelsey, David H. "The Human Creature." In *The Oxford Handbook of Systematic Theology*, edited by John Webster, Kathryn Tanner and Iain R. Torrance. Oxford, UK: Oxford University Press, 2007.

Moltmann, Jürgen. *The Trinity and the Kingdom: The Doctrine of God*. Translated by Margaret Kohl. San Francisco, CA: Harper & Row, 1981.

Pohl, Christine D. *Making Room: Recovering Hospitality as a Christian Tradition*. Grand Rapids, MI: W.B. Eerdmans, 1999.

Rogers, Carl R. "The Necessary and Sufficient Conditions of Therapeutic Personality Change." *Journal of Consulting Psychology* 21 no.2 (1957) 95–103.

Russell, Letty M. *Just Hospitality: God's Welcome in a World of Difference*. Louisville, KY: Westminster John Knox, 2009.

Sampson, Edward E. *Celebrating the Other: A Dialogic Account of Human Nature*. Boulder, CO: Westview, 1993.

Stockitt, Robin. *Imagination and the Playfulness of God: The Theological Implications of Samuel Taylor Coleridge's Definition of the Human Imagination*. Eugene, OR: Pickwick Publications, 2011.

Sullivan, Paul. "Examining the Self-Other Dialogue through 'Spirit' and 'Soul'." *Culture & Psychology* 13 no. 1 (2007) 105–28.

Sullivan, Paul, and John McCarthy. "Toward a Dialogical Perspective on Agency." *Journal for the Theory of Social Behaviour* 34 no. 3 (2004) 291–309.

Vice, Sue. *Introducing Bakhtin*. Manchester, UK: Manchester University Press, 1997.

Volf, Miroslav. *After Our Likeness: The Church as the Image of the Trinity*. Grand Rapids, MI: Eerdmans, 1998.

———. *Exclusion and Embrace: A Theological Exploration of Identity, Otherness, and Reconciliation*. Nashville, TN: Abingdon, 1996.

White, Michael. *Narratives of Therapists' Lives*. Adelaide, Australia: Dulwich Centre, 1997.

Winslade, John. "Utilising Discursive Positioning in Counseling." *British Journal of Guidance & Counselling* 33 no. 3 (August 2005) 351–64.

3

Creating Space for Faith
Relationality and Dialogical, Incarnational Integrative Method

SIOBHAN HUNT

As a young person, my desire to help other people was awakened during my personal experiences of distress and the nature of the help I received during those times. The path through these experiences and towards feelings of wholeness was hugely influenced by my faith and relationships with other people who shared this faith. The relationships with these people gave me a sense of a personally invested God who sees all people as precious. As a result of my connection with this personally-invested God, I decided to engage in study that would equip me to effectively help people. Yet, upon entering my studies in psychology, I found that my faith was not only unwelcome, but something of which to be ashamed. This left me with a sense of fragmentation between two important values in my life: connecting with God and helping people. It also left me feeling confused, as for me these two values were connected, and my study created a divide between them. Thus, I found myself faced with the task of trying to create a bridge between these two areas of my life so that I could engage in the work of helping people with a sense of integrity about both my purpose for being there and my methods of helping. Some way along my journey towards this place of integrity, I encountered Entwistle's writing on integration and found it provided some helpful language to my experience.

Entwistle[1] argues that the academic disciplines of theology[2] and psychology can be likened to two books written by the same author—God. One book, theology, is about how God works in the world, and the other, psychology, is about how God's world (specifically, people) works. He defines integration as the faithful reading of both books. While this is a helpful metaphor, as it gives respect and value to both disciplines, I find it difficult to directly apply, as learning to read these books does not occur in a vacuum. Rather, we learn to read in the midst of a cacophony of voices that speak about what knowledge is, how we come to know, which types of information are legitimate, and the nature of the people who are doing the reading. The ideas associated with modernism, for example, suggest that people are individual, autonomous selves on the quest to discover objective, empirical truth. Postmodern thinking, on the other hand, offers the view that there are many truths and that meaning is not discovered, but created. Furthermore, there is also a broad philosophical (and theological) movement towards relational ways of understanding people, the world, and knowledge. These different schools of thought lead to different conclusions about the best way to read the "two books." How then, is one to go about "faithfully reading" the two books of psychology and theology and hearing the stories that they *both* tell?

In this chapter, I tell my story of finding a satisfactory way to draw from psychological thought, my faith experience, and my theological position when thinking about how to care for people. First, I look at three epistemological trends: modernism, postmodernism, and relationality, as well as theological ideas, and explore how they have shaped the way I "learned to read" the two books. I then describe six elements of the approach I took to integration, or reading the two books, as a counseling student in a relational philosophical and social trinitarian theological context. Throughout this discussion, I trace the path that I took from a modernist understanding and practice of integration, in which rejection and assimilation are paramount, to an understanding of integration grounded in relationality, lived experience, story, and community.

WHY TWO BOOKS?

The church has a lengthy tradition of engaging with psychological issues, through reflection on the problems humanity faces, as well as caring for its

---

1. Entwistle, *Integrative Approaches*.
2. A slightly different emphasis to the lived experience of relationship with God, which I refer to in this chapter as "faith."

people. In the western world, the church was seen as a primary place for people to seek emotional and spiritual care; however in the last two hundred years, with the advent of modern psychology, there has been a shift away from pastors and towards psychologists when caring for those in mental or emotional distress.[3] In 1979, Carter and Narramore argued that:

> Christianity is in the throes of an encounter with psychology. On academic and popular levels alike, psychology is making inroads into areas traditionally considered the domain of Christianity . . . Increasingly, our society is looking to psychology to shed new light on the problems of human existence.[4]

Perhaps this shift from pastors to psychologists is a reflection of changes in the wider philosophical climate and the resulting epistemological differences.

The shift from pastors to psychologists as people who provide emotional and psychological care occurred in the context of a dominant modernist philosophy in popular culture. In modernist thinking, knowledge tends to be rational and objective, and "suspect are all beliefs that seem to curtail autonomy or to be based on some external reality other than reason."[5] In a modernist, post-Enlightenment world, it then follows that knowledge that comes from faith tends to be de-valued and knowledge coming from scientific method is upheld. Therefore, approaches to care which are empirically and statistically supported, such as many of those prominent in the domain of psychology, tend to be more valued and trusted in modernist-influenced cultures than those based upon theological and philosophical reflection. Further enhancing the perceived gap between Christian faith and science, of which psychology is a sub-discipline, is a common perception that the church is anti-scientific, owing to historical examples such as the sentencing of Galileo in the seventeenth century, as well as the increasing prominence of anti-intellectualism within western Christian faith.[6] Thus, whilst theology and psychology are speaking on similar topics regarding the nature of humanity, problems, and health, there is difficulty in holding open discourse between the two disciplines; they are written in *two* books, not one. This was reflected in the environment that I encountered during my psychology study. The legitimacy that modernism lends to the divide between theology and psychology hints at the impact that this school of thought has on integration between psychology and faith, to which I will now turn.

3. See: Johnson, "Brief History"; Entwistle, *Integrative Approaches*, 18–34; Holeman, *Better Counseling*, 39.
4. Carter and Narramore, *Integration*, 9.
5. Grenz, *Primer on Postmodernism*, 4.
6. Moreland and Matlock, *Smart Faith*.

A MODERNIST APPROACH TO INTEGRATION OR "READING THE TWO BOOKS"

Modernism, with its scientific, rationalistic epistemology, encapsulates ideas about persons and knowledge which impact on the valuing of psychology and theology. The ideal modern person is "the autonomous self, the self-determining subject who exists outside any tradition or community."[7] Knowledge is certain, rational and objective. To reiterate what I stated earlier, this leads to a preference for empirically-based evidence, discovered by an objective individual. This could also be referred to as a paradigmatic approach, with an emphasis on truth over meaning.[8] Furthermore, in this view of knowledge, psychology and science would be given priority over faith in the conversation regarding care and wellbeing, because, within a modernist culture, faith-based sources of information are viewed as less legitimate as they rely on ways of knowing other than objective rationalism. The influence of modernist thinking was seen early on in my integration journey, when my primary goal was to discover the one, verifiable "truth" into which psychology and faith would both fit, as well as my sense that objective, empirical data would hold more weight in the search for truth than my experiences of faith. These modernist ideas about epistemology align with two of Eck's[9] categories of integration: non-integrative and manipulative, which I will now explore.

Modernist assumptions about knowledge correlate with approaches to reading the two books such as those Eck[10] describes as "non-integrative." Eck claims that in non-integrative paradigms, the integration of knowledge drawn from diverse ways of knowing does not really occur, because a process of "rejection" is applied to the data from the other discipline, and so they remain separate. Consider, for example, Freud's[11] hypothesis that God is an illusion that people create in reaction to a sense of their own helplessness. Freud posits that the need for this illusion is gone now that people are able to use science in order to gain knowledge about the world they live in. Thus, Freud completely rejects God, seeing him as some kind of wish fulfillment, and places science as "the only road which can lead us to a knowledge of reality outside ourselves."[12] In addition to outright rejection, modernism,

---

7. Grenz, *Primer on Postmodernism*, 4.
8. Parry and Doan, *Story Re-visions*, 2.
9. Eck, "Integrating the Integrators."
10. Ibid., 103.
11. Freud, *Future of an Illusion*.
12. Ibid., 50.

which elevates the significance of science and rational thinking, could lead to approaches to integration which require one discipline to be assimilated.

That is, a modernist approach to knowing could also lead to methods like those seen in Eck's[13] category of "manipulative" integrative models, which are based upon a paradigm of data manipulation. Here, there is a degree of acknowledgement of the validity of data from other ways of knowing and disciplines, however, the data are manipulated to fit within the paradigm of one's own discipline, or forced to pass through a filter before becoming more acceptable. For example, for an integrator with a worldview heavily focused on science and modernism, ideas from theology or the realm of faith may need to be passed through a scientific or empirical filter before holding any credibility. One example of how this might look in the context of counseling is neuroscience research that examines brain physiology during religious experience, and thereafter speaks about religious experience in terms of neural activation and not relationship. In summary, modernism is likely to lead to a reading of the two books which results in separation between disciplines or some kind of assimilation of disciplinary contributions that are not primarily based on its epistemological preference. This affects the story the two books tell, as one voice is not heard on its own terms, and is in some way distorted. As such, while I valued aspects of modernist philosophy, I found that it did not lend itself to an approach to integration which helped me to satisfactorily bridge the divide between psychology and faith. Many of the challenges which modernism presents to integration are rejected by the postmodern school of thought. In contrast to modernism, postmodernist philosophy places value on the plurality of knowledge, or hearing from different voices. I move to now introduce this philosophy because it opens space for a more inclusive approach to integrating knowledge about human wellbeing gained from psychology and theology.

A POSTMODERN APPROACH TO READING THE TWO BOOKS

In recent years, the emergence of postmodernist thought opened space for many sources of knowledge, including that of faith or theology, in the making of meaning and knowledge. Postmodernism arose in reaction to modernism, rejecting the idea of objective knowing of truth, the ideal of rationality, and universal truth.[14] While I do not completely agree with this rejection, as I believe the scientific method is a legitimate epistemology,

13. Eck, "Integrating the Integrators," 104.
14. Gannon and Davies, "Postmodern, Post-structural, and Critical Theories."

postmodern ideas about epistemology raise important hermeneutical issues, and they made an important contribution to my integration journey and are thus worth discussing. Rather than assume that we can know things as they are in themselves (*noumena*), postmodern thought posits that we can only know them as they appear to us (*phenomena*).[15] Here, there is more emphasis on the subjectivity of knowing, as well as on the role of language in constructing reality or identity.[16] Indeed, "the postmodern ethos resists unified, all-encompassing, and universally valid explanations. It replaces these with a respect for difference and a celebration of the local and particular at the expense of the universal."[17] It could be described as a narrative way of knowing, with an emphasis on meaning over truth.[18] This emerging postmodern philosophy also offers new possibilities for the inclusion of faith and theology in conversations about care. Where conversation was once difficult in the modernist climate due to a lack of importance given to knowledge arising from faith, history, and tradition, there is now increasing space at the table for values-based knowledge, like that of faith. I am not suggesting that reading the two books of theology and psychology only began with the introduction of postmodern epistemologies, but that new possibilities were created.

However, while postmodern thinking helped me to feel that my faith could make a legitimate contribution to the conversation, it still left me without a clear path for how to approach integration. Perhaps this was in part a personal reaction to the ideas presented by postmodernism. After being steeped in modernist thinking for most of my life, the ideas of postmodernism took some time to adjust to. Though I appreciated the creation of space for faith and the valuing of different ways of knowing, I did not feel that it was a place in which I could confidently stand as I approached integration. Although I now have a more nuanced and appreciative understanding of postmodernism and see how it fits within Eck's "non-manipulative"[19] integrative approaches, at the time of my counseling study this was not the philosophical paradigm that resonated most deeply with me. Instead, I connected with the ideas represented within the philosophical "turn" to relationality.[20]

---

15. Shults, *Reforming Theological Anthropology*, 20.
16. Burr, *Social Constructionism*.
17. Grenz, *Primer on Postmodernism*, 12.
18. Parry and Doan, *Story Re-visions*, 2.
19. Eck, "Integrating the Integrators," 108.
20. Shults, *Reforming Theological Anthropology*.

A RELATIONAL APPROACH TO READING THE TWO BOOKS

A key feature of my philosophical context for approaching integration is relationality. I am influenced by modernism, due to its pervasiveness in the culture in which I am embedded, and even more influenced by postmodernism, due to its emphasis on language and the social context aligning with my values. However, encountering the idea of knowing through relationship was a key step in the journey towards bridging the divide between faith and psychology, because it both created space for difference and promoted connection. Shults traces the recent philosophical "turn" to relationality, to which I am referring, from the privileging of substance over relationality as "a new appreciation of relationality as an explanatory category."[21] That is, rather than primarily defining something in terms of the substance of which it is comprised, within this view it is now defined in terms of the relationships in which it is embedded. From this perspective, people are not primarily considered as individuals, but as beings in relationship. The epistemology represented by this relational philosophy aligns closely with Eck's "non-manipulative" paradigms of integration. It is within these approaches that I finally found a place to begin creating a bridge between my faith and psychology.

In Eck's[22] non-manipulative integration paradigms, which fit with a relational approach to knowing, data is integrated through a process of correlation, or unification. Correlation allows the data to remain within the context of its discipline to retain its integrity, and the process of integration involves finding connections between the disciplines, either through seeing them as different levels of explanation, or by creating links between the data of each discipline. In these approaches, information from both disciplines is valued, including the uniqueness or difference of those ideas, and integration is the process of making connections. This non-manipulative process of unification seeks to combine the best from each discipline into a unified set of understandings; a process that I suggest can be seen to reflect the unity and diversity of God's creation. Therefore, a relational approach to knowing leads to an integration process that values both unity and diversity. It allows both disciplines to be heard, but also asks that they find a way to join their voices in unity. Though this is perhaps only subtly different to the approaches arising from postmodernism, it creates quite a different picture

---

21. Ibid., 11.
22. Eck, "Integrating the Integrators," 108.

to the modernist approach discussed above, where there was separation between the disciplines or assimilation of one.

Thus far in my integration journey, modernist philosophy has given me a value for the individual self, empirical knowledge, and the search for truth, but has not allowed space for faith in the integrative process. In contrast, postmodernism has taught me the value of many voices and of the role of language in creating knowledge, and has created a space for faith to join the integrative discussion about how to care for people. The relational approach has given me a way to bridge these two extreme philosophical positions, as well as a starting place for the integration of psychology and faith. The differences between these philosophical positions can be summarized as emphasizing truth and paradigms (modernism), or meaning and narrative (postmodernism), or unity and diversity (relationality). I have now provided a fairly detailed overview of the philosophical and epistemological context in which I approached integration.

As I acknowledged earlier, integration does not occur in a vacuum—we are influenced by the ideas around us, whether we acknowledge them or not—and so examining one's philosophical assumptions is a crucial step when thinking about integration. Before I turn to outline some of the specific aspects of my approach to integration, I will briefly describe my theological standing place, which is another key aspect of my context for integration.

OUTLINING MY THEOLOGICAL CONTEXT

The theological context in which I approached the task of integration as a counseling student was shaped by my understanding of the biblical narrative,[23] which includes ideas about personhood, suffering and hope, and God's work in the world. While not a full account of my theological context, I will provide a brief overview of some of the features that played a part in my particular integration journey. First, I am influenced by the idea that people are created by God in his image, meaning that the nature of persons reflects something of his nature. Secondly, God was made incarnate in Jesus, and through his death and resurrection a new kingdom was inaugurated, one which exists in part now, but which will exist one day in fullness. In the meantime, Christians participate in God's kingdom work to create glimpses of his kingdom and anticipate its full arrival.[24] Third, as a result of the "now but not yet" nature of God's kingdom, people live in a reality where there is

---

23. Here I am referring to the biblical narrative as I learned it during my study at an evangelical Christian college.

24. Wright, *Surprised by Hope*.

both suffering and hope. The particular theological idea of suffering which I align myself with is that described by Wright.[25] Rather than interpret suffering as good and part of God's will or plan,[26] or as an inescapable part of existence,[27] Wright suggests it is relatively meaningless, and a part of the old reality that is being replaced with God's new kingdom. This positions working against suffering as a part of the church's calling to anticipate God's kingdom, rather than viewing it as an act of defiance against God or an act of futility. It is through working against suffering and for hope that Christians may anticipate the new creation in the midst of a world still subjected to the old way of suffering. Furthermore, as I mentioned above, there has been a philosophical turn towards relationality in recent years. Since there is a "reciprocity between theological conceptions and the philosophical and scientific conceptions of any given culture and time,"[28] there is also a move towards relationality in theological thinking. All this to say, I align myself with this relationally-informed theology.

The move towards emphasizing the central role of relationality in discipline of theology is reflected in a shift from unitarian to trinitarian concepts of God. Grenz describes this as a movement "from the centrality of the one divine subject, indicative of substantialist philosophical orientations, to the concern for the three trinitarian persons."[29] If humans are created in the image of this relational God, then it follows that humans image God relationally. Rather than the modernist autonomous individual self, people can instead be viewed as persons-in-relation, held together in mutually reciprocating relationships and embedded in social contexts. These relationships are best characterized by I-Thou relating,[30] and include separation and binding,[31] or differentiation and connection.[32]

Having outlined the context in which I read the two books, I will now turn to explore the impact of this context on my epistemology. To illustrate this, I will explore six key aspects of my experience of integration which I noticed while I was a counseling student in this relational theological and philosophical context.

---

25. Ibid.

26. Boice, "Sure, I Believe"; Piper, "We Can Rejoice in Suffering"; Paul II, "Savifici Doloris"; Trueman, "Luther's Theology."

27. Suchocki, *What is Process Theology?*, 9.

28. Shults, *Reforming Theological Anthropology*, 11.

29. Grenz, *Social God and the Relational Self*, 24.

30. Buber, *I and Thou*.

31. Volf, *Exclusion and Embrace*.

32. Schnarch, *Passionate Marriage*, 53–74.

FEATURES OF MY RELATIONAL APPROACH TO READING THE TWO BOOKS

Feature One: Relational

As I have discussed, my approach to reading the two books was impacted by the implications the theological and philosophical turn towards relationality had for knowing and the nature of reality. From a social trinitarian perspective, knowing changes from impersonal, explicit statements and proofs, to something more interpersonal, as the "paradigm of all knowing [is] the interpersonal, covenantally constituted, relationship."[33] Here, reality is seen as constituted by relationships, and as persons-in-relationship, we come to knowledge relationally. This relational perspective led me to value the role of a community of colleagues in the integrative process, moving integration away from an individual, abstract process of combining concepts, to a collaborative process undertaken by real people. Although I must confess to being somewhat influenced by the idea of individualism, I found that a key aspect of my integration journey was my connection with lecturers and other students as we grappled with how to make sense of our faith. This relational aspect of reading the books refers to the connection between people, but it is also reflected in the way an individual might engage with two differing sets of ideas. This relational nature of knowing is further emphasized in the next feature of my integration process: dialogue.

Feature Two: Dialogic

Within this relational context, a dialogue between the two integrative parties is a key approach to integration, because it reflects the idea of two distinct identities held together in mutual reciprocity. Dialogic approaches allow both distinctiveness and integrity of ideas, and foster connection. Since psychology and theology, and more broadly, the scientific community and the church, have been estranged at times, it is helpful to consider theologian Miroslav Volf's ideas about the reconciliation of people in a state of conflict or rejection. Volf[34] offers the view that exclusion of those who are different occurs either through a violation of separation, or a violation of binding. That is, separation is violated when the distinctiveness of the other is not recognized, and he or she is assimilated or subjected. These dynamics can be seen in Eck's "manipulative" approaches to integration—the

---

33. Meek, *Loving to Know*, 395.
34. Volf, *Exclusion and Embrace*.

distinctiveness of one paradigm is lost as it is forced to be re-interpreted in light of the other discipline's paradigm. Binding is violated when the right of the other to be in connection is not recognized, and thus he or she is cast as an enemy that must be pushed away, or a nonentity to be disregarded. A similar phenomenon is reflected in Eck's non-integrative approaches,[35] where the data from one discipline is rejected by the other. This exploration of what can happen between two parties that are in conflict holds some clues for how a relational, dialogical approach to integration between two allied disciplines might look. This approach requires respect for each party (Volf's "separation"), and the right of each party to enter into relationship, to be part of the conversation (Volf's "binding"). This view was particularly helpful when I was trying to answer the question: "What is a person?" It helped me to overcome some of the reductionism I encountered in the past and arrive at the understanding that people are multi-faceted, embodied beings, held together in mutually reciprocating relationships, and shaped by social discourses. I found that when integration is located within the relational metaphor, the invitation is to encounter and cherish the stranger's differences, not to assimilate or reject them.

Feature Three: Formational

The type of encounter where difference is cherished relies upon a person who is not closed off to difference, out of fear, but rather a person who is open and "willing to give [themselves] for others and to receive others in [themselves]."[36] This is what Volf refers to as a de-centered center of self-giving love. Integration that occurs within a relational climate and is based upon dialogue therefore involves an element of being open to being changed. When the integration journey is viewed from the relational perspective it is not merely an academic journey, but a deeply personal one that invites the integrator to grow and change as he or she encounters people and ideas. For example, I was impacted in my counselor education by a lecturer who challenged us to examine our theological understanding of suffering. As I engaged with different Christian interpretations of suffering and hope and how they fit with wider biblical narratives,[37] I found that more was being formed than my ideas; *I* was being shaped as I allowed space for new ideas and considered my position in relation to suffering. In other words, this was not a simple academic exercise as it held implications for my actions

---

35. Eck, "Integrating the Integrators," 103.
36. Volf, *Exclusion and Embrace*, 71.
37. McConnell, *Disruptive Power*.

in the counseling room and the meaning my counseling work held. Like with Kierkegaard's "pre-theoretical commitments," these were not ideas that were seen, but ideas that I saw through, like looking through a lens.[38] Thus I noticed that there was a formational element to my approach to integration; engaging with integration shaped me. In turn, who I was then impacted on the integrative process.

Similar to the way that the philosophical context impacts the reading of the two books, as I discussed earlier, who I am as a person also impacts the reading of the two books. Heidegger, working in the field of phenomenological hermeneutics, proposed that "understanding is never without presuppositions or preformed prejudices, for there is no neutral or unbiased starting place from which one may begin to understand. There is only the place and situation in which we always already find ourselves."[39] Just as I was formed by the integration process, so I, in turn, shaped the integration process. My experience of integration, then, was reflexive.

Feature Four: Reflexive

As a result of this recursive element in my experience of integration, rather than conceptualize integration as a straight line from disintegration to wholeness, I conceptualized it as a spiral that twists and turns into ever deeper levels of understanding. This hermeneutical principle is sometimes applied to understanding text, including biblical text. For example Osborne writes that a spiral is a good metaphor for hermeneutical biblical interpretation "because it is not a closed circle but rather an open-ended movement . . . I am not going round and round a closed circle that can never detect the true meaning but am spiraling nearer and nearer to the text's intended meaning."[40] A dynamic back-and-forth process occurs. As someone who likes to create a cohesive "big picture" I found the uncertainty of this uncomfortable, but I could also see the benefit of it; each cycle of the feedback loop took me a little deeper into the mystery and brought a little more clarity. In fact, it brought more than clarity, because, as I mentioned before, *I* was shaped, not just my thinking. I found that, as I was shaped by each turn of the cycle—as I engaged more deeply with my faith and then acted from my new understanding—I was beginning to think and act in ways that echoed the nature and works of Christ. One place I saw this was in an increasing awareness of and desire for ethical relating. It could be said

---

38. John, *Truth and Subjectivity*, 13.
39. Porter and Robinson, *Hermeneutics*, 60.
40. Osborne, *Hermeneutical Spiral*, 6.

then, that the formational, recursive cycle was forming and maturing me as a person in-Christ. Through engaging with my faith and theology in this process of integration, I was growing up "in every way into him who is the head, into Christ."[41] Thus, in my experience, the result of the spiral of integration was much wider than deeper cognitive understanding, the result was a journey towards Christlikeness, or "Christian living."[42] One way to think about this recursive, formational aspect of integration is to link what I have been saying with the Christian notion of incarnation; to embody and live on behalf of Christ in life and in the counseling room.

Feature Five: Incarnational, Embodied or Lived

The idea of Christian living or Christlikeness suggests that I can be a counselor who is in Christ, not through overt "Christian" acts such as explicitly speaking about God, praying for my client, or giving out Bible verses, but through the way that I relate as a person. Therefore, integration is about much more than bringing my theology, ideas, or counseling theories into the room, it is about bringing *Christ* in to the room in the way that I embody and live out his teaching, and as I am formed in his image. We could say then, that integration is, or at least has the potential to be, incarnational: "God's truth lives through us as we live as Jesus lived."[43] There are several ways we can "live as Jesus lived" and so wholeheartedly integrate faith into our counseling work, for example: through the way we enter into the client's suffering, through the way we offer relationship, and by challenging the prevailing culture. I will now explore each of these three expressions in more detail.

Suffering and empathy as incarnational presence. Just as Jesus is believed to have entered into the suffering of humankind, taking the pain upon himself, and in overcoming that suffering provided a hopeful glimpse of a redeemed way of living, so we as Christian counselors can enter into the suffering worlds of our clients and journey with them to wellness. In this way, we can represent or embody Christ in the counseling room. Benner writes that one of the ways counselors enter the client's suffering worlds is through "empathic involvement."[44] That is, engaging empathetically with a client expresses something of the nature of God's entrance into our lives, and his humble journeying with us. Looking at empathy through an in-

---

41. Eph 4:15, NIV.
42. Farnsworth, *Wholehearted Integration*, 78.
43. Ibid., 108.
44. Benner, "Incarnation as a Metaphor," 291.

carnational lens, we see that this engagement with the client is not merely intended to soothe or comfort; it also includes an element of creating a shift for the client towards a more hopeful, whole way of being. We could draw some links between this incarnational journey through suffering and the core condition of empathy in person-centered therapy.

Person-centered therapy (PCT) was founded by Carl Rogers in the 1950s and has its roots in humanism. Like with Maslow's hierarchy of needs, the theory of therapeutic change that lies behind PCT is that, given the right conditions, the person will move towards growth. Although this theory does not fully align with the concept of persons-in-relationship, PCT is welcome as a partner in the integration dialogue. PCT can contribute much to the current discussion due to its focus on providing empathy in therapy. Writing with regards to empathy, Mearns and Cooper say that the person-centered therapist:

> May begin to develop an in-depth, advanced empathic sense of what the client is experiencing; and this will not just be a cognitive understanding, but one that is also emotional and embodied . . . when therapists share something of what they are experiencing at this level with clients, this can often have the very powerful effect of helping clients deepen their understanding of how they experience their world.[45]

Hence we see that empathy is not providing surface-level comfort to the client, it is a true entering-into the client's experience. It is a whole-person engagement with the cognitive, emotional and embodied other. Furthermore, just as Christ's engagement with humanity gave a glimpse of a new way of living, something about this empathic engagement in PCT helps the clients to see their world in a new way. One mechanism by which this change occurs is through focusing on the "edge of awareness": "Simply focusing on the known surface feelings may only be going over old ground, whereas focusing on the edge (the felt sense) can be the door to the unknown."[46] The therapist has entered the person's experience to the point that she is able to tentatively help the client to focus on that which is just beyond his or her current awareness. Exploring this unknown area can lead to a new way of understanding the person's experience. Thus, while not an exact analogy for the work of Christ, this therapeutic task echoes something of his personal, incarnational engagement with humankind. This engagement with suffering in service of finding hope and wholeness, illustrated through the example of empathy, is one way that Christian counselors incarnate Christ in

---

45. Mearns and Cooper, *Working at Relational Depth*, 130.
46. Mearns and Thorne, *Person-Centred Counseling in Action*, 65.

their practice. I will now turn to discuss a second element of incarnational therapy: the way counselors offer connection or relationship to the counseling client.

Relationship as incarnational presence. The second incarnational element of therapy is the quality of relating between the therapist and client. As I have discussed, relationship is at the very core of God's triune nature. The three beings are bound together in a relationship that perfectly balances unity and difference in the "dance" known as *perichoresis*.[47] This relationship within the Trinity is typified by "full equality, glad submission, joyful intimacy and mutual deference."[48] Relational—as opposed to functional or structural—interpretations of the *imago Dei* posit that it is through love-orientated relational connection with others that we image God.[49] It follows then, that connecting with other humans in loving relationships is an incarnational act, as we echo, embody, or reflect the nature of Christ. Therefore, it is possible for therapy to be incarnational when the Christian counselor offers to the client the type of relationship that Christ offers humanity. Speaking about this relationship in the language of counseling theory, one could perhaps draw some links to PCT, particularly that branch of PCT known as *two*-person-centered therapy.

In contrast to earlier iterations of PCT, the focus of the two-person or dialogical branch of PCT, is "on encountering the client in an in-depth way and sustaining such a depth of relating."[50] The therapist hopes to create a particular type of relationship with the client, as well as facilitate particular experiences of interpersonal connection. This connection is typified by co-presence,[51] where both the therapist and the client "come together in a wholly genuine, open and engaged way,"[52] both are open to being impacted by the other, and willing to share of themselves. Thus, we see here an echo of the relationship between the persons of the Trinity. For the Christian counselor schooled in trinitarian theology, offering this relationship is an invitation to step into his or her identity as a person-in-relationship. Furthermore, offering this relationship can help to facilitate therapeutic change for the client[53] through entering into suffering and providing hope. That is, as the therapist enters into relationship with the client, he or she is open

---

47. Grenz, *Theology for the Community of God*, 68.
48. Mark Shaw, as cited in Seamands, *Ministry in the Image of God*, 35.
49. Grenz, *Social God, Relational Self*.
50. Mearns and Cooper, *Working at Relational Depth*, xiii.
51. Ibid., 134.
52. Ibid., 37.
53. Terrell, *Intentional Incarnational Integration*, 162.

to experiencing the client's unhealthy ways of relating. The therapist takes on the pain in these moments of encounter by not responding in the way in which the client is used to, for example, not responding to anger with aggression and instead engaging in a way that reflects the self-giving heart of the triune God. In doing this, the hope of the therapist is to give the client an experience of a new way of relating to others, which can be healing in itself and can potentially help the client to engage differently in his or her everyday relationships. My point here is that there is a transformational element to connecting in relationship.

Justice-making as incarnational presence. So far, the incarnational elements of therapy I have discussed reflect my understanding that Jesus meets with people in a personal, relational way. However, during his time on earth, he also engaged with wider social and political contexts and he invites us to participate in these activities. Jesus demonstrated a particular interest in justice for the oppressed and marginalized, and he often challenged the prevailing cultural and religious structures. Some examples of this are: healing a crippled man on the Sabbath,[54] his response to the teachers of the law and the Pharisees regarding a woman caught in adultery,[55] the story of the Good Samaritan,[56] and healing a man with leprosy.[57] Through Jesus' example, we see that he was not just concerned with the spiritual wellbeing of the people he interacted with, but also with their physical, emotional, relational, and social wellbeing. We can conclude that "the kingdom of God works from within the existing social and cultural matrix of each person to bring liberation and healing, especially from the forms inflicted by that person's own social setting."[58] This suggests that working for justice in wider social contexts is an aspect of "Christian living," and thus another legitimate incarnational element of counseling.

This incarnational act of working for justice can be expressed within the counseling room. Narrative therapy, which is based in the idea that people are socially constructed through a dynamic interplay of power and language, is a particularly useful modality for attending to issues of power. From the narrative therapy perspective, problems occur when people are subjected to dominant discourses and so lose their voice and agency in the writing and telling of their story according to their preferred cultural norms.[59] The role of

---

54. Mark 3:3–6, NIV.
55. John 8:1–11, NIV.
56. John 4, NIV.
57. Matt 8:1–4, NIV.
58. Anderson, *Shape of Practical Theology*, 234.
59. White, *Maps of Narrative Practice*.

power in the construction of identity and problems means that any attempt to deconstruct "personal" problems cannot help but be "political." That is, in narrative therapy, personal transformation is social transformation, and vice versa. Thus, the narrative therapy room can become a site of resistance as the injustices of society are exposed.[60] This exposure happens as therapists help clients to: separate the problem from their identity, deconstruct the problem by exposing the discourses that support it, and increase their agency by repositioning themselves in an alternate story.[61] Although the role of a counselor is typically confined to the counseling room, turning the room into a site of resistance guards against adjusting the person to injustice, which can happen when the therapist "does therapy" to the person without considering the wider social issues. However, the tales of Christ's involvement with people, as well as my experiences of engaging with the wider school context of the children I counseled during my counseling degree, led me to wonder whether Christian living calls me to take this work for justice outside the traditional walls of the counseling room. For me, this aspect of incarnational therapy is about engaging with the community, not just the individual. While I am still working on how I can add this element of incarnational therapy into my counseling work and my way of life, there are others who are already doing so, such as Waldegrave et al. in their *Just Therapy* work.[62] There is another example of this later in this volume in Mike Williams's chapter on *Undercover Anti-Bullying Teams*. This desire to look outside the walls of the counseling room hinted at another aspect of what it means to be a Christian counselor: that of participating in God's works in the wider world.

The elements of my approach to integration which I have outlined so far are that it is: relational, dialogical, formational, recursive, and incarnational. I will now briefly consider a sixth aspect: participation.

Feature Six: Integration as Kingdom Participation and Anticipation

My integration journey moved me from a place of fragmentation to considering how who I am becoming as a person embodies the nature and teachings of Christ, making him incarnate in the counseling room. For me, this question of who I am becoming and how I live as a result is seated in the wider context of my purpose or place in the world. Once again, following engagement with lecturers and students in my course of study, I was introduced to the ideas of participation in and anticipation of God's kingdom. Torrance writes of Jesus

60. See Waldegrave et al., *Just Therapy*.
61. White, *Maps of Narrative Practice*.
62. Waldegrave et al., *Just Therapy*, 6.

that "by his Spirit he draws men and women to participate both in his life of worship and communion with the father in his mission from the Father to the world."[63] From this perspective, true worship and communion is that of the Son with the Father, and through Christ we as Christians are able to participate in that. Likewise, Christians can see their work, be it counseling, agriculture, teaching, and so on, as participation in God's ongoing work in the world.[64] This participation in God's work is one way to anticipate the eventual coming of his kingdom in full: "we [the church] must work in the present for the advance signs of that eventual state of affairs when God is "all in all," when his kingdom has come and his will is done "on earth as in heaven.""[65] The idea that we are living out of God's story, participating in his work, and anticipating the eventual restoration of his kingdom, helps me to integrate theology and counseling as it provides a wider context for my work and my purpose in life, as well as shaping my idea of "success." It challenges me to question the way that I work and live, as I consider whether the way I practice counseling, run my business, and practice my faith are acting as glimpses of the new way of life within God's kingdom.

CONCLUSION

To conclude, I return to my opening paragraph where I introduced my desire to find a sense of integrity between my faith and the study I hoped would equip me to meet my God-inspired desire to help people. I now find that my goal of being more equipped to help people has been achieved through my engagement with both psychology/counseling and theology/faith. Furthermore, I am in a place where I can have a sense of integrity while I help people in any sphere of my life, not just within the counseling room. The relational philosophical context in which I chose to locate myself and the theological ideas I aligned myself with meant that the result of my engagement with the task of integration does not look like a formulaic description of how counseling and theology fit together. My journey has been one of moving from paradigmatic or "truth" based ways of knowing and valuing information, towards those based in relationships and narrative or meaning, a stance I believe to be consistent with the story of Jesus. I found that integration could be better described as a story describing my steps towards becoming more like Christ in his engagement with humanity, and participation in his work in the world.

63. Torrance, *Worship, Community, Triune God*, 31.
64. Bartholomew and Goheen, *Drama of Scripture*, 202–205.
65. Wright, *Surprised by Hope*, 211.

References

Anderson, Ray S. *The Shape of Practical Theology: Empowering Ministry with Theological Praxis*. Downers Grove: InterVarsity, 2001.

Bartholomew, Craig G., and Michael W. Goheen. *The Drama of Scripture: Finding Our Place in the Biblical Story*. Grand Rapids: Baker Academic, 2004.

Benner, David G. "The Incarnation as a Metaphor for Psychotherapy." *Journal of Psychology and Theology* 11 no.4 (1983) 287–294.

Boice, James M. *Sure, I Believe—So What!* Scotland, U.K.: Christian Focus, 1994.

Buber, Martin. *I and Thou*. New York: Scribner, 1970.

Burr, Vivien. *Social Constructionism*. 2nd ed. East Sussex: Routledge, 2003.

Carter, John D., & Bruce Narramore. *The Integration of Psychology and Theology: An Introduction*. Grand Rapids: Zondervan, 1979.

Eck, Brian E. "Integrating the Integrators: An Organizing Framework for a Multifaceted Process of Integration." *Journal of Psychology and Christianity* 15 (1996) 101–115.

Entwistle, David. N. *Integrative Approaches to Psychology and Christianity: An Introduction to Worldview Issues, Philosophical Foundations, and Models of Integration*. Eugene, OR: Wipf and Stock, 2004.

Farnsworth, Kirk.E. *Wholehearted Integration: Harmonizing psychology and Christianity through Word and Deed*. Grand Rapids, MI: Baker Book House, 1985.

Freud, Sigmund. *The Future of an Illusion*. Translated by W.D. Robson-Scott. Edited by James Strachey. Garden City, NY: Anchor, 1964.

Gannon, Susanne, and Bronwyn Davies. "Postmodern, Post-structural, and Critical Theories." In *Handbook of Feminist Research: Theory and Praxis*, edited by Sharlene Nagy Hesse-Biber, 65–91. Thousand Oaks: Sage, 2007.

Grenz, Stanley J. *A Primer on Postmodernism*. Grand Rapids: William B Eerdmans, 1996.

———. *The Social God and the Relational Self: A Trinitarian Theology of the imago Dei*. Louisville, KY: Westminster John Knox, 2001.

———.*Theology for the Community of God*. Grand Rapids, MI: Wm. B. Eerdmans, 2000.

Holeman, Virginia T. *Theology for Better Counseling*. Downers Grove: InterVarsity, 2012.

John, Varughese. *Truth and Subjectivity, Faith and History: Kierkegaard's Insights for Christian Faith*. Eugene, OR: Pickwick, 2012.

Johnson, Eric L. "A Brief History of Christians in Psychology." In *Psychology and Christianity: Five Views*, edited by Eric L. Johnson, 9–48. Downers Grove: InterVarsity, 2010.

McConnell, T. Mark. "The Disruptive Power of Christian Hope: Suffering, Cancer, and Theological Meaning." In *Spirituality and Cancer: Christian Encounters*, edited by Tim Meadowcroft and Caroline Blyth, 149–162. Auckland: Accent, 2015.

Mearns, Dave, and Mick Cooper. *Working at Relational Depth in Counseling and Psychotherapy*. London: Sage, 2005.

Mearns, Dave, et al. *Person-Centred Counseling in Action*. 4th ed. London: Sage, 2013.

Meek, Esther L. *Loving to Know: Covenant Epistemology*. Eugene, OR: Cascade, 2011.

Moreland, J.P., and Mark Matlock. *Smart Faith: Loving Your God With All Your Mind*. Colorado Springs: TH1NK, 2005.

Osborne, Grant R. *The Hermeneutical Spiral: A Comprehensive Introduction to Biblical Interpretation*. Downers Grove, IL: InterVarsity, 1991.

Parry, Alan, and Robert E. Doan. *Story Re-visions: Narrative Therapy in the Postmodern World*. New York: Guildford, 1994.

Paul II, John. "Savifici Doloris (Christian meaning of human suffering)." *Catholic Information Network* (July 1995). http://www.cin.org/suffer.html

Piper, John. "Why we can rejoice in suffering." *Desiring God* (October 23 1994). http://www.desiringgod.org/resource-library/sermons/why-we-can-rejoice-in-suffering

Porter, Stanley E., and Jason Robinson. *Hermeneutics: An Introduction to Interpretive Theory*. Grand Rapids, MI: William B. Eerdmans, 2011.

Schnarch, David. *Passionate Marriage: Keeping Love and Intimacy Alive in Committed Relationships*. Victoria, Australia: Scribe, 2009.

Seamands, Stephen A. *Ministry in the Image of God: The Trinitarian Shape of Christian Service*. Downers Grove, IL: Intervarsity, 2006.

Shults, F. Leron. *Reforming Theological Anthropology: After the Philosophical Anthropology*. Grand Rapids, MI: William B. Eerdmans, 2003.

Suchocki, Marjorie. *What is Process Theology? A Conversation with Marjorie*. Claremont, California: Process and Faith, 2003.

Terrell, Jeffrey C. "A Discussion of Intentional Incarnational Integration in Relational Psychodynamic Psychotherapy." *Journal of Psychology & Christianity* 6 no.2 (2007) 159–165.

Torrance, James B. *Worship, Community and the Triune God of Grace*. Downers Grove, IL: IVP Academic, 1996.

Trueman, Carl R. "Luther's theology of the cross." *New Horizons* (October 2005). http://www.theologian.org.uk/churchhistory/lutherstheologyofthecross.html

Volf, Miroslav. *Exclusion and Embrace: A Theological Exploration of Identity, Otherness and Reconciliation*. Nashville: Abingdon, 1996.

Waldegrave, Charles, et al. *Just Therapy—A Journey: A Collection of Papers from the Just Therapy Team, New Zealand*. Adelaide, Australia: Dulwich Centre, 2003.

White, Michael. *Maps of Narrative Practice*. New York: Norton Professional, 2007.

Wright, Tom. *Surprised by Hope*. London: SPCK, 2007.

SECTION TWO

Stories of Counseling Practice

4

Uniqueness and Belonging
Healing through Relationship

JAYME KOERSELMAN

This chapter presents a description of how the analogy of the members of the Trinity relating with uniqueness and a unified belonging has shaped my thinking and practice as a psychotherapist. I will briefly outline Christian trinitarian thought and how I understand this to integrate with philosophical and psychological ideas of relationship. In particular, I will explore how the dynamics of power appear in relationships. Based on how power is configured, relationships can be used to empower people to create a relationship of presence, vulnerability, and trust, or it can result in a battle for control causing isolation and a loss of both "self" and "other." I believe the ideas of social trinitarianism are especially relevant in understanding how this occurs in a counseling relationship. Authors such as Grenz, Volf, Zizioulas, and Gunton have argued that it is vital to see that God is a social being and that each member of the Trinity relates to one another with particularity and inclusiveness. Taking these ideas forward, Balswick, King, and Reimer suggest that this is central to a theological anthropology and how we were created to develop as human beings within loving "reciprocating relationships."[1] These insights mirror the recent findings within psychology that speak to the importance of healthy attachments and how our interactions with others have the power to shape, and change our development.[2] While the social trinitarian analogy has come under significant critique, it has allowed for much more constructive conversation between theology,

---

1. Balswick, et al., *Reciprocating Self*.
2. Siegel, *Developing Mind*; Thompson, *Anatomy of the Soul*.

philosophy, and psychology because of the renewed relational focus. Finally, to show how this integration has developed into my theory of practice, I will discuss the importance of using the interpersonal process of the therapeutic relationship as a vehicle for change.

IT ALL STARTS WITH RELATIONSHIP

Even for Christians, the concept of the trinitarian relationship between Father, Son, and Spirit can be befuddling. Recently, when I was trying to explain this rich theological concept to my five-year-old son, I asked myself how a rational person could believe, let alone explain, the notion of one substantive God in three distinct persons. Growing up in the Christian tradition, the Trinity was one of those difficult concepts that I naively accepted as part of my faith without much contemplation. It was only when I trained as a therapist at a graduate school intent on grappling with the integration of theology with psychology that the concept started to be transformed into a complex yet foundational tenet of relationality. This learning continued as I moved into teaching counseling at a similar institution which focused even more on these things.

From my study, it became evident that the God we are made to reflect is truly relational. Each member of the Trinity has a mutual and reciprocating love and acceptance for the other and lacks any fear of being overpowered. We similarly are made to connect and relate to others and ourselves in this way. I suggest that this yearning to connect is in our DNA and we can no more rid ourselves of this than our need for oxygen or water. Unfortunately in our current world, I believe that relationships often result in heartache and pain, rather than empowerment and thriving. When this is the case, we tend to respond by trying to relieve the pain and protect ourselves by gaining power over the situation. Instead of entering back into the vulnerability of relationships, we try to take care of our needs *alone* through other means. These means may include seeking escape through addiction, numbing our desire and emotion, controlling or dismissing others, or even creating a facade of success that masks our shame, anxiety, and emptiness. These problematic ways of coping are often what drive people to seek out therapeutic help.

While these are definite areas of concern for any therapist or client, the foundation of these problems is in our difficulty relating to others. Many therapists (and clients) are focused on solving the symptoms or "presenting problems" in their lives. The aim is to reduce the depression or anxiety, eliminate problem behaviors or phobias, deal with trauma and its effects, or become more comfortable with oneself and one's desires. The focus on these things may reduce the symptoms but, much like a doctor who only treats the symptoms of the disease and not the disease itself, the root cause may go untreated. I would argue that the root cause of distress lies in the yearning for close relationship and these needs and desires not being met. It is this relationship hunger that can drive people towards therapy. This also seems to reinforce the common western idea that one of the main goals in life should be finding a method which allows us to be self-sufficient and without pain or difficulty. Contrary to this is Jesus' greatest commandment which speaks to a different goal born out of a relational invitation—to love God, one another, and ourselves.[3] His command reminds us that our purpose and fulfillment comes in the form of connection with others and in turn ourselves.

A CORE DILEMMA

In my teaching roles, I often refer to my conviction that the core dilemma people face as humans is to have a clear sense of both "self" and "other" in our relationships; that is, not to diminish or over-emphasize either. It seems that we constantly wrestle with our desire to be valued and distinctly seen while *also* being part of a caring community. We want intimate connections with others, but the fear of being rejected and vulnerable is overwhelming. We want relationship, but we also want control. In other words, we want our personal freedom and independence from others, but we also want to ease the loneliness that can seem ever-present.

To manage this primary dilemma, I observe that what often happens in our relationships is an erosion and eventual destruction of the self and/or other. The differences that make us separate and unique individuals are either ignored or forcibly homogenized and the natural interdependence we share becomes severed. As a result, we seem to create hierarchies of power to feel in control and work to be as independent as possible. What we are left with are severed relationships and the "most basic human loneliness that threatens us and is so hard to face."[4] In Martin Buber's well-known terms, the "I" (me) and "Thou" (the other) become diminished "its," objects to be used, rather than a subject to be known.[5]

---

3. Matt 22:36–40, NIV.
4. Nouwen, *Reaching Out*, 26.
5. Buber and Kaufmann, *I and Thou*.

To describe these dynamics, I often use a Dr. Seuss story about the Sneetches.[6] As the story goes, there are two kinds of Sneetches, some with stars upon their bellies and some with none. The Sneetches with stars believe they are better and more important until Sylvester McMonkey McBean comes to town with a machine that will put a star on anyone's belly for a price. This, of course, causes much confusion as everyone starts to have stars and there is now no way to distinguish between the two groups. Luckily, McBean has a machine that will take stars off of their bellies for an even heftier price. McBean ends up swindling the Sneetches out of all their money as they alternately add and remove their stars. Finally, the Sneetches come to their senses and realize their folly, ultimately learning an invaluable lesson "that Sneetches are Sneetches, and no kind of Sneetch is the best on the beaches."[7]

The story reveals how each group's sense of self and other becomes warped. Each group struggles with inferiority, and consequently the "other" becomes a sort of enemy to be overpowered in some way. Hierarchies of power are formed to try to stay in control, and in this case stars become the way of measuring whether the self or other is inferior or superior. Those with the stars mask their own sense of inferiority by making something they naturally have as the defining value factor and viewing the others without stars as inferior. Those who don't have stars buy into this view that they have an inferior self and work to try to attain value by what the group in power has defined as valuable. Both view the other as an enemy and two groups are formed, an "us" and a "them." One group looks to uniformity, believing it will provide community and belonging, making what they perceive as a flawed uniqueness irrelevant. The other, in turn, depends solely on their uniqueness to define their worth and exert power while dismissing any notion of a unified belonging with others. Volf describes this as exclusion, and argues that both distance and belonging are essential as "belonging without distance destroys . . . but distance without belonging isolates."[8] He argues that without distance we try to shape everyone to be like ourselves through assimilation and without belonging we simply eliminate them from our world because they don't fit into our schema (this parallels clinical definitions of how narcissism functions[9]). As the trinitarian analogy I introduced earlier suggests, without both uniqueness and belonging happening

---

6. Seuss, *Sneetches*.
7. Ibid., 26.
8. Volf, *Exclusion and Embrace*, 50.
9. Payson, *Wizard of Oz*.

simultaneously and reciprocally, we lose a clear sense of both the self and the other.

One could argue this is at the root of the fall of humanity in Genesis 3. The serpent initiates the erosion of the "other" by changing the title he uses for God in his approach to Eve. In the ancient near Eastern world, names were significant with regard to a person's character. In the opening description given by the narrator in the first verse of Genesis 3, the term YHWH (LORD God) is used (interestingly, it is remarking on the craftiness of the serpent YHWH had made). Throughout the Jewish scriptures, YHWH is used to connote God's personal presence and involvement. The serpent, however, calls God by the title Elohim which is associated with God as the powerful one who creates and judges. While both titles are used often through the Jewish and Christian scriptures, the shift in focus from the present and relational God to the one who powers over is significant, and subtly reminds Eve and the reader of God's power and authority rather than his loving desire for relationship. Immediately for Eve, the communal relationship of belonging is changed into an adversarial threat. Eve is complicit in adopting this title in the rest of the pericope.

The serpent continues to question Eve's connection to and knowing of God by the phrase *"Did God really say . . . "*[10] Eve's memory of who God is even seems to fade in her amended recollection of God's command to not eat the fruit, as she adds the prohibitive phrase "and you must not touch it" which does not appear in the initial command of Genesis 2:16–17. These changes in how Eve views God and herself are furthered when the serpent tells her that if she eats the fruit, she too "will be like God, knowing good and evil."[11] The serpent suggests that Adam and Eve's uniqueness compared to God is a defect; uniqueness becomes inferior. At this point, the reader can almost feel Eve's sense of entitlement and belief that God (*Elohim*) is an enemy trying to keep her from power and knowledge or even just a good-looking and nutritious meal![12] The serpent's seed of doubt grows to fear as the intention of God and whether he is loving or excluding through his withholding of the fruit is questioned. The couple's response to this fear of inferiority is to try to gain power through nullifying any difference between themselves and God. Their choice only further disconnects them from their own identity as beloved (destruction of self) and belonging with God.[13] I

---

10. Gen 3:1, NIV.

11. Gen 3:5, NIV.

12. Gen 3:6, NIV.

13. This is important to note, as whenever the "other" is eroded our own sense of self is also damaged, and vice versa.

believe their story is representative of what we do as humans today when we too choose the tree of knowledge in hopes of gaining power and safety rather than the vulnerability of mutual and authentic relationships with God and others.

THE RECIPROCATING LOVE OF THE TRINITY

The relationality associated with the social analogy of the Trinity stands in stark contrast to this vying for power in order to protect our individualism at all costs. The relationship between Father, Son, and Spirit is one of perfect love which we are told in 1 John 4:18 drives out any fear. Because of the perfect nature of shared love, the aspects of uniqueness and belonging co-exist among each member of the Trinity, and any fear of who has power is precluded. King describes this quality as reciprocity which is "the glue that holds the relational polarities of uniqueness and unity together."[14] Many examples of this can be found in the gospel of John where love, power, authority, words, and life itself are reciprocally shared between Father and Son. In the context of love, there is no loss of the distinctness of the members or the roles of each. Nor is there any doubt about the kind of unity and oneness represented by Jesus repeatedly saying that the Father is in Him and He in the Father[15] and that they "are one."[16] This indwelling of one another is extended to the Spirit whom the Father sends in the name of the Son to teach and be an advocate on behalf of the Father and Son. The term *perichoresis* is often used to describe a mutual interpenetration or indwelling that is characterized by each member existing "with one another, for one another and in one another. They exist in one another because they mutually give each other space for full unfolding."[17] It is precisely because they are in a unified relationship that their particularities are revealed, and these particularities in turn contribute to their unified purpose. Gunton likens the unified relationship to love and the particularities to freedom and contends that these two qualities should be exemplified in all social systems.[18] He goes on to say:

> The theology of God conceived to exist in the interrelationship of persons in which neither the one nor the many has priority over the other provides an alternative to the two poles of modern

---

14. Balswick, et al., *Reciprocating Self*, 35.
15. John 14:11; 17:21, NIV.
16. John 17:11, NIV.
17. Moltmann, *Coming of God*, 298.
18. Gunton, *Promise of Trinitarian Theology*.

political thought, individualism, which elevates the many over the one, and collectivism, which does the reverse.[19]

While we can't presume to think human relating can be an equivalent to the trinitarian relationship, the Trinity does give us a model that can inform our therapeutic practice, especially in the areas of power, individuation, and belonging.

A RELATIONAL TURN

Interestingly, the renewed focus on the social aspects of the Trinity has occurred parallel to an "intersubjective turn" from individualism to relationality in some areas of philosophy and psychology.[20] For those of us that live in a "first world" or "western" society, individualism has been an undergirding principal which guides many of our actions, ideals, and ontological assumptions. Starting with the dualism of Greek philosophers and cemented by René Descartes' famous axiom "I think, therefore I am," most modern ontological theories and culture focus on the mind and conclude that our conscious (or unconscious) thoughts and emotions propel our actions and make us who we are. From this viewpoint, while we are capable of relating to one another, it is as two individually separate, autonomous entities that interact the way two billiard balls knocking together would. This individualistic philosophy also influenced the initial development of psychotherapy and continues to do so regardless of modality. From Freud's psychoanalysis to Rogers's self-actualization to the cognitive behaviorism of Skinner, Ellis, and Beck, most psychotherapeutic theory assumes the goal is a self-regulated, self-aware, self-determining individual that is free from problematic symptoms or neurotic thinking and behavior.

Early in the 20th century, philosophers such as Heidegger, Bakhtin, and Buber initiated what has become known as the intersubjective turn. Their ideas moved away from the notion that people develop separately from others, and instead worked upon the premise of our existence being based in encounter. Mearns and Cooper described this important ontological change as "we do not exist as individuals first and then come together with others to form relationships," but rather "we exist with others first, and only after that come to develop some notion of individuality or separateness."[21] Soon after this philosophical shift, early psychoanalysts such as Fairbairn,

---

19. Ibid., 171.
20. For a detailed discussion, see Mearns and Cooper, *Working at Relational Depth*.
21. Ibid., 5.

Sullivan, and Winnicott set about exploring how interpersonal relationships effect development and how they might be both the cause and remedy of our problems. Much of their work went unnoticed until the later part of the century when it was rediscovered and influenced the relational movement within psychoanalysis. Sometimes referred to as a "relational turn"[22] this change focused more on the therapeutic relationship and its interactions and less on an individual's symptoms, history, and drives/motivations.

These developments in psychoanalytic theory were paralleled with the start of transformative studies in attachment theory developed by John Bowlby and Mary Ainsworth. Ainsworth's "Strange Situation" study of how human infants formed relationships and dealt with the stress of separation[23] was the start of a significant amount of research that has suggested that children not only need care and attention but *interaction and communication* with others in order for healthy development.[24] Studies in neuroscience also support the relational thesis, and have shown that even our physical well-being is affected by our interpersonal relationships. Cardiovascular function, sleep and hormonal rhythms, immunity, breathing, and emotional states are all influenced by the brains' limbic system interacting with others which is called limbic regulation.[25] The connection between brain science and relationality has been taken up by many including Dan Siegel and Allan Schore who developed Interpersonal Neurobiology (IPNB). IPNB posits that our brains are continually changing and growing (neuroplasticity) through our experiences and that interacting with an empathic, understanding, and regulating therapist actually changes the brain. Biological science, like theology, is showing that while we have our own individual selves, we are meant to be in connected reciprocating relationships and greatly impacted by them.

All of these theological, philosophical, and psychological ideas are at the heart of the style of psychotherapy that has shaped my own theory of practice. The importance of the therapeutic relationship and specifically how power is used to encourage both individual particularity and a mutual belonging has become a primary interest of mine. Many therapeutic approaches focus around resolving symptoms or personal issues through insight, information, or certain techniques (cognitive restructuring, meditation, trauma resolution, etc.). While these are useful techniques, I believe it is essential to pay close attention to and use the therapeutic relationship

22. Mitchell, *Relationality*; Reynolds, "How Does Therapy Cure?"
23. Salter, Ainsworth, and Bell, "Attachment, Exploration, and Separation."
24. Siegel, *Developing Mind*; Stern, *Interpersonal World*.
25. Lewis et al., *General Theory of Love*.

itself. The purpose of this is twofold. First, if we view the therapeutic relationship as a social microcosm,[26] the interpersonal problems of the client outside of therapy will eventually surface inside and can be explored. Secondly, and most importantly, once these interpersonal difficulties surface, the *experience* (rather than just insight) of a loving and reciprocal therapeutic relationship provides a corrective emotional response[27] or "moments of meeting"[28] that provide the foundation of any effective change in therapy. Eventually, if this happens consistently in therapy, a client is able to transfer this way of being to his or her outside relationships.[29]

THERAPEUTIC RELATIONSHIP: EXPLORING THE "SPACE IN-BETWEEN"

The focus and discussion of the relational "space in-between" therapist and client has been variously described. Examples include the "here and now,"[30] relational encounter,[31] and interpersonal process.[32] One common theme in these discussions is how the therapist is not just a neutral/professional role or learned advisor, but a human being with unique differences and styles of relating that intersect with those of the client. The therapeutic process involves acknowledging and exploring both the client and therapist's individual differences and styles of relating (particularity) within the context of how they contribute to the relational encounter (belonging). When both the particularity of self/other and the reciprocal sense of belonging are valued, I find that it transforms the experience and use of power for both therapist and client.

Throughout the development of psychotherapy, there has been a consensus that a good therapeutic alliance must be present in order for a successful therapeutic outcome. An example is Rogers' (1957) influential idea that the core conditions of empathy, congruence, and unconditional positive regard need to be present so the client is free to grow and change.[33] While Rogers moved towards more of a relational therapy, especially later in his life, his ideas still focused on the therapist providing these core conditions

26. Yalom, *Theory and Practice*; Yalom, *Gift of Therapy*.
27. Mangis, "Kicking the Patient."
28. Lyons-Ruth et al., "Implicit Relational Knowing."
29. Teyber, *Interpersonal Process in Therapy*, 28.
30. Yalom, *Gift of Therapy*.
31. Mearns and Cooper, *Working at Relational Depth*.
32. Teyber, *Interpersonal Process in Therapy*.
33. Rogers, "Necessary and Sufficient."

to the client while exploring the client's individual feelings and experiences in life. The Rogerian therapist was to understand and experience the client's world and authentically encourage self-development through autonomy and self-direction. From the perspective of my commitment to therapeutic presence, the problem with Rogers' approach is that it allows the therapist to stand outside of the discussion. Because of this, the work still has the feel of the "blank screen" approach of classical psychoanalysis. While it may not be as dominant, the individual particularities of the therapist (or the connection or need for it) are not typically considered, and a power hierarchy that positions the client beneath and the therapist as "off-limits" is set up.

The potential danger I see with this stance is that it does not consider how the therapist is continually impacting the client in the encounter itself. Wachtel speaks to this from the therapist's perspective cautioning:

> If the therapist is not alert to her influence on what is being observed, she denies or minimizes it, then it is difficult to take it into account, to understand that she is not really observing "the patient," but the patient *in relation to a particular kind of interpersonal relationship with a particular individual who has particular qualities and is responding to the patient's own qualities in particular ways* (italics original).[34]

Even the roles themselves of "therapist" and "client" can change the interaction and what becomes the normative way of being for both. The roles can diminish the personhood of the other and change the encounter from the I-Thou potential, to an it-it. In practice, I find that if both people rigidly keep to only their "professional" relationship, it reduces the effectiveness and can even mislead the therapeutic direction. As one client of mine initially said, "I view you primarily as a therapist performing a role in my life, not really as a person." As we explored this, he realized that viewing me this way protected him from feeling the full impact of my reactions, emotions, or thoughts, and so kept him from the full vulnerability of sharing himself with another human. He also realized it kept him from realizing the full potential of healing his shame within our relationship. He was much more comfortable putting me in a neutral "detective" role whose job it was to analyze a problem and give clear suggestions on how to change it. Later, when he began to view me as a real person, a scary and sobering thought occurred to him: that I knew his life with intimate detail, his inner and mostly hidden world of desires, fears, and vulnerabilities, in a way that no one in his life, not even his wife, did. To view me more as a real person and not just a role, changed the influence I was able to have on his reshaping of identity. Prior

---

34. Wachtel, *Relational Theory*, 17.

to this, my statements of empathy and care for him were dismissed because they were assumed to be simply part of the professional role he believed I was playing. If he chose rather to receive my presence and view me as a knowing and caring human being, it meant letting my words and presence matter more which for him was extremely vulnerable, but ultimately more healing.

When people choose to relate vulnerably, power and the possibility of shame are also more present. These vulnerable moments are when one of us is seen by the other in a way that feels exposing, risky, and out of control; we have given our power to the other and await his or her response. Will they see our fragility and desire to connect and respond similarly, or will they use the power to elevate themselves over us through judgment and shame? Brene Brown, argues that shame is the most powerful and master emotion.[35] She defines shame as the fear of disconnection due to a perceived core flaw in our being (ironically this fear of disconnection is often what creates it as we move away to protect ourselves). Because shame can be so powerful, it often dictates how we are in relationships. In defense of our shame, we move away from others through the masks of competence, strength, and control. If really challenged, we use the power of shame to blame others when faced with our own vulnerability or failures. The reciprocal power of empathy, care, and ultimately love which draws us together turns into the isolating power of control, shame, and apathy.

Based on all of this, I assume that from the first moment a client makes contact, vulnerability, power, and shame are all at work. Most clients will be feeling quite vulnerable and shameful initially because of whatever struggle brings them. There can be the immediate feeling of being "less than" and the need of someone who is more wise, stable, and has life figured out, which moves the power balance immediately to the therapist. This often is one of the first inherent difficulties of therapy, but I believe can also be one of the most healing. Most clients have had plenty of experiences where this relational power has been harmful, and these continually reinforce their shame and inclination to hide, blame, and disconnect. This soon becomes an expected occurrence in relationships from which the idea of transference originates. The true healing of therapy comes from what Alexander[36] first called a "corrective emotional experience." This happens when the therapist provides a different and potentially healing response in the moments a client is expecting a repetition of old relational patterns.[37] We all develop

---

35. Brown, *Gifts of Imperfection*.
36. Alexander and French, *Psychoanalytic Therapy*.
37. Teyber, *Interpersonal Process in Therapy*; Yalom, *Theory and Practice*.

a relational lens for how we interpret the actions, feelings, and unspoken thoughts of others by what we have experienced in the past. Our brains anticipate and interpret future experiences through the lens of past experiences. As this lens becomes more entrenched, we are prone to interpret most relational interactions according to what we expect and have experienced rather than what may actually be occurring. If our experiences have taught us that vulnerability will be used against us to disempower and shame, our natural tendency will be to expect this in all relationships and to defend against it.

What takes place in a successful therapeutic relationship is a reworking of this lens through corrective emotional experiences.[38] This is a process that starts with paying close attention to what Yalom[39] calls the "here and now" or the present interactions between the therapist and client in the therapeutic hour. I find that much can be learned by how the client interacts in the normal course of therapy *and by how I respond*. I emphasize this last part because it is vital to how power is experienced and used in the relationship. As I stated above, the role of therapist almost always comes with the privilege of power especially at the beginning stages. It can be tempting to withdraw into the safety of the role through analyzing and "fixing" the client's issues or ways of being and forget Wachtel's reminder; that the client interaction is with us and we have a significant role in the client's way of being. We bring our own lens of relating to the interaction which, like the client, is a mixture of what we have experienced in the past and the current moment. This is one of the reasons Yalom says personal psychotherapy is the most important part of psychotherapy training.[40] He goes on to say that the most significant tool the therapist has is the therapist's own self. If there isn't a good understanding of why we feel or respond the way we do in relationships (our own particularity), we will not be able to decipher the client's or the interpersonal space-in-between (belonging) that is so vital to working in this way.

It is at this point that the theological ideas discussed above can really inform clinical work more directly. The call of love is for the therapist to be appropriately vulnerable in the therapeutic relationship. Disclosure of the here and now brings the therapist's emotions, thoughts, and reactions into the permissible realm of discussion and can humanize the therapist from the blank screen analyst role. If framed appropriately, process comments

---

38. Accordingly, when the therapy is stagnant or conflicted, one of the first questions to ask is if a past problematic relational pattern is being enacted.
39. Yalom, *Gift of Therapy*; Yalom, *Theory and Practice*.
40. Yalom, *Gift of Therapy*, 40.

also open up the possibility of both parties in dialogue together formulating ideas about the interaction and relationship. The particularities of each are honored as well as forming a sense of belonging within the relationship. Personal disclosure has historically been discouraged in therapy but Yalom argues that to have an authentic encounter means sharing something of yourself especially when questioned and that not sharing can hinder everything else in the session.[41] The American Psychological Association also listed therapist self-disclosure as "promising and probably effective" as part of its empirically based study on effective therapy relationships.[42] Too often, our role as therapist can seduce us into a lack of vulnerability; we hide behind a professional non-emotive stance.[43] This is especially true because it intersects with our human propensity for being in control and hoarding personal power in order to protect ourselves. If we choose this way, I argue, we will never authentically connect with clients and our work will stagnate and lack meaningful change for both the client and ourselves. If we instead have the courage to choose vulnerability, the individual power that separates and divides is transformed into a mutual power of presence.

Paul's metaphor of the body in 1 Corinthians 12 is a poignant picture of how we all are unique yet connected. Paul's argument is that diversity is required, for "if the whole body were an eye, where would the sense of hearing be?"[44] Without difference and uniqueness, we wouldn't function. What's more, belonging cannot be questioned as each individual part is a member of the whole even if that part tries to deny it, "Now if the foot should say, 'Because I am not a hand, I do not belong to the body,' it would not for that reason stop being part of the body"[45] (Paul even repeats this in the next verse suggesting it is worth reflection). We are secure in our belonging no matter our particularities. In fact, we belong *because of* our particularities, each having a different part to play.

CONCLUSION

In summary, as therapists that work from a Christian worldview, we have the opportunity to invite our clients to experience an empowering love that cherishes difference and assures belonging. While much of this chapter has

41. Ibid., 90–93.

42. Norcross, ed., *Psychotherapy Relationships*.

43. I am not suggesting professionalism is not important and appropriate, only that it needs to be combined with vulnerability.

44. 1 Cor 12:17, NIV.

45. 1 Cor 12:15, NIV.

outlined how our therapeutic presence, based on the social analogy of the Trinity, is the vehicle for change, I would be remiss not to say that relational healing is ultimately possible because of the presence of the Trinity. Jesus' incarnational act of becoming human and giving up his own life and power in order to invite us into the presence of the triune God is what allows us to be vehicles of this presence for our clients. Through Jesus and in the power of the Holy Spirit, God seeks us out in our brokenness and forever solves our core dilemma of particularity and belonging. We are invited (not forced which suggests our particularity is important) to join the presence of the Trinity with the promise that nothing we do or reveal will ever change our belonging. Andrei Rublev was the painter of a famous icon called "The Trinity" which shows three figures sitting at a communal table. There is an open spot at this table waiting for us to join the intimate circle of relationship. This to me is the opportunity therapy can provide for both therapist and client. In being a part of the healing and transformative love, we are empowered to invite others to join the ever-expanding circle of belonging.

References

Alexander, Franz, and Thomas Morton French. *Psychoanalytic Therapy: Principles and Application*. Lincoln: University of Nebraska Press, 1980.

Balswick, Jack, et al. *The Reciprocating Self: Human Development in Theological Perspective*. Downers Grove: InterVarsity, 2005.

Brown, Brene. *The Gifts of Imperfection: Let Go of Who You Think You're Supposed to Be and Embrace Who You Are*. Center City, Minn: Hazelden, 2010.

Buber, Martin, and Walter Kaufmann. *I and Thou*. New York: Scribner, 1970.

Gunton, Colin E. *The Promise of Trinitarian Theology*. 2nd ed. London: T&T Clark, 2003.

Lewis, Thomas, et al. *A General Theory of Love*. Toronto: Random House Inc., 2000.

Lyons-Ruth, Karlen, et al. "Implicit Relational Knowing: Its Role in Development and Psychoanalytic Treatment." *Infant Mental Health Journal* 19 no. 3 (1998) 282–289.

Mangis, Michael W. "Kicking the Patient: Immediacy in the Consulting Room." *Journal of Psychology & Theology* 35 no.1 (2007) 43–51.

Mearns, Dave, and Mick Cooper. *Working at Relational Depth in Counseling and Psychotherapy*. London: Sage, 2005.

Mitchell, Stephen A. *Relationality: From Attachment to Intersubjectivity (Relational Perspectives Book)*. New edition. Routledge, 2003.

Moltmann, Jürgen. *The Coming of God: Christian Eschatology*. 1st Fortress Press ed. Minneapolis: Fortress, 1996.

Norcross, John C., ed. *Psychotherapy Relationships That Work: Therapist Contributions and Responsiveness to Patients*. New York: Oxford University Press, 2002.

Nouwen, Henri J. M. *Reaching Out: The Three Movements of the Spiritual Life*. Garden City, N.Y: Image, 1986.

Payson, Eleanor. *The Wizard of Oz and Other Narcissists: Coping with the One-Way Relationship in Work, Love, and Family*. Julian Day, 2002.

Reynolds, Robert. "How Does Therapy Cure? The Relational Turn in Psychotherapy." *Counseling, Psychotherapy, and Health* 3 no.2 (2007) 127–50.

Rogers, Carl R. "The Necessary and Sufficient Conditions of Therapeutic Personality Change." *Journal of Consulting Psychology* 21 no.2 (1957) 95–103.

Salter Ainsworth, Mary D., and Silvia M. Bell. "Attachment, Exploration, and Separation: Illustrated by the Behavior of One-Year-Olds in a Strange Situation." *Child Development* (1970) 49–67.

Seuss. *The Sneetches, and Other Stories*. New York: Random House, 1961.

Siegel, Daniel J. *The Developing Mind: How Relationships and the Brain Interact to Shape Who We Are.* New York: Guilford, 2001.

Stern, Daniel N. *The Interpersonal World of the Infant: A View from Psychoanalysis and Developmental Psychology.* New York: Basic, 1985.

Teyber, Edward. *Interpersonal Process in Therapy: An Integrative Model.* 6th ed. Australia: Brooks/Cole Cengage Learning, 2011.

Thompson, Curt. *Anatomy of the Soul: Surprising Connections between Neuroscience and Spiritual Practices That Can Transform Your Life and Relationships.* Carol Stream, IL: Salt River, 2010.

Volf, Miroslav. *Exclusion and Embrace: A Theological Exploration of Identity, Otherness, and Reconciliation.* Nashville: Abingdon, 1996.

Wachtel, Paul L. *Relational Theory and the Practice of Psychotherapy.* New York: Guilford, 2010.

Yalom, Irvin D. *The Gift of Therapy.* New York: HarperCollins, 2002.

———. *The Theory and Practice of Group Psychotherapy.* Basic, 1995.

5

Designed for and by Love
Working with Families from an Attachment and Interpersonal Neurobiology Framework

Dr. Ruth McConnell

In this chapter I present an overview of my parent consulting work incorporating research from attachment theory and interpersonal neurobiology framed within a trinitarian, incarnational, theological anthropology. My original training as a counseling psychologist, in Aberdeen, Scotland, has been further supplemented by my training with Gordon Neufeld,[1] a Vancouver-based psychologist who uses an attachment-based developmental paradigm to understand parent/caregiver-child relational dynamics.

Attachment theory and interpersonal neurobiology can, I believe, offer helpful insights into human relationality. Before I address these fields of research, I will present a trinitarian, incarnational theological anthropology as the ontological foundation to the work that I do with clients.

A TRINITARIAN INCARNATIONAL THEOLOGICAL ANTHROPOLOGY

Trinitarian, incarnational theological anthropology offers insights into what it means to be made in the image of a triune relational God, *imago Dei*, providing a basis for understanding love, an appreciation of the distinctiveness and particularity of persons, as well as their relatedness and embodiment in communion or community. In Gunton's words, "to be human is to be

---

1. Neufeld and Mate, *Hold On*; Neufeld, "Power to Parent Parts 1–3."

created in and for relationship with divine and human others."[2] Boff highlights the relational communion found in the Trinity:

> For there to be true communion there must be direct and immediate relationships, eye to eye, face to face, heart to heart. The result of mutual surrender and reciprocal communion is community. Community results from personal relationships in which each is accepted as he or she is, each opens to the other and gives the best of himself or herself.[3]

Boff refers to the Trinity's mutuality and reciprocity, in terms of what I understand to be a non-judgmental, emotionally safe attachment, as well as adding an embodied dimension.

A trinitarian incarnational anthropology celebrates the uniqueness of persons where "self is never lost in the face of the other."[4] As Moltmann explains, "the three divine Persons exist with one another, for one another and in one another. They exist in one another because they mutually give each other space for full unfolding."[5] This mystery of unique particularity as well as mutual indwelling of the persons of the trinity has been described as the Greek word, *perichoresis;* it describes the reciprocity of giving and receiving found in the perfect and eternal trinitarian relationship.[6] The word *perichoresis* has been translated as a circle dance,[7] or the mutual interpenetration of relationships.[8] Rohr goes so far as to contend that "the unending flow of giving and receiving between Father, Son, and Spirit is the pattern of reality. God is not only a dancer, but the Dance itself! We as Christians are invited to participate in rhythms of this dance of New Creation."[9]

When we take these suggestions as the basis of our anthropology, we can also see that we are made in the image of a relational God who characterizes perfect love (absence of fear and defensiveness), respect and reciprocity, glad submission, mutual deference, and joyful intimacy;[10] who both wills the good of the others and is humbly open to her influence too. These characteristics are reflected within a good counseling relationship

---

2. Gunton, *One, Three, Many*, 222.
3. Boff, *Trinity and Society*, 3.
4. Balswick et al., *Reciprocating Self*.
5. Moltmann, *Coming of God*, 298.
6. Goff, "Measuring the Clergy/laity."
7. Rohr and Morell, *Divine Dance*.
8. Kruger, *Great Dance*.
9. Rohr and Morell, *Divine Dance*.
10. Shaw as cited by Seamands, *Ministry*, 35.

and a healthy adult-child attachment, for the full unfolding of each person's growth into wholeness.

Trinitarian anthropology values the doctrine of the incarnation which emphasizes holism, including the role of embodiment (our physiological and mental structures) as well as our relational nature (including our desire for meaning making and storied identities). This trinitarian emphasis on the incarnation, in my opinion, can be applied to counseling practice with the aid of insights from inter-personal neuroscience as well as attachment theory, which places the desire for relationship, or attachment hunger,[11] at the core of our embodied humanity. This can be particularly relevant when we reflect on the role our embodied selves play in the emotional healing experienced in therapy. Participation in the trinitarian life has an effect in and on our embodied existence; I would posit that this is mirrored in the effect that attachment has on our neurological development. In counseling, especially, there is relational potential to heal wounded minds, at the embodied level, involving brain process (i.e., mirror neurons, synaptic connections, and neural networks) as well as at the emotional and relational level. Could this be one way the incarnational reality of the Trinity appears in the counseling encounter? Could this be one way we get to participate in the Divine Dance of the Trinity? I posit that whenever there is neuronal healing through secure attachment (healthy love), this is the work of the Trinity and a movement towards our true humanity in Christ. As the Apostle Paul says, where there is love, there is God, for God is love.[12]

Having established that trinitarian incarnational anthropology offers an analogy of persons centered on loving reciprocal relations between embodied individuals, I will now highlight insights from attachment theory and interpersonal neurobiology which resonate with the view that the Trinity invites us to participate in relational lives that are shaped by cruciform, other-centered giving and receiving love.[13] I believe that the Trinity offers more than just a helpful template for humans to emulate if they want to love well, it also includes participating in the divine nature of the Triune God, in whom we live and move and have our being.[14]

---

11. Neufeld, "Power to Parent 2." Neufeld has coined the term "attachment hunger" to describe the instinctual basis of our emotional and psychological need to connect; it follows similar laws of nature to natural physical hunger.

12. 1 John 4:7, KJV.

13. Volf, "Social Program."

14. Acts 17:28, KJV.

ATTACHMENT THEORY

Now let us turn our attention to attachment theory and how it may fit within this outlined theological anthropology. Attachment theory has become a crucial paradigm for the study of parent-child and adult romantic relationships,[15] offering a scientifically grounded basis for understanding how we become who we are as relational beings.[16] To put it more poetically, attachment theory highlights, "the primal dance of finding ourselves in another, and another in ourselves."[17] We can hear echoes of the divine dance metaphor here. It provides a powerful account of the formation of relational bonds that ensure our physical survival and psychological security throughout our lifespan.[18] Attachment theory has also led to new perspectives on thinking about and approaching our clients' spirituality.[19]

Attachment theory provides insights in to the suffering, vulnerabilities, and common feelings like anxiety, anger, grief, and sadness that our clients bring to us.[20] It has an exceptionally strong empirical base, providing a lifespan developmental framework often absent in current treatment models.[21] I have found that attachment theory has helped me bridge the gap between research and practice as it underscores the centrality of relationships not just for healthy human well-being, but also the core relational dynamics central in therapeutic healing. It focuses on the need for physical and emotional proximity to an emotionally attuned caregiver in childhood, and a romantic partner in adulthood[22] who provides a sense of security and a "safe base" from which to explore and emerge into the world.

A caregiver's sensitivity to a child's distress appears to be a significant factor in determining the "attachment style" that the infant develops,[23] identified as secure (representing about 70 per cent of the general population), and three insecure patterns—avoidant, anxious, and disorganized (representing approximately 10 percent each).[24] Insecure attachment styles have been understood to be "survival strategies" to adapt to suboptimal caregiv-

---

15. Johnson, "Attachment Perspective"; Holmes and Johnson, "Adult Attachment."
16. Robert, *Becoming Attached*.
17. Saltman, "Attachment Theory."
18. Bowlby, *Attachment and Loss*; Bowlby, *Secure Base: Parent-Child*; Lewis et al., *General Theory*.
19. Hall, "Psychoanalysis," 14.
20. Wallin, *Attachment in Psychotherapy*.
21. Connors, "Attachment Theory."
22. Finkel and Eastwick, "Attachment and Pairbonding."
23. Weinfield et al., "Individual Differences."
24. Ainsworth et al., *Patterns*.

ing environments; however, they can have an adverse effect on adjustment in later relationships, increasing one's vulnerability to psychopathology.[25] According to Bowlby, the therapeutic relationship can be construed as an attachment relationship; effective therapy can repair early attachment failures by engendering "earned security."[26] He conceptualized the major goal of therapy to help the client move from insecure to more secure attachment by providing a "corrective emotional experience."[27] Since Bowlby's seminal paper,[28] authors from a range of different therapeutic schools have developed these ideas further but, to date, there have been no systematic reviews of how attachment theory can inform the practice of psychotherapy.[29]

One of the tenets of attachment theory is that attachment hunger, or our longing to experience a deep emotional connection to an "other," is universal and as valid as physical hunger and as vital for our psychological well-being as food is for our physical wellbeing.[30] Rather than being a pathological childhood dependency that we outgrow, the desire to be attached in relationships is normal and remains with us throughout our lives.[31] This inherent dependency also set us up for vulnerable wounding. Bowlby argued that more universally than the trauma of separation and loss, it was the ongoing, everyday interactions of children and their parents that shaped their psychological development.[32]

Another important principle in attachment theory is the concept of Internal Working Models (IWM), or mental representations/schemas, which develop from early relationships, guiding our feelings, thoughts, and expectations in later relationships.[33] If a child is securely attached to his or her caregiver then his or her IWM would predispose him or her to see him or herself as lovable and others as trustworthy and accessible to care for him or her[34] If insecurely attached, the child's IWM may lead him or her to believe he or she is not worthy of love (often resulting in low self-esteem) and

---

25. Goodwin, "Relevance of Attachment Theory."
26. Bowlby, "Affectional Bonds II."
27. As cited in Berry and Danquah, "Attachment-Informed Therapy," 18.
28. Bowlby, "Affectional Bonds I."
29. Berry and Danquah, "Attachment-Informed Therapy."
30. Neufeld, *Aggression*.
31. Greenberg and Johnson, *Emotionally Focused Therapy*.
32. Bowlby, *Secure Base: Clinical Applications*.
33. Main and Solomon, "Insecure Disoriented Attachment."
34. Beardselee et al., "Affectively Ill Parents"; Main and Solomon, " Insecure Disoriented Attachment."

is not able to trust others.[35] These internal thought processes and relational dynamics are now being able to be studied in greater detail due to recent advances in the field of neuroscience.

Before I progress, I need to clarify that I would not consider myself a classical attachment therapist for a number of reasons: firstly, I am not inclined to offer a diagnostic classification as rigidly defined by the four classically labelled attachment styles. I do not administer the AAI (Adult Attachment Inventory[36]) and I resist diagnosis due to its reductionist, totalizing potential. Secondly, my preference is to understand attachment along a continuum from secure to insecure[37] as I believe there to be more fluidity in relational styles across the lifespan and even within daily interactions; changes in attachment patterns can happen in either a positive or a negative direction, due to life stressors and changes in key relationships.[38] When I encountered Neufeld's attachment-based developmental approach (which is applied to parenting and teaching relationships) I could see its applicability to my therapeutic work as a children's counselor, a family therapist and psychotherapist with adults suffering from anxiety, depression, and relational distress.

The more I learn about attachment theory the more I believe that when secure attachment is shaped in terms of triune love it has the potential for intrapsychic, interpersonal, and spiritual healing. Attachment theory can be helpful for making sense of not just inter-personal relational dynamics,[39] but also the intra-psychic elements and transcendent (spiritual) elements of our lived experience. My interpretation and application of attachment theory includes three dimensions: *inter-personal attachment* (how I relate to the other), *intra-psychic attachment* (how I relate to my "self"; e.g. the nature of my self-talk, the view I have of my identity and self-esteem, which form the basis of our Internal Working Models[40]) and a *transcendent dimension* (which includes the spiritual, our relationship to God, our view of our place in the cosmos and our relationship to land and creation, which resonates with indigenous and especially a *Māori*[41] worldview).

35. Bowlby, *Affectional Bonds*.
36. Griffin and Bartholomew, "Models of the Self," 430; Besharat, "Adult Attachment Inventory."
37. Cowan and Cowan, "Seven Unresolved Issues."
38. Waters et al., "Attachment Security."
39. Robert, *Becoming Attached*.
40. Bretherton, "Updating"; Macfie et al., "Intergenerational Transmission."
41. *Māori* are the indigenous people of Aotearoa/New Zealand. *Māori* cosmology holds to an understanding of the land as being the placenta or the mythical place of the origin of humankind, therefore they do not introduce themselves from an individualistic Western identity position, but rather in relation to the land of their forebears.

INTERPERSONAL NEUROBIOLOGY

Since the 1990s, scientists greatly advanced understanding of the brain, developing powerful tools to move from the study of neurons to circuits and, ultimately, to behavior and emotional distress.[42] How attachments change the architecture and functioning of the brain are questions examined by the field of interpersonal neurobiology[43] which involves the application of neuroscientific data to parenting, psychotherapy, and education.[44]

Research into the neuroscience of attachment sheds light on the embodied nature of human relationality. There is mounting evidence that seems to suggest that we are hardwired for connection;[45] it is the power of being with others that shapes our brains;[46] our relationships shape our biology as well as our experiences.[47] Early nurturance plays a vital role in the development and integration of the diverse systems within our brains. Our embodiment, in the form of our brain-to-brain link (mirror neurons) allows our strongest relationships to shape us[48] and certain relationships can continue to repair our wounded minds throughout our lifespan.[49] So we can see that the fields of interpersonal neurobiology and attachment theory are very closely related.

HEALING THROUGH RELATIONSHIP: INTRODUCING NEUFELD'S MODEL OF ATTACHMENT

Now that I have introduced some of the basic tenants of classical attachment theory, I will now introduce a second significant factor in the development of my attachment-based psychotherapeutic approach. I was introduced to Neufeld's work at a time in my life when I had two young daughters whom I was parenting with traditional behavior-modification techniques, which I had been taught in my psychological training and had used in my work as a child and family counselor for years. However, when it came to the

---

42. Insel, "Decade."
43. Cozolino, *Neuroscience of Human Relationships*.
44. Siegel, *Developing Mind*; Siegel and Hartzell, *Parenting*; Siegel and Goleman, *Mindsight*.
45. Cozolino, *Neuroscience of Human Relationships*; Tatkin, *Wired for Love*; Goleman, *Social Intelligence*.
46. Cozolino, *Neuroscience of Human Relationships*.
47. Goleman, *Social Intelligence*; Siegel and Goleman, *Mindsight*.
48. Goleman, *Social Intelligence*, 56.
49. Badenock, *Brain-Wise*; Cozolino, *Neuroscience of Psychotherapy*.

application of these principles to my own precious daughters, not only was I finding them less and less effective as they grew older, but I realized that I was causing damage to my relationship with them. One day a friend introduced me to Neufeld and Mate's book *Hold On to Your Kids*[50] which gave me insights into an attachment based understanding of parenting that revolutionized not only my relationship with my children, my partner and God, but also how I practiced counseling.

Like myself, I found that Neufeld has synthesized many developmental theories and has come up with a model which helped me make sense of my own human relationships and my relationship with God. Neufeld presents a model of how healthy attachment may develop in the early years and continues to develop and strengthen across the lifespan. He outlines six ways that children attach to their caregivers (see figure one), but it also applies to how all attachment forms across the life stages. Neufeld notes that "although [attachment] begins in infancy, the hunger for physical proximity never goes away."[51] I would add that our hunger for spiritual and emotional intimacy also never goes away.

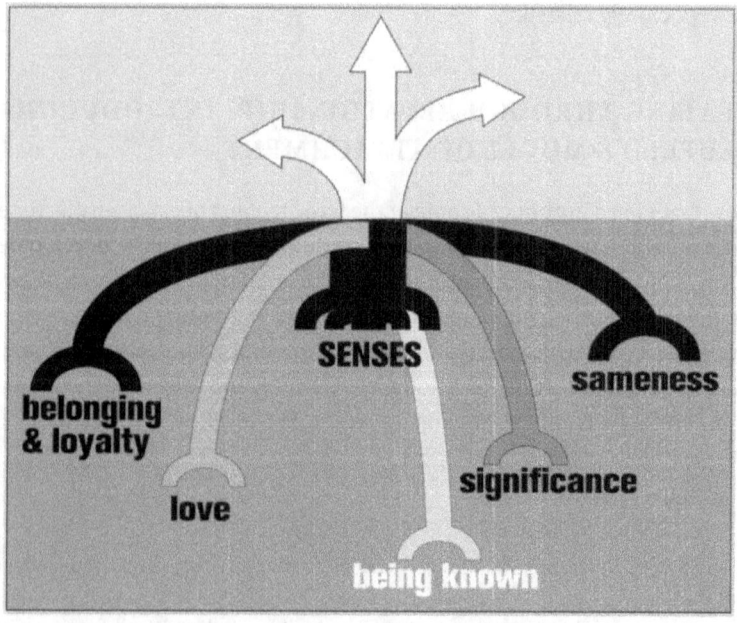

Figure one. *Neufeld's six levels of attaching.*[52]

50. Neufeld and Mate, *Hold On*.
51. Ibid., 21.
52. Neufeld, "Power to Parent Part 1." Used with permission.

Neufeld's six levels of attaching progress sequentially involving increasing depths of intimacy and greater capacity for vulnerable, authentic relating. The levels move from being physically present (the least vulnerable form of connection), to emotional and psychological intimacy (the most vulnerable forms of relating). As the child develops increasing capacity for relational connection, by deepening their "attachment roots," or having more "ways to hold on" to another, as Neufeld[53] says, so too does he or she develop greater capacity for emotional and psychological maturity.

Attachment Level One: Senses

Attachment *through the senses,* involves physical proximity, or being with the attachment figure. This form of attachment begins from birth[54] through the first year of life and is mediated through the five senses. When the infant can't be with their attachment figure, or closeness is threatened or disrupted, she will naturally express alarm, anxiety, and protest.[55]

Infants who are able to attach through the senses in their first years develop enough trust[56] and can start to internalise their relationships.[57] This also develops their capacity to progress in their developmental journey. I work with many parents who feel that their children have not securely attached to them or have detached due to some stress or emotional misattunement. My focus is to help them become the parent to whom their child will securely reattach. The kind of nurture a child at this stage of psychological development needs is primarily sensory-rich attachment: lots of hugs, lots of reassuring eye contact, a deeply reassuring tone of voice that doesn't trigger displeasure (which might be perceived as a precursor to further rejection, emotional distancing or separation) and allowing the child to "shadow" (hover very close to) the caregiver.

Many foster parents I work with have noticed this need in their foster children. I remember a foster parent of a twelve-year-old girl,[58] who had experienced extreme neglect and multiple attachment disruptions in her

---

53. Neufeld and Mate, *Hold On*, 21.

54. Some would argue that attachment actually begins in utero; Pollock and Percy, "Antenatal Attachment."

55. Bowlby, *Affectional Bonds*; Bowlby, *Attachment and Loss* 3; Neufeld and Mate, *Hold On*, 20.

56. Erikson, *Identity*.

57. Bazzano, "Intersubjectivity"; Bowlby and Salter Ainsworth, *Child Care*.

58. Examples throughout this chapter are composite clients based on work with a variety of clients in different contexts and in different times.

short life. In one of our sessions the foster mum expressed exasperation that her foster child was extremely clingy; she said she was starting to feel "really crowded" and didn't know what to do. I explained that this is "normal" for a child who has had such deep attachment ruptures and neglect from early infancy. If we perceive her according to her chronological age, we may get alarmed and interpret her clinginess as a sign of pathology. We may be inclined to push her away to help her "stand on her own two feet." However, in this case, pushing her away would be disastrous as it may lead to more attachment wounding and further detaching.

Neufeld contends that we all grow older but we all don't necessarily grow up: he calls this developmental stuckness.[59] In the case of this twelve-year-old girl, the educational psychologist's assessment of her cognitive and emotional development was at the level of a six-year-old. According to Anda and colleagues, the neglected, maltreated child is all too often an infant emotionally, who requires the kind of one-to-one interaction that normally only babies get.[60] This level of attachment may have been missing in this foster child's infancy. In order to unfold into her natural developmental potential, she needed to be "fed" metaphorically, at this level from a safe attachment figure, in order to become "satiated"[61] and be able to progress to the next level of attachment.

The foster mother came to reframe this clingy behaviour as legitimate attachment hunger which had not been satiated (rather than "attention-seeking"), so she turned to try and meet these needs rather than turning the child away. According to Neufeld, children will naturally progress to the next level of development once they have had their attachment hunger satisfied at those earlier levels of attachment.[62] The key to satiating a child's attachment hunger is to give more than is being pursued.[63] From my perspective, the foster mother needed to lean into the child's hugs and offer an even bigger hug so that the child comes to psychological rest, feeling satiated in the provision of healthy attachment. Over time the foster mother found that the child became less clingy and "let go" of her spontaneously. Together we witnessed the process of maturation that was fuelled by a child's attachment hunger being satisfied at this first level of attachment, by keeping someone we love close. However, "out of sight, out of mind" is a very fragile way of being attached so as the child develops (starts walking, following after the

---

59. Neufeld, "Power to Parent Part 2."
60. Anda et al., "Enduring Effects."
61. Neufeld, "Power to Parent Part 2."
62. Ibid.
63. Ibid.

attachment) the child progresses onto the next level of attaching so that they have more than one way of staying attached.

Attachment Level Two: Sameness

The second level of attaching is through *sameness*, "usually in evidence by toddlerhood . . . the child seeks to be like those she feels closest to."[64] She attempts to copy and be as similar as possible to whom she is attaching, which features "prominently in learning language and in the transmission of culture."[65] To attach by wanting to be like the attachment figure is what Neufeld refers to as identification: "to be one with that person or thing."[66] This involves one's sense of self merging with the object of identification (e.g. parent, a hero, a group, a role, or a country/nationalism). The more "dependent a child or person is, the more intense these identifications are likely to be."[67]

When I work with parents and caregivers of children who are insecurely attached, once they have mastered level one, attaching by *senses: being with*, I then encourage the parents to work at level two, *attaching through sameness*. By getting the parent to be able to find as many areas of similarity or sameness ("me too") as possible with the child, reinforces this level of attachment: for example: "oh, you like that kind of music . . . me too!" or "you like watching that show . . . me too!" or "you and I both have blue eyes."

Attachment Level Three: Belonging and Loyalty

If all is going well with the child's attachment system, by the third year of life a child is able to have a third way or level of attaching: through *belonging and loyalty*. This is characterised by possessiveness, as well as desiring to be obedient to whom they are attached.[68] Neufeld states that "the attaching toddler will lay claim to whomever or whatever he is attached to—be it mummy, daddy, teddy bear or baby sister."[69]

The desire *to belong* and *be loyal* to one another is a natural attachment instinct; loyalty can be intense (e.g. gang-members' behaviour) but it

64. Neufeld and Mate, *Hold On*, 22.
65. Ibid.
66. Ibid.
67. Ibid.
68. Ibid.
69. Ibid.

merely follows attachment instincts.[70] The key intervention to get a child re-attached is to have established levels one and two and then work at helping the child to develop a deep sense of *belonging* to the *whānau*[71] or family unit. Pre-schoolers are often fascinated by stories of what it was like for them to join the family: were they anticipated or a surprise? Were they welcomed? They get great pleasure looking through baby photos and hearing early stories of their inclusion in the family unit. Once a child has securely attached to the caregiver at this level, he or she offers incredible loyalty, which manifests itself as being willing to be instructed (obedience rather than rebellion and secrets) and willingly following the caregiver's values and ideals.

Attachment Level Four: Significance

The fourth way of attaching is to seek to *be significant* or to matter to the one we are attaching to, which ensures emotional closeness, not just physical proximity.[72] If all is going well with the other levels of attachment, then this stage usually happens at around age four to five. The attaching pre-schooler "seeks ardently to please and to win approval . . . is extremely sensitive to looks of displeasure and disapproval."[73] The problem with this way of attaching is that it makes a child vulnerable to being hurt, because to want to be significant to someone who makes us feel that we don't matter results in an attachment wound. A sensitive child can be easily crushed "when the eyes he is scanning for signs of warmth and pleasure do not light up in his presence, be they the eyes of parent or peer."[74]

One of the phrases Neufeld uses to describe what attachment is all about is "being invited to exist in the presence of the other"[75] connoting hospitality, acceptance and love, and here we see another connection with trinitarian incarnational anthropology, which Jesus so concisely describes in the parable of the lost son.[76] Children who are attaching at level four (wanting *to be significant*) are constantly looking for signs that they matter to the caregiver (e.g. "Did you miss me when I was gone?" "Am I special to you?").

---

70. Ibid.
71. *Māori*: extended family unit.
72. Neufeld and Mate, *Hold On*, 23.
73. Ibid.
74. Ibid.
75. Neufeld, "Power to Parent Part 1."
76. Luke 15, KJV.

I was working with a mother whose eight year old daughter was very anxiously attached to her. The mother was preparing to go on a business trip and knew that this would be hard for her daughter so we focused on how to help her daughter keep a sense of connection even while separated from her mother. The mother decided that she would put a note in the daughter's diary for each day that she would be away (level four: *significance*), as well as one of her t-shirts with her perfume on it (level one: *senses*—smell) and daily phone calls home (level one: *senses*—hearing), saying lots of "I miss you too" (level two: *sameness* and acknowledging emotional connection). For anxiously attached children, tangible and sensory object (notes in lunch boxes, little gifts to be unwrapped each day, a stone or a shell from a walk together to keep in child's pocket to touch regularly, a handkerchief or item of clothing with the caregiver's scent/perfume on it) keep the sense of connection and significance strong even in times of physical separation.

Attachment Level Five: Love/Emotional Intimacy

By the fifth year of life, a child is expected to be able to develop the fifth way or level of attachment: *through loving feelings* (emotional intimacy). If attaching via *the senses,* the first and most primitive way, is the short arm of attachment; *emotional intimacy or love,* would be the long arm.[77] For a five year old, who can feel deeply and vulnerably, the pursuit of emotional intimacy becomes intense. Experiencing this level of emotional intimacy with the parent results in higher resilience; the child can tolerate much more physical separation and yet hold the parent close, metaphorically, in his heart. The child carries the image of the loving and beloved parent in his mind (as an Internal Working Model), and finds support and comfort.[78] This is why Schore describes attachment theory as an Emotional Regulation Theory.[79]

Consider another example from my parent-consulting work: a mother who had an extremely anxious eight year old daughter who was defensively detached[80] from her. She would often dictate to her mother rather than comply with her requests, becoming an *Alpha* child.[81] Neufeld describes the *Alpha complex* as the dynamic where a very anxiously attached child will go

77. Neufeld and Mate, *Hold On.* 23.
78. Ibid.
79. Schore, "Attachment and Regulation."
80. Defensive detachment describes flight from vulnerability, see Neufeld and Mate, *Hold On*, 98.
81. Neufeld, *Alpha Children.*

into a dominant, bossy and often bullying stance to try to regain power and take the lead in the child-caregiver relationship. In this case, the daughter's dominance of the mother disempowered her, which further exacerbated her daughter's anxiety. When an *Alpha* child sees her caregiver as impotent to protect her from a scary world, she often moves into the lead rather than the dependent follower role. The daughter had taken the lead in the relational dance to the point of terrifying her mother with her aggression and overwhelming emotional "meltdowns." The focus of our work was to help the mother reclaim her rightful, benevolent, *Alpha* leader position in order for her daughter's anxiety levels to reduce.

Over a few months we worked at re-establishing a secure attachment, firstly by removing all the extra-curricular activities that were exhausting them both and over-stimulating their highly sensitive natures.[82] A simplified life with more time to connect at home after school was my recommendation (*level one—attaching through the senses/being with*). Next we worked on level two, finding lots of way to attach through *sameness;* they both loved crafts and quietly reading together. With level one and two in place, the daughter felt a more secure attachment to her mother, which moved her to level three: *attaching through belonging.* As the daughter let her mother take the lead more in the relationship, she moved to a more dependent position and came to more psychological rest in the relationship, which meant her anxiety levels reduced.

As the daughter's *Alpha dominance* abated, so too did the mother's hyper-aroused amygdala, the fight-flight response centre of the brain, which was always scanning for danger, expecting a "meltdown" with her daughter. A core part of my therapeutic work is attending to the embodied aspects of the care-giver's attachment dynamics. Much of my work with the mother was to help her regulate her own anxiety levels (which were a residual aspect of her own attachment needs not being met in her childhood).[83] The mother's more calm demeanour helped the daughter self-regulate so her outbursts and tantrums diminished. At the neurological level the mother was able to regulate the child through limbic resonance and attunement.[84]

---

82. Both the mother and daughter would describe themselves as Highly Sensitive Persons; Aron, *Highly Sensitive Person*.

83. This is the intrapsychic attachment healing work that I do with the parent/caregiver as well as the focus on interpersonal attachment healing work between caregiver and child. For more on the subject of intergenerational transmission of attachment wounds see Macfie et al., "Intergenerational Transmission"; Clarke and Dawson, *Growing Up Again*.

84. Schore, "Attachment and Regulation"; Schore, *Affect Regulation*; Lewis et al., *General Theory*.

This meant the daughter felt less alarmed and anxious, so was able to relinquish her *Alpha* lead position in the dance, becoming more dependent and able to receive care rather than dictating how to be taken care of.

Within a few months the mother reported that the eight-year-old's bossy, aggressive behaviour and anxiety levels had reduced significantly and that she was receiving drawings of hearts and little "I love you" notes. This was an outward sign of an inward change: a sign of a child *attaching through love, or emotional intimacy* (level five) and coming to more psychological rest in the secure attachment with her mother.

Attachment Level Six: Being Known/Psychological Intimacy

Finally, the sixth way or level of attaching is through *being known* (psychological intimacy), which is usually observable by the time a child enters school. To feel close to someone is to be known by them; this is a recapitulation of level one attaching (*by the senses/being with*), except that being seen and heard are now experienced psychologically instead of strictly physically.[85] This emotional and psychological intimacy can involve sharing secrets, making the attachment bond very close and exclusive. Some of these secrets may even involve aspects of the self that may be seen as shameful, so when they are offered to the other and received with non-judgemental acceptance, this deepest level of attachment is secure.[86] Along with psychological intimacy come increased feelings of vulnerability if this bond is broken or secrets are betrayed. As a result, this is the rarest of intimacies; many of us are reluctant to share even with loved ones our deepest concerns and insecurities about ourselves, or our most shameful shadow side. Yet there is no closeness that can surpass the sense of feeling known and still being liked, accepted, welcomed, and fully, unconditionally invited to exist.[87]

When we are able to relate at this depth of intimacy, in a therapy session or in our own relationships, this for me, is like walking on holy ground. This can be seen as a reflection of the Trinity's joyful intimacy.[88] When we reach this level of depth and safety in human relationships it provides a fertile ground for our full psychological and emotional maturation.[89] This

---

85. Neufeld and Mate, *Hold On*, 23.
86. Ibid.
87. Ibid.
88. Shaw as cited in Seamands, *Ministry in the Image*.
89. Neufeld, "Power to Parent Part 2"; Neufeld and Mate, *Hold On*.

echoes Moltmann's description of how the members of the trinity "give each other space for full unfolding."[90]

With each new level of attachment, deeper vulnerability is involved. However, this increased capacity for vulnerable attaching leads to greater psychological maturity. The less mature the child is the more infantile his attaching. If there is only one way of holding on (i.e. *through being with/senses*) then the clinging is likely to be intense and desperate. The quest for *sameness (level two)* and *being with each other (level one)* are among the least vulnerable ways of attaching. If development of the attachment is healthy, these six strands become interwoven into a strong rope of connection that can preserve closeness even under the most adverse circumstances.[91] A securely attached child has many ways of staying close and holding on, even when physically apart.

Along with vulnerable attaching come many vulnerable feelings. In my work with parents, I find that much of their unresolved childhood attachment dynamics often start to heal, through the attachment that is created between us, the therapist, and the client. For example, I saw this kind of healing with a mother who had been eroded by her eleven-year-old son's *Alpha* dominance: bullying her, threatening her with a knife, erupting in aggression, impulsivity and displaying obsessive tendencies. She had sought help in the adolescent mental health system but had mostly been given diagnoses. Then she "fell out of the system" and came to see me. She became aware of Gordon Neufeld's work when she attended a day seminar on *Making Sense of Anxiety*.[92] She came to realize that many of the behaviors that she saw her son displaying could be due to anxiety, and the answer may lie in his attachment with her. Sadly, she did not believe that she would be enough of an answer for him: she had lost her *Alpha* lead in the relationship. For a few sessions we focused on what it would look like for her to *become an answer* for her son, not necessarily *to have all the answers*; taking care of her son's attachment needs, especially for contact and closeness (level one: *senses*) when he was most anxious.

After a few sessions I could see an internal shift had taken place; she seemed more confident, less anxious and more grounded. She was moving into her legitimate *Alpha* position. I asked her if she had noticed this in herself and she beamed and nodded. "Where did you get your beautiful *Alpha* from?" I asked. She replied without missing a beat: "From you; you have become my safe place." She went on to say that she had come to realize that she needed to help her son feel safe in the world: "I try to be safe for

---

90. Moltmann, *Coming of God*, 298.
91. Neufeld and Mate, *Hold On*, 23.
92. Neufeld, *Anxiety*.

him as you have been to me." This is an example of the power of a corrective emotional experience in the therapeutic encounter which leads to a secure attachment within the client-counselor relationship. This, in turn, emanates into the parent-child subsystem in the family, offering hope for the next generation, to be loved well and to go on to loving well.

CONCLUSION

In my counseling and parent-consulting work I believe I love others through helping them parent from a healthy attachment base, mirrored in the secure attachment I offer in therapy. My ability to love and metaphorically "hold" my clients in a secure attachment comes from my experience of the love at the heart of the Trinity. This love ripples out incarnationally as I love my clients and they love their children.

According to Wallin, if early relationships "promoted an insecure attachment pattern then subsequent relationships can offer us second chances, perhaps affording us the potential to love, feel and reflect with the freedom that flows from secure attachment. Psychotherapy, at its best, provides just such a healing relationship."[93] I posit that this is an example of the power of incarnated love in relational healing; through embodied love, even after neglect or abandonment in early life, synaptic connections can be rewired if a child receives secure attachment in later life, or an adult client in a therapeutic encounter.

Thus, love in its embodied form (neural connections and attachment dynamics) is present in each counseling encounter. Love embodied leads to healing hearts, minds, and relationships, as we are "invited to exist in the presence of the other."[94] In counseling, we love as a reflection of the Trinity's relational dance, characterized by reciprocity, mutuality, particularity, separateness as well as in emotionally safe community, offering hospitality and embrace for the healing and restoration of our clients. The Trinity loves through incarnation, through embodiment. We have all been invited into the divine dance; to share the divine privilege of partnering with the Trinity in this beautiful Kingdom project of healing love.

---

93. Wallin, *Attachment in Psychotherapy*, 14.
94. Neufeld, "Power to Parent Part 1."

References

Anda, Robert, et al. "The Enduring Effects of Abuse and Related Adverse Experiences in Childhood: A Convergence of Evidence from Neurobiology and Epidemiology." *European Archives of Psychiatry and Clinical Neuroscience* 256 (2006) 174–86.
Aron, Elaine. *The Highly Sensitive Person.* London: Harper Collins, 1999.
Badenock, Bonnie. *Being a Brain-Wise Therapist: A Practical Guide to Interpersonal Neurobiology.* New York: Norton, 2008.
Balswick, Jack, et al. *The Reciprocating Self: Human Development in Theological Perspective.* 2nd ed. Downers Grove, IL: InterVarsity, 2016.
Bazzano, Manu. "Intersubjectivity Revisited." *Person-Centered and Experiential Psychotherapies* 13 no. 3 (2014) 206–16.
Beardselee, William R., et al. "Children of Affectively Ill Parents: A Review of the Past 10 Years." *Journal of the American Academy of Child and Adolescent Psychiatry* 37 no. 11 (1998) 1134–41.
Berry, Katherine, and Adam Danquah. "Attachment-Informed Therapy for Adults: Towards a Unifying Perspective on Practice." *Psychology and Psychotherapy: Theory, Research and Practice* 89 no.1 (2016) 15–32.
Besharat, Mohammad. "Development and Validation of Adult Attachment Inventory." *Procedia-Social and Behavioural Sciences* 30 (2011) 473–79.
Boff, Leonardo. *Trinity and Society.* Orbis, 1988.
Bowlby, John. *A Secure Base: Clinical Applications of Attachment Theory.* London: Routledge, 1988.
———. *A Secure Base: Parent-Child Attachment and Healthy Human Development.* New York: Basic, 1988.
———. *Attachment and Loss.* New York: Basic, 1969.
———. *Attachment and Loss. Vol. 3 Sadness and Depression.* London: Hogarth, 1980.
———. *The Making and Breaking of Affectional Bonds.* London: Tavistock, 1979.
———. "The Making and Breaking of Affectional Bonds. I. Aetiology and Psychopathology in the Light of Attachment Theory." *The British Journal of Psychiatry* 130 (1977a) 201–10.
———. "The Making and Breaking of Affectional Bonds. II. Some Principles of Psychotherapy." *The British Journal of Psychiatry* 130 (1977b) 421–31.
Bowlby, John, and Mary Salter Ainsworth. *Child Care and the Growth of Love.* Harmondsworth, England: Penguin, 1965.

Bretherton, Inge. "Updating the 'Internal Working Model' Construct: Some Reflections." *Attachment & Human Development* 1 no. 3 (1999) 343–57.

Clarke, Jean Illsley, and Connie Dawson. *Growing Up Again.* 2nd ed. Minnesota: Hazelden, 1998.

Connors, Mary. "Attachment Theory: A 'Secure' Base for Psychotherapy Integration." *Journal of Psychotherapy Integration* 21 no. 3 (2011) 348–62.

Cowan, Philip A., and Carolyn Pape Cowan. "Attachment Theory: Seven Unresolved Issues and Questions for Future Research." *Research in Human Development* 4 no. 3–4 (2007) 181–201.

Cozolino, Louis. *The Neuroscience of Human Relationships.* New York: W.W. Norton, 2006.

———. *The Neuroscience of Psychotherapy: Healing the Social Brain.* 2nd ed. New York: W.W. Norton, 2010.

Erikson, Erik. *Identity, Youth and Crisis.* New York: W.W. Norton, 1968.

Finkel, Eli J., and Paul Eastwick. "Attachment and Pairbonding." *Social Behavior* 3 (2015) 7–11.

Goff, Christopher Wyatt. "Measuring the Clergy/laity Gap and Its Effect on Church Health and Outreach." PhD diss., Asbury Theological Seminary, 2008.

Goleman, Daniel. *Social Intelligence: The New Science of Human Relationships.* New York: Bantam Books, 2006.

Goodwin, Isabel. "The Relevance of Attachment Theory to the Philosophy, Organization, and Practice of Adult Mental Health Care." *Clinical Psychology Review* 23 (2003) 35–56.

Greenberg, Leslie S, and Susan M Johnson. *Emotionally Focused Therapy for Couples.* New York: Guilford Press, 1988.

Griffin, Dale, and Kim Bartholomew. "Models of the Self and Other: Fundamental Dimensions Underlying Measures of Adult Attachment." *Journal of Personality and Social Psychology* 67 no. 3 (1994) 430.

Gunton, Colin. *The One, the Three and the Many: God, Creation and the Culture of Modernity. The 1992 Bampton Lectures.* Cambridge, England: Cambridge University Press, 1993.

Hall, Todd. W. "Psychoanalysis, Attachment and Spirituality Part 1: The Emergence of Two Relational Traditions." *Journal of Psychology and Theology* 35 no. 1 (2007) 14–28.

Holmes, Bjarne M., and Kimberley Johnson. "Adult Attachment and Romantic Partner Preference: A Review." *Journal of Personality and Social Psychology* 26 no. 6–7 (2009) 833–52.

Insel, Thomas. "A Decade after the Decade of the Brain: Understanding Mental Disorders as Circuit Disorders." http://dana.org/Cerebrum/2010/A_Decade_after_The_Decade_of_the_Brain__Compilation/.

Johnson, Susan M. "The Attachment Perspective on the Bonds of Love: A Prototype for Relationship Change." In *The Emotion-Focused Casebook: New Directions in Treating Couples,* edited by James Furrow, et al., 31–58. New York, NY: Routledge, 2011.

Kruger, C. Baxter. *The Great Dance: The Christian Vision Revisited.* Vancouver: Regent College Publishing, 2005.

Lewis, Thomas, et al. *A General Theory of Love.* Toronto, Canada: Random House, 2000.

Macfie, Jenny, et al. "Intergenerational Transmission of Role Reversal between Parent and Child: Dyadic and Family Systems Internal Working Models." *Attachment & Human Development* 7 no. 1 (2005) 51–65.

Main, Mary, and Solomon, Judith. "Discovery of an Insecure Disoriented Attachment Pattern: Procedures, Findings and Implications for the Classification of Behaviour." In *Affective Development in Infancy,* edited by T. Berry Brazelton, 95–124. Norwood, NJ: Ablex, 1986.

Moltmann, Jürgen. *The Coming of God: Christian Eschatology.* Minneapolis: Fortress, 1996.

Neufeld, Gordon. *Alpha Children,* Videocourse. (2011; Vancouver, Canada: Neufeld Institute.), DVD.

———. *Making Sense of Aggression.* Videocourse. (2010; Vancouver, Canada: Neufeld Institute.), DVD.

———. *Making Sense of Anxiety.* Videocourse. (2014; Vancouver, Canada: Mediamax Interactive Productions.), DVD.

———. *The Power to Parent Part 1: Attachment the Vital Connection.* Videocourse. (2008; Vancouver, Canada: Neufeld Institute.), DVD.

———. *The Power to Parent: Part 2 Helping Children Grow Up.* Videocourse. (2008; Vancouver, Canada: Mediamax Interactive Productions.), DVD.

———. *The Power to Parent: Part 3 Common Challenges.* Videocourse. (2009 Vancouver, Canada: Mediamax Interactive Productions.), DVD.

Neufeld, Gordon, and Gabor Mate. *Hold on to Your Kids: Why Parents Need to Matter More than Peers.* Toronto, Canada: Vintage, 2004.

Pollock, Philip H., and Andrew Percy. "Maternal Antenatal Attachment Style and Potential Fetal Abuse." *Child Abuse & Neglect* 23 no. 12 (December 1999) 1345–57.

Robert, Karen. *Becoming Attached: First Relationships and How They Shape Our Capacity to Love.* New York: Oxford University Press, 1994.

Rohr, Richard, and Mike Morell. *The Divine Dance: The Trinity and Your Transformation.* New Kensington, PA: Whitaker House, 2016.

Salter Ainsworth, Mary D., et al. *Patterns of Attachment: A Psychological Study of the Strange Situation.* Hillsdale, NJ: Erlbaum, 1978.

Saltman, Bethany. "Can Attachment Theory Explain All Our Relationships?" *New York Magazine* (June 2016). http://nymag.com/thecut/2016/06/attachment-theory-motherhood-c-v-r.html.

Schore, Allan. "Attachment and the Regulation of the Right Brain." *Attachment & Human Development* 2 no. 1 (2000) 23–47.

———. *Affect Regulation and the Repair of the Self.* New York: W.W. Norton, 2003.

Seamands, Stephen. *Ministry in the Image of God: The Trinitarian Shape of Christian Service.* Downers Grove, IL: InterVarsity, 2005.

Siegel, Daniel J. *The Developing Mind: How Relationships and the Brain Interact to Shape Who We Are.* 2nd ed. New York, NY: Guilford, 2012.

Siegel, Daniel J., and Daniel Goleman. *Mindsight: The New Science of Personal Transformation.* New York, NY: Bantam, 2011.

Siegel, Daniel J., and Hartzell, Mary. *Parenting from the Inside Out: How a Deeper Self-Understanding Can Help You Raise Children Who Thrive.* Penguin Putnam, 2005.

Tatkin, Stan. *Wired for Love: How Understanding Your Partner's Brain and Attachment Style Can Help You Defuse Conflict and Build a Secure Relationship.* Oakland, CA: New Harbinger, 2011.

Volf, Miroslav. "'The Trinity Is Our Social Program': The Doctrine of the Trinity and the Shape of Social Engagement." *Modern Theology* 14 no. 3 (1998) 404–21.

Wallin, David J. *Attachment in Psychotherapy*. New York: Guilford Press, 2007.

Waters, Everett et al. "Attachment Security in Infancy and Early Adulthood: A Twenty-Year Longitudinal Study." *Child Development* 71 (2000) 684–89.

Weinfield, Nancy, et al. "The Nature of Individual Differences in Infant-Caregiver Attachment." In *Handbook of Attachment: Theory, Research, and Clinical Applications*, edited by Jude Cassidy & Phillip Shawer, 68–88. New York, NY: Guilford, 1999.

6

The Impact of the Concepts of *Perichoresis* and *Hesed* for Teaching and Family Relationships

Dr. Barbara Bulkeley

After considerable experience as a family therapist, the change to working full-time in a Christian tertiary counselor education program has proved challenging. In this chapter, I will explore two key theological ideas which have considerably influenced my teaching of family therapy over the past seven years. I will present these concepts of *perichoresis* and *hesed* and discuss how they have impacted on my teaching of two foundational papers about families as well as reflecting on some links that have been made visible between these concepts and my practice of family therapy. I will also include ideas that some families have discussed in therapy and students in classes. In particular, these examples include ideas that families found helpful in their understanding of what constitutes "family" in today's society. The idea of *hesed (chesed)* as a basis for family virtues is very different from having the western belief of "romantic love" as the central tenet of a marriage partnership. The concept of this family virtue of *hesed*—loving kindness, faithfulness, solidarity—means that we talk with families in a different way. As a teacher, along with my students, I have been challenged to think about what I view as a theological basis for marriage and family. The impact of these ideas on my understanding and teaching about family has taken a much more relational stance.

When I came to Bethlehem Tertiary Institute (BTI) in 2009 as a family therapist and counselor educator, I was given responsibility for teaching the three papers about families in the Bachelor of Counseling program. So I "inherited" *The Family*[1] as the set text for the first year paper. The themes and topics covered in this BTI first year course had an emphasis on theological concepts of family and understanding of how these ideas influenced the family system. It was in this way that I was introduced to the idea of *perichoresis*.

Balswick and Balswick[2] present a trinitarian model that reflects the nature of relationship, and build on the concept of covenant relationships with the fundamental principle of unconditional love at its center. This trinitarian relationality enables distinction and unity to exist in the family like we see them in the Trinity of Father, Son, and Spirit. However, "unlike God, we are not perfect."[3] As a Christian, this idea really caused me to explore how I had worked with hurting and struggling families, and how this would change in the future. However, as an educator, I now had the opportunity to seek to teach my students in an authentic, unconditional way. This concept of *perichoresis* (mutual indwelling in complete unity) as presented by Volf changed the way I "saw" family, and thus how I worked relationally with families.[4]

The first chapter of Balswick and Balswick's book is entitled "A trinitarian foundation for family relationships." Their analogy of basing the theology of family relationships on the relationality within the Holy Trinity and descriptions of God in relationship was a new concept to me. I found the idea that "relationships between family members are to reflect the relationality within the Holy Trinity"[5] to be powerful and, on reflection, led to changes in my thinking. In endeavoring to explain this concept of relationality, Balswick and Balswick clearly state that we should not be "picking out key verses" that sit well with how we see the Bible's view of family. This fits with my preference to use biblical themes and understandings rather than simply individual verses.

The social trinitarian model that Balswick and Balswick introduced to me presents a trinitarian model that reflects the nature of relationship, and builds on the concept of covenant relationships with the fundamental principle of unconditional love at its center. This trinitarian relationality enables distinction and unity to exist in the family as are seen in the Trinity of Father, Son, and Spirit. This vision of relationality that is often referred to as *perichoresis*, or the mutual indwelling in complete unity, changed the

---

1. Balswick and Balswick, *Family*.
2. Ibid., 19.
3. Ibid., 19.
4. Volf, *After Our Likeness*.
5. Balswick and Balswick, *Family*, 18.

way I "saw" family, and now I conceptualize family work in a much more relational way. This will be explored in detail below.

The key argument associated with this view of God, that I wish to discuss, is that human beings reflect God's image in relationality. As the Father, Son, and Spirit mutually indwell in a trinitarian relationship, so humans should be mutually indwelling in family relationships. I am arguing that the notion of *perichoresis* can be applied to a human family or community as an analogy because as creatures of God, humans relate to God as creatures to their creator.[6] However, the idea of Gunton that the "persons in the Trinity do not simply enter into relations with one another, but are constituted by one another in relations"[7] suggests that *perichoresis* describes the sort of unity in which plurality is preserved rather than erased. So the persons of the Trinity act as themselves, yet the others are present in that person. The point I want to highlight here is that there is a balance of the separateness yet togetherness, with the inter-dependence of family relationships. Humans are not perfect, so are not able to live in perfect relationships. As I began to better understand this notion of what is the ideal in God's eyes, I began to explore how I could work with and also teach about families in a different way. This new way was in contrast to much literature which often treats individuality and relationality as two separate categories, almost seen as in opposition.

As a systemic family therapist, I am familiar with assessing the impact of one member's behaviors or experiences on the family unit. I teach about notions of homeostasis, of systems being organic and inter-related, so these concepts are certainly not new to me. I have taught about circular causality, implying that in a system every member both influences the others and is influenced by them. I know that the family system is co-evolving and so teach about the influence of the development of family members and their relationships with each other.[8] Additionally my personal experience as an educator and family therapist has taught me that family relationships are inter-dependent and never static. Furthermore in terms of human development, children and adolescents, while developing their own unique selves through the process of differentiation, seek to find a new identity while still remaining connected to the family.[9] I was, therefore, delighted to see the concept of *perichoresis* leading to the analogy of relationships between fam-

---

6. Volf, *After Our Likeness*.
7. Gunton, *One, Three, Many*, 114.
8. Hayes, "Re-introduction to Family Therapy"; Nichols and Schwartz, *Family Therapy*.
9. Bartle-Haring, "Parent-adolescent Differentiation."

ily members who are seen as reflecting the distinction and yet the unity that exists in a family, as modelled perfectly in the Trinity of Father, Son, and Spirit. To recognize the link between key concepts in my profession and my faith just made sense to me when I first encountered them. I realized that my way of thinking about families had been much more influenced by secular training and concepts than by theology. I determined to endeavor to change my thinking and let *perichoresis* transform my thinking and practice.

Making these links though, did raise some important professional challenges, both for my work as an educator and as a therapist. For example, if I now think of the mutuality of the members of a family, could I continue to teach about the notions of Minuchin and his Structural School?[10] How would such ideas as boundaries, sub-systems, hierarchies and alliances work, if instead of a prescribed structure in a family, relationality was seen as key? If a key way of working structurally involves the therapist taking charge of family sessions and being the instructor, director, and leader, I wondered how these concepts and ways of working could possibly fit into this new way of envisaging families that instead emphasizes mutual indwelling in unity. However, I came to conclude that for me there is little conflict. I think of God as a parent who relates to his children and where a covenant relationship exists, it is underpinned by *perichoresis*. This helps me to be able to understand that the strength of the family is its oneness *and* its interdependence. However, while relationality is the key to family relationships, I still believe that some structural ideas such as hierarchy and systems can be useful ways to work with families where they are having some difficulties in relating to each other.

Individuals who may be very different in personality, outlook, as well as age and stage, somehow are bound together in a "family" (however this is defined in terms of relationships). Below I will discuss this further in reference to *hesed*. As children enter and move through the transition period known as adolescence, generally they still do share their parents' values and beliefs.[11] It is these family beliefs that organize internal and external familial experiences. Edgar-Smith and Wozniak emphasize that an important part of this involves the values that the family holds regarding how the members relate together.[12] These relational values help organize and give meaning to experiences within the family. So as I think in terms of relational aspects of family life, organized around shared views and values, *perichoresis* provides me with a "value template" to ensure support for both the personal aspects

10. Hayes, "Re-introduction to Family Therapy."
11. McGoldrick and Gerson, "Genograms."
12. Edgar-Smith and Wozniak, "Family Relational Values," 188.

of family life, as well as the interdependence that exists in the concept of the family as a system. Gunton's words give me a way of understanding perichoresis more specifically, and therefore a new way of seeing relationality in my work:

> An account of relationality that gives due weight to both one and many, to both particular and universal, to both otherness and relation, is to be derived from the one place where they can satisfactorily be based, a conception of God who is both one and three, whose being consists in a relationality that derives from the otherness-in-relation of the Father, Son and Spirit.[13]

PERICHORESIS IN FAMILY LIFE

The idea of *perichoresis* invites me to explore both how I work with hurting and struggling families, and how I teach my students in an authentic, unconditional way. I move on now to discussing these two aspects of my life and work, and how my work in these two domains is impacted by the ideas of *perichoresis*. Reflecting on my previous work as a family therapist, I realize that many families with whom I worked found it very difficult to understand the ideas of the family being one and interdependent, and had considerable difficulty coping with transition periods in the family life cycle. Duvall considers that the tasks of family development occur at each stage of the family life cycle and must be successfully negotiated for ease of transition to the next stage.[14] Yet all families are different and so their life circumstances will dictate the timing and duration of each "stage."[15] Duvall reminds us that members need to re-evaluate their familiar roles and positions in order to cope with the new stage. I suggest that re-evaluation of such values and ways of relating are key, especially concerning the balance between independence and inter-dependence, or in the terms of Gunton, as mentioned above, "otherness" and "relation."

Discussion of the values which families hold about independence and the role of adolescents or young adult children in a family is essential in family therapy. I worked with a family where the parents had strong Christian faith. They had two teenagers, a son aged sixteen and a daughter who was nearly fifteen. The daughter was climbing out of the window, meeting her boyfriend and staying out all night, thus causing a major problem for her

---

13. Gunton, *One, Three, Many*, 6–7.
14. Duvall, "Family Development."
15. Ibid.

parents and their hopes for their family. The members of this family talked at length about the value they placed on independence, but it seemed that the impact of emerging young adults had not been fully considered. When I mentioned that in this family there were two adults and two adolescents, I was interrupted immediately by the mother and told I was wrong. She stated that there were four adults in the family. Reflecting on this recently, I wonder if an understanding of the mutuality of the family members could have been helpful. I would now talk with them about what mutual relationships mean. The idea expressed by Hui about personhood emerging gradually through dialogue seems to fit in this situation.[16] In practice this may have challenged the notion that mutuality means equality. If this had been the case, the family may well have begun to see things in a different way and a discussion of how this shift to the next stage could have been more successfully managed. My point is that the concept of *perichoresis* is not rigid and fixed at any one stage of family development, but can change as the system changes and understanding deepens.

I believe that with the emphasis in family therapy that each family is a system, I would argue that the stability of family could be seen as related in this way of mutual being-together. As humans we do not and never can "indwell each other" in the same way the persons of the Trinity do, but such mutuality and giving up of each other to the others in the family/relationship adds strength to those relationships. This is in contrast to how many family systems theorists understand the stability of family as existing in the overall quality of family interactions[17] and as shown in qualitatively different types of families.[18] Even as family systems reorganize during the transition to another stage of family life, they try to maintain homeostasis (balance) and adhere to the rules of the respective family type, as stated by Olson some years ago.[19] Hence the emphasis is clearly that it is the rules of the family rather than relationship that determine the stability. In complete contrast to this very structural way of understanding families, some years ago one of our final-year BTI students wrote that "The intention seems to be that humans would be meaningfully connected relationally while holding a distinct and empowered sense of personhood."[20] It is this understanding of personhood—believing in such ideas as mutuality and inter-dependence—that families can cope more effectively with challenging situations.

16. Hui, "Jen and Perichoresis."
17. Favez et al., "Development of Family Alliance."
18. Lindblom et al., "Dynamic Family System Trajectories."
19. Olson, "Circumplex Model," 144.
20. Julian, personal communication, May 2013.

I worked for some time with another family who had several children, including triplets. They faced the issue of how to adequately balance shared personhood and individuality when their daughters reached adolescence. As a family of faith they believed their children were indeed a gift from God, but daily life was difficult and it often seemed much easier to treat the girls in similar ways to each other. As I now think about *perichoresis*, I wonder if discussions about the relationship of independence and interdependence as a basis for family life might have been more effective than trying to use a solution-focused way of working that was more concerned with the practical ways of making changes in this situation. Such conversations would certainly have been effective as I envisage that these parents could have accepted such a concept as fitting into their system of beliefs, yet may well have struggled with the practical outworking of *perichoresis* in their family system.

I understand *perichoretic* relationality to mean a belief in this way of thinking about familial independence, interdependence, and mutuality rather than individuality. I propose that this understanding invites a style of family relating in which individuality is cherished by self-giving love, and leads to consideration of what we mean by the word "family". If we think of *perichoresis* as a model for family, then how is family defined? I will now move to an overview of how family is understood in the Bible and connect briefly with some key Old Testament ideas of ways of considering viewing family.

FAMILY IN THE OLD TESTAMENT

In the Old Testament, a common word used is *Mishpach or mispaha* (clan). This is the most common term for a group made up of a number of households. It could be as small as a village or as large as a tribe. Moynagh states that *mispaha* "blurs the distinctions between family and tribe and between family and nation."[21] However the term *beth 'ab* (father's house) is also used to signify a family grouping.[22] This did not refer simply to a nuclear family, but included married children and their families, as well as servants and slaves. This concept of family being much wider than simply parents and their children, seems to fit well with the understandings I had gained through living in central Africa for many years. If family is considered by a high proportion of the world's population much more in terms

---

21. Moynagh, *Family*, 72.
22. Bulkeley, "What is a family?"

of relationality rather than structure, then this emphasis on relationality, connectedness made sense.

CHANGING VIEWS OF FAMILY

Over many years, my views on what is family and how I, as a family therapist, work and now teach about family, have been shaped by a wide range of life circumstances. In this section I will discuss some of these, and lead on to some aspects of culture and society in *Aotearoa* New Zealand.[23] My first introduction to non-western ways of "being" or "doing" family started when I studied anthropology as a minor subject at university in Belfast. A few years later, I spent nearly ten years living in Kinshasa, Congo in the 1980s. There I first observed, and then got to know Congolese families who operated in ways that were very different to me and my European understanding of family, formed as I grew up in Northern Ireland. Knowing that such a different concept of family existed was invaluable to me, both then and now. For example, when Kapita, our gardener, asked for additional money to pay for medical bills for his nephew, who was living as a son with Kapita and his wife, how could we refuse? This meant that at times we had to challenge the "rules" of our mission agency, which took a distinctly western view of who was and perhaps more importantly to them, who was not "family" in terms of those for whom we were responsible for as relatives of those people we employed to assist us in our house and garden. In this very poor country, employers assisted with healthcare and education costs for their workers' families. To us, it was the "right" thing to do; for if children or other adults were living in a household and dependent on their relative (uncle, aunt, cousin, brother, sister or whoever) then they were in our eyes, family.

Another aspect of Congolese society helped to change my western idea of family as based very much along structural lines. This was learning that Congolese spoke of being brothers with the same mother "*mama moko*" even when they had different fathers. There was no categorizing of half-brothers and sisters, or step-brothers and sisters, even cousins, nephews and nieces. My journey to further embrace Hebrew concepts of family, such as *mispaha* and *beth 'ab*, rather than continuing with the "nuclear" concept I had grown up accepting as the norm, was further re-enforced when we moved to New Zealand in the 1990s.

In the contemporary *Aotearoa* New Zealand context, *whānau* or perhaps *hapū*, words that are well-known and understood by both *Māori* and

---

23. This name, *Aotearoa* New Zealand, is in keeping with our bicultural identity as a nation.

non-*Māori* living here, are the nearest equivalents to a Biblical "family." *Te Ara*: The encyclopedia of New Zealand defines *whānau* as "an extended family group spanning three to four generations, [that] continues to form the basic *whānau* unit of *Māori* society."[24] Those of us living and working in *Aotearoa* New Zealand cannot but be influenced by the concept of *whānau*. Thus, for me, the western understanding of a nuclear family as being "the family" with other relatives categorized and distanced as "extended family" seems much less biblical because of this strong sense I have developed of seeing families being so much more than a mother, father, and their children. This comes, I believe, from my life experience and new learnings about both family and faith, and integration of these into my practice.

So now having lived for some decades in a variety of settings, in three very different continents, as I reflect on my work with many families, I am aware that this has certainly been influenced by these practical experiences and my changing belief in what is "family." An example of this is when I extend an invitation to a client's family members to come to a family therapy meeting and am asked "Who can come?" I have made a point of saying "whoever is family to you." To me this fits with the trinitarian relationality and invitation to a new way of envisaging family—in a *perichoretic* way.

The same broad definition of family is also evident in the New Testament. One of the words used for family is *patria*, which I understand to mean something more like a tribe, since all are descendants of one often-distant ancestor, e.g. "the Christ will come from David's family."[25] The other common word used in the New Testament to refer to family groups is *oikos* (household). However, what is clear is that family in the biblical narrative is important because of their function and not structure. Tim Bulkeley helpfully argues that while there is no model family structure described in the Bible, and that, in fact, most of the families might well be described as far from functional, there are clear virtues identified.[26] I believe that such ideas are vital in today's world for constructing a Christian understanding of family, as they offer a normative view of family flourishing.

HESED

Having discussed *perichoresis* and biblical terms for family such as *mispaha, beth 'ab, patria* and *oikos*, as well as *Māori* concepts of *whānau* and *hapū*, I am now turning to discuss virtues as encapsulated by the Hebrew word

24. Taonui, "Tribal Organization."
25. John 7:42
26. Bulkeley, "What is a family?"

hesed (chesed). I think it is important not just to think about the people who make up a family, but also to consider how those individuals relate to each other. It is this relational being towards the other that is key to *perichoresis*, but *hesed* gives us insight into how those relationships were to be enacted. In the Old Testament, God shows us what families ideally should be like, with the virtue of *hesed* being fundamental to family relationships. No one word in English adequately describes *hesed*. It can helpfully be translated as loving-kindness, love, loyalty, commitment, constancy, mercy, faithfulness, grace, and reliability.[27] Phanon[28] goes so far as to say that "the word *hesed* cannot be explained in one English word because it includes all the aspects of the positive attributes of God."

Hesed is exemplified in God's loving relationship with the Israelites. In family relationships, such virtues as faithfulness, love, mercy, and grace are what is expected. However, *hesed* also has the implication that within a family there is the expectation of mutual support and protection, solidarity and sticking-together-through-thick-and-thin. In the story of Ruth, *hesed* is displayed by Ruth and later Boaz who both show solidarity to the family. The character of Boaz is likened to God by his action as a redeemer who "acts with chesed, kindness."[29] So when people act with *hesed*, there is the clear sense that God is acting in them. Clark emphasized that *hesed* is not merely an attitude or an emotion. It can be more richly described as a "beneficent action performed in the context of a deep and enduring commitment between two persons or parties."[30]

It is important to recognize that God expresses *hesed* to His people because of who He is, not because of what people need, desire, or deserve. His motivation is benevolent grace. Hesed offers a sense of family mutuality and solidarity, which moves us away from the western notion of "romantic love" as being at the center of marriage. If *hesed* is at the center, the defining attribute of family values, this is then clearly linked to reliability and dependability, doing what is best for the family. Think of siblings who may bicker among themselves when playing together, but once someone from outside the family criticizes or attacks one of them, the others immediately rally around and join forces. They show solidarity, *hesed*. Ideally, in terms of *hesed*, a family is about faithfulness and solidarity, about obligation, protection and trust, and not about rights.[31]

27. Bulkeley, "What is a family?"; Clark, *Hesed*; James, *Gospel of Ruth*.
28. Phanon, "Double Hesed," 23.
29. Ostriker, "Book of Ruth," 350.
30. Clark, *Hesed*, 267.
31. Bulkeley, "What is a family?"

As mentioned earlier, if *perichoresis* talks of how family members relate towards each other with mutual indwelling and inter-dependence, then I see *hesed* as complementing this by giving a clear indication of how family behave towards each other. Practicing family therapy with a commitment to a *perichoretic* and *hesed* understanding of family relationships has led to many conversations over recent years as families try to understand what family means, how a family stays strong and together, and what helps in the sometimes difficult shift to the next developmental stage. Obligation or solidarity may be important in discussions with couples who are having severe difficulties in their relationships. For example, having the realization that marriage vows, "for better or worse, for richer or poorer" mean just that, even if romance seems a distant memory, can bring an understanding that there still is commitment to the relationship and their spouse. However, this can only be the starting point for working with those who want to make their marriage work despite often enormous challenges. So these virtues of solidarity, trust, loyalty, and mutual dependence and inter-dependence seem a solid foundation for teaching about and understanding families in the twenty-first century.

CHANGES IN MY TEACHING

Now that my work with families is shaped by understandings of *perichoresis* and *hesed*, I have moved away from teaching a purely systemic approach to family functioning and structure. I have become much more aware of the inter-dependence of members. I am interested in the statement of Witterborn et al.: "Life is spent in a wide variety of personal relationships including those with friends, romantic partners, grandparents, parents, children, siblings, supervisors, therapists, and clients."[32] They discuss how family therapists and researchers have long recognized the linked nature of human lives and, so far as methodological and statistical advances have allowed, have used a variety of methods to study interdependence within family relationships.

In western cultures there has been considerable emphasis on independence, in particular the notion of teenagers becoming independent from their families, almost to the extent that they do not need ongoing parental relationships. However, research in New Zealand in the *Youth* 2000, *Youth* '07 and *Youth* 12 surveys, each with almost 10,000 High School students, clearly shows that for New Zealand teenagers, parents continue to play a very important role beyond childhood, into and throughout the teenage

32. Witterborn et al., "Dyadic Research," 5.

years, and even beyond.[33] Expressed in a different way, this indicates that caring and connected relationships with parents are important for teenagers and these relationships are also predictors of good outcomes for young people. The majority of students surveyed in 2007 reported having good relationships with their parents.[34] This close and caring relationship with a parent is described as being one of the most important predictors of good health and wellbeing. Students who have strong positive relationships with their parents are better able to cope with challenges and changes in their lives. They may also achieve better at school and have healthier and happier relationships with others.

If the concept of *perichoresis* is taken into account, it could appear that families and society should not be promoting independence, but rather inter-dependence. Increasingly, I emphasize the need to question the western view that within families, young people are somehow seeking independence from the family. Instead I now practice and teach about considering the meaning of mutuality, where in a family each continues to be a part of the whole.

FIVE IMPLICATIONS FOR PRACTICE

Before coming to *Aotearoa* New Zealand, as I mentioned earlier, I had opportunity to consider the role of the extended family in Congo. Now in New Zealand, I have been impacted particularly by *Māori* ideas of *whānau, hapū,* and *iwi*. However, the notion of mutual indwelling as well as solidarity goes further than simply thinking of an extended family.

Implication One

I now consider families as being a different type of organism, one that emphasizes the mutuality and yet the individuality of its members.

Implication Two

The concept of *perichoresis* and *hesed* taken together mean that while the concept of "extended family" goes part way to conceptualizing a change from the more westernized idea of "nuclear family," it is only partial. "Extended

---

33. Adolescent Health Research Group (AHRG), *New Zealand Youth;* AHRG, *Youth* '07; Clark et al. *Youth* '12.

34. AHRG, *Youth* '07, 4.

family" does not specify a way of relating within families. In families where the virtues of both mutuality and solidarity are included, there is a difference. Such families are likely to see results such as increased experiences of wellbeing, where children and adults together experience safety, and enjoyment of the possibility to make unique contribution both to their family life as well as to the wider community and society.

Implication Three

The ideas of *perichoresis* and *hesed* and their impact have caused me to change the way these papers are scheduled within the counselor education program. The "theological understanding of family" section of the year one *Families and Whānau* paper, now comes right at the start of the course. I believe it is critical to provide emerging practitioners with an ethical vision of family relationships that is rooted in Christian tradition. Without this, they risk being vulnerable to other views of "Christian families" which could make them ill-prepared for the complex family relationships that they will encounter during practicum and when training is finished. This is critical to give a real understanding of the different ways of thinking about Biblical views of family. Students now read the first chapter from the fourth edition of *The Family*[35] with the purpose of introducing to them such ideas as the social trinitarian vision of relating. Then they discuss these very new ideas, either in class or in on-line forums. *Hesed* and biblical family values are introduced, and students are encouraged to think about what this means to them in terms of their understanding of God's plan for families.

Implication Four

One clear learning appears to be the idea that God's perfect plan for families is rarely seen in the biblical narrative. We therefore need to be able to stop ourselves thinking of "an ideal" which does not always exist. Instead we move towards an understanding of the imperfections that exist in a fallen world and realize that as God works with families who are not perfect, he invites us to do the same. In providing students with an ethical or virtue-based vision of family relating, we seem to disrupt some of their taken-for-granted theological assumptions. On many occasions students have discussed how in some churches they have seen ways which are less than accepting of families who do not fit the "norm" of a mother and father who are married and

---

35. Balswick and Balswick, *Family (4th ed.)*.

have the requisite 2.4 children. In fact, Statistics New Zealand's projections for 2001 to 2021[36] suggest that two-parent families are likely to decrease by around 5 percent, while one-parent families are projected to increase by 21 percent. The largest change is that "couples without children" are now likely to be the largest group nationwide. So what we may have believed to be the ideal or typical family is no longer the norm. A key point made by Tim Bulkeley, who comes each year to lecture to this class, is that "God is at work in the messy realities of family life." This saying is often mentioned by students in discussions, and even in assignments, as having been a change-point for them.

Implication Five

If I see *perichoresis* as a life-changing concept with the Father, Son, and Spirit mutually indwelling, and now consider the year three *Working with Couples and Families* paper, then it invites a different teaching approach. I say this because if family members are seen to be in this *perichoretic* relationship, then ways of considering the family as a system and concepts such as hierarchy will not necessarily fit. These are ideas on which I am still pondering. If the Triune God comes as a family and has a heart for families, then I need to consider the center of family relationships. The idea of *hesed* as the basic value for a family is easier to understand and teach. For me, the notion of working with whatever type of family is presented does not pose a problem. Seeing solidarity/trust/loving faithfulness as being at the core of their existence means I can be freed from somehow holding on to notions of an "ideal family." I see that God is there and if He can work in a broken world and in a "non-ideal" family then so can I. If my students, with some knowledge of these concepts, see *perichoresis* and *hesed* as ways of increasing understanding, this may lead to them working more relationally with hurting families. So, if they see these families in a different way, and thus work in a more relational way, I will be pleased. I hope that the ideas from Year One can be recapped in Year Three and the difficult issues that are tackled in that paper (such as conflict, separation and divorce, and blended families) may be viewed differently.

Overall my hope is that when individuals begin to consider these concepts, something within their thinking and being will change and they may "see" differently those individuals and families with whom they live, and those with whom they will be working as counselors.

---

36. Statistics New Zealand, *Family and Household Projections.*

References

Adolescent Health Research Group. *New Zealand Youth: A Profile of their Health and Wellbeing.* Auckland, New Zealand: The University of Auckland, 2003.

Adolescent Health Research Group. *Youth '07: The Health and Wellbeing of Secondary School Students in New Zealand. Initial Findings.* Auckland, New Zealand: The University of Auckland, 2008.

Balswick, Jack, and Judy Balswick. *The Family: A Christian Perspective on the Contemporary Home.* 3rd ed. Grand Rapids, MI: Baker, 2007.

Balswick, Jack, and Judy Balswick. *The Family: A Christian perspective on the contemporary home.* 4th ed. Grand Rapids, MI: Baker, 2014.

Bartle-Haring, Suzanne. "The Relationships Among Parent-Adolescent Differentiation, Sex Role Orientation and Identity Development in Late Adolescence and Early Adulthood." *Journal of Adolescence* 20, 5 (1997) 553–56.

Bulkeley, Tim. "What is a Family?" http://www.nzchristiannetwork.org.nz/family/233-what-is-a-family.html

Carter, Elizabeth A., and Monica McGoldrick. *The Expanded Family Life Cycle: Individual, Family, and Social Perspectives.* Boston: Allyn and Bacon, 1999.

Clark, Gordon R. *The Word "Hesed" in the Hebrew Bible.* Sheffield, England: JSOT, 1993.

Clark, Terryann, et al. *Youth '12 Overview: The Health and Wellbeing of New Zealand Secondary School Students in 2012.* Auckland, New Zealand: The University of Auckland, 2013.

Duvall, Evelyn Millis. "Family Development's First Forty Years." *Family Relations*, 37 no.2 127–134.

Edgar-Smith, Susan and Robert H. Wozniak. "Family Relational Values in the Parent-Adolescent Relationship." *Counseling and Values*, 54 no.2 (2010) 187–200.

Favez, Nicolas, et al. "The Development of Family Alliance from Pregnancy to Toddlerhood and Child Outcomes at Five Years." *Family Processes*, 51 no.4 (2012) 542–558.

Gunton, Colin E. *The One, the Three and the Many: God, Creation and the Culture of Modernity.* Cambridge: Cambridge University Press, 1993.

Hayes, Heather. "A Re-introduction to Family Therapy: Clarification of Three Schools." *Australian and New Zealand Journal of Family Therapy*, 12 no.1 (1991) 27–43.

Hui, Edwin. (2000). "Jen and Perichoresis: The Confucian and Christian Bases of the Relational Person." In *The Moral Status of Personhood: Perspectives on Bio-ethics*, edited by Gerhold K. Becker, 95–117. Amsterdam: Rodopi, 2000.

James, Carolyn Custis. *The Gospel of Ruth: Loving God Enough to Break the Rules*. Grand Rapids, MI: Zondervan, 2008.

Lindblom, Jallu, et al. "Dynamic Family System Trajectories from Pregnancy to Child's First Year." *Journal of Marriage and Family*, 76 no.4 (2014) 796–807.

McGoldrick, Monica, and Randy Gerson. "Genograms and the Family Life Cycle." In *The Changing Family Life Cycle: A Framework for Family Therapy*, edited by Elizabeth Carter and Monica McGoldrick, 164–189. 2nd ed. New York, NY: Gardner, 2003.

Moynagh, Michael. "Family." In *New dictionary of Christian Ethics and Pastoral Theology*, edited by David J. Atkinson, et al., 372–75. Downers Grove, IL: InterVarsity, 1995.

Nichols, Michael P., and Schwartz, Richard C. *The Essentials of Family Therapy*. 2nd ed. Boston, MA: Pearson, 2005.

Olson, David H. "Circumplex Model of Marital and Family Systems." *Journal of Family Therapy*, 22 no.2 (2000) 144–167.

Ostriker, Alicia. "The Book of Ruth and the Love of the Land." *Biblical Interpretation*, 10 no.4 (2002) 343–359.

Phanon, Panthakan. "Double *hesed* of God in Naomi's life (Ruth 1:19–22)." *Asian Journal of Pentecostal Studies*, 13 no. 1 (2010) 20–39.

Statistics New Zealand. "Subnational Family and Household Projections: 2001 (Base) to 2021 Update." http://www.stats.govt.nz/browse_for_stats/people_and_communities/Families/SubnationalFamilyandHouseholdProjections_HOTP01-21update.aspx

Taonui, Rāwiri. "Tribal Organization—*Whānau*." http://www.teara.govt.nz/en/tribal-organisation/page-4

Volf, Miroslav. *After Our Likeness: The Church as the Image of the Trinity*. Grand Rapids, MI: Eerdmans, 1998.

Witterborn, Andrea K., et al. "Dyadic Research in Marriage and Family Therapy: Methodological Considerations." *Journal of Marital and Family Therapy*, 39 no.1 (2013) 5–16.

7

Christian Hope
Ethical Responses to Trauma

Lisa Spriggens

I considered starting this chapter with a personal story of trauma, or a small anecdote which might allude to the nature of this particular chapter. However, stories of trauma seldom suit being collapsed into pithy anecdotes. Traumatic events have always been a part of the human experience; however, now more than ever trauma, and the effects of it, is being noticed, shared, and talked about. Numerous media platforms mean that I can sit in my living room and witness horrific scenes of terror, destruction, and death, sometimes as they are happening. I have been blessed, so far, with a life relatively free of significant trauma experiences, however in my work as a counselor I have experienced, and carry the effects, of witnessing countless stories of others' trauma.

A significant body of research now exists in the area of trauma[1] including its impact on the individual,[2] the witness to the trauma, and the collective.[3] This chapter explores some ways in which a relational trinitarian theology might inform our response to those who have experienced trauma.[4] It draws on counseling practices that I observe reflect something of trinitarian thinking about the way love invites us to respond to trauma. In

---

1. For example, Briere, *Child Abuse Trauma*; Briere and Scott, *Principles of Trauma Therapy*; Herman, *Trauma and Recovery*; Rothschild, *Body Remembers*.
2. Rothschild, *Body Remembers*.
3. Weingarten, *Common Shock*, 15–8.
4. Moltmann and Moltmann-Wendel, *Passion for God*.

particular, it draws on witnessing practices[5] which honor the stories people bring and response-based practices[6] which honor the responses people have to trauma. This chapter will also explore collaborative practices[7] which reach out into communities in practices of justice and connection. These practice responses stand against isolation and work to draw people back into relationship with themselves and others, while honoring what they survived. The thinking here is that noticing responses, rather than effects, directs us to the skills and resilience survivors have drawn upon in their story. As trauma survivors are invited back into relationship, identity is able to be re-shaped in ways which bring forth preferred ways of knowing themselves and reflect the journey they have travelled.[8] Thus, this chapter will show how theology and ethics are experienced in the practice of trauma counseling.

DEFINING TRAUMA

In its broadest sense I understand trauma to be any events which are "out of the ordinary and are directly experienced as threats to survival and self-preservation."[9] These threats can be real or perceived.[10] Weingarten helpfully pays attention to the "common shock" experienced by people in the unintentional witnessing of routine, everyday violence.[11] Whatever shape trauma takes, it challenges a basic human assumption in the goodness of life.[12] As such it threatens to interrupt experiences of *shalom*; that is subject-to-subject relationships with self, other, God, community, and environment, and can often bring shame, isolation and relational disconnection as survivors endeavor to make sense of their experience.

---

5. Weingarten, *Common Shock*, 191–224; Weingarten, "Witnessing, Wonder and Hope."
6. Wade, "Despair, Resistance, Hope."
7. Reynolds, "Resisting Burnout."
8. White, "Working with People," 26–8.
9. Janoff-Bulman, *Shattered Assumptions*, 53.
10. Pearlman and Saakvitne, *Trauma and the Therapist*, 60.
11. Weingarten, *Common Shock*, 3.
12. Janoff-Bulman, *Shattered Assumptions*.

THEOLOGICAL FOUNDATIONS FOR WORKING WITH TRAUMA SURVIVORS

Trauma can bring with it a myriad of existential and theological questions. In response to trauma counselors often hear "Why do bad things happen to good people?" "Why me?" "What have I done to deserve this?" Making meaning of trauma, resolving the "why" of trauma, can be seen as a part of the healing process. There is an urge, on the part of the survivor, for the story of the trauma to be, somehow, integrated in to the meta-narrative of a person's life.[13] However these questions can also become sites where trauma is perpetuated. In other words, there is a struggle to find answers to events which defy logic. This perpetuation of trauma has unfortunately often been supported by theology and the church.

A THEOLOGY OF TRAUMA AND SUFFERING

In spite of arguing that it has a role to play, theology and practical teaching in the church have often been very unhelpful to the trauma victim. For example, transactional understandings of atonement typically construct a narrative of the cross which focuses on the crucifixion as the mode of payment for sin.[14] Under these models of the atonement humanity is witness to Jesus paying the cost for human failure, to fulfil the law as determined by God. This theology can be very destructive for people when they are suffering. It can lead to explaining suffering as a "test of faithfulness," or a "result of a lack of faith," or of "sin," or as "spiritual attack," and it can portray an image of God who has decided for us to experience suffering. Furthermore, theology which supports the understanding that all events are ordained by God may invite counselors to make meaning of trauma in ways which are more likely to have the survivor searching for the "reasons" why God chose for them to go through this traumatic experience,[15] rather than working with the client to alleviate the suffering caused by the trauma. In circumstances where trauma has occurred as a result of another's actions attention can be drawn away from the responsibility the other might hold and towards searching for an ultimate reason why God chose, or allowed, these events to happen. It can also result in a judgmental stance on the part of the counselor, who may respond from understanding suffering in the ways mentioned above. These assumptions and ways of working with trauma

13. Neimeyer et al., "Grief Therapy."
14. Bondi, *Memories of God*, 120–1.
15. Boyd, *Is God to Blame?*; Jones, *Trauma and Grace*, 23–42.

risk the survivor experiencing blame and responsibility for the experience. Boyd offers some critique of what he terms this "blueprint worldview"[16] and reflects on the ultimate love we see in the story of the Cross. He argues that if the Cross is the centerpiece of the Gospel story it is not logical that God would allow, or ordain, tragedy and evil as this would challenge the ultimate love evidenced in the Cross. It seems to me that we have an ethical responsibility to notice the effects of the theology we engage with, and in the light of this pay attention to how, as counselors, we are making meaning of the trauma stories we hear in our work. My point is that anything in the counseling context that separates either the client, or the counselor, from the compassion of God is unhelpful. I say this along with Olthuis who suggests that it is compassion which "transforms suffering"[17] and brings life. This aligns with theological positions which describe Christ as being "with" us in our suffering.

SUFFERING "WITH"

There has been a theological turn, over the last generation, towards an understanding of the atonement that is centered on love rather than the law. Sometimes referred to as incarnational atonement, it centers on how humanity is invited to participate with Christ in this. The incarnation, as the realization of God entering our humanity, becomes the site of atonement.[18] In the incarnation God enters our humanity fully in the life of Christ. The Cross is not, then, a symbol of a payment for sin, but an act to bring humanity back in to Love.[19] In this shift away from the transactional model of atonement, through the story of the Cross, it becomes possible to see suffering as a part of the world we live in, rather than an act ordained, or at least not interrupted, by God.

Moltmann, as one of the earliest non-transactional theologians in the western tradition, has a particular way of expressing Christ being with us in suffering. Moltmann suggests that as people start to explore existential questions, like those mentioned above, we come to a summative question of God's character: "Is God the transcendent and untouched stage manager of the theater of this violent world, or is God in Christ the central engaged figure of the world tragedy?"[20] Victims of trauma are offered either a God—or counselor—

16. Boyd, *Is God to Blame?*, 41.
17. Olthuis, *Beautiful Risk*, 45.
18. Tanner, "Incarnation, Cross, and Sacrifice," 48–56.
19. Bondi, *Memories of God*, 141–4.
20. Moltmann and Moltmann-Wendel, *Passion for God*, 72.

who watches dispassionately, or one who, through Christ, is required to take on, and risk being overwhelmed by, suffering. Moltmann suggests there is another alternative, "active suffering,"[21] which asks for a willingness to be open to, and affected by others suffering. This suffering reflects "passionate love"[22] and is a suffering which, rather than coming from a place of incapability, arises from the abundance of God's love for creation. The Trinitarian relationship is reflective of this love. Rather than the Father dispassionately witnessing the Son's death at the crucifixion, the Trinity experiences this trauma collectively. The Father witnesses and grieves passionately. It is in light of this act of "suffering with" that the Cross can be read as representing, counselors are invited to "active suffering," being with, and encountering people in ways which open us up to being affected and changed by the relationship. This is a vastly different position to that of searching for "reasons" for the trauma. In recognition of this relational engagement with trauma it is worth exploring a theology which invites a focus on relationship.

TRINITARIAN THEOLOGICAL ANTHROPOLOGY

It is a belief that, above all else, God is love, and a strong sense of ethical responsibility to embody this love in my work has me engaging with a theology which reflects this commitment. Trinitarian theology invites this engagement with a relational anthropology. The Trinity reflects the nature of what it means to be a person.[23] If we are *imago Dei*, then we are created to be beings in relationship, reflective of the nature of the Trinity.[24] This way of understanding people as persons-in-relation[25] participating in the life of the Trinity makes available a theological position from which to engage in counseling work on behalf of love and compassion, rather than a judgment of the reasons why a client has arrived in my room. Given that we are relational beings and trauma works to rupture relationship, working to restore relationship is an entirely appropriate response to trauma.[26] I see this as incarnational in nature, inviting others back in to relationship. How we understand suffering and hope will shape what happens in this relationship.

21. Ibid., 74.
22. Ibid., 74.
23. Grenz, *Social God*.
24. Balswick et al., *Reciprocating Self*.
25. Grenz, *Social God*.
26. Janoff-Bulman, *Shattered Assumptions*.

THEOLOGY OF HOPE

In the face of trauma, hope can be what holds us. As Christians, how we understand hope will strongly inform what meaning we make of trauma and suffering. Christian theology often looks to the resurrection as the source of hope. Resurrection hope draws us forward towards life and new beginnings.[27] In this common metaphor, however, there is a risk that in holding on to hope, the very real pain of the trauma becomes invisible. As Christians we are so often told that we are to have hope, that where there is life in Christ there cannot be death. These triumphalist notions of hope can also mean those living with trauma have no place of acceptance. An experience of trauma can rupture life in such a way that it will not ever be the same again.[28] The trauma survivor is faced with the challenge of continuing to live, while experiencing the death of a life that was. Trauma is not just an event, it is the "ongoing crisis of living" which often persists long after the event.[29] Critically, questions emerge about whether there is room for both death and life in the aftermath of trauma, or even the possibility of life. A theology of hope that encompasses both is needed.

The story of the crucifixion is a powerful story of trauma. It is complex and multifaceted, offering space for death and life in the aftermath of trauma. Rambo[30] engages with the crucifixion story through the lens of trauma theory. She challenges theological positions on the resurrection which hold to the separation between the death of Good Friday and the life of Easter Sunday. In her exploration of Easter Saturday she invites us in to the mysticism and silence of the in between, where both life and death exist. This, I suggest, is the realm inhabited by compassionate counselors. Rambo goes on to argue that a lived experience of trauma holds both death and life, and that Easter Saturday is the theological equivalent of this trauma experience. Some Christian theology requires the believer to forsake death for life. But this does not often fit the experience of trauma. In the aftermath of trauma there is death which lingers. This could be the literal experience of death, or a more meta-physical death which might look like Janoff-Bulman's[31] death of some fundamental assumptions about the world. Rambo suggests Easter Saturday as a starting point for witnessing, and holding the tension of both death and life existing simultaneously. As counselors we are invited to enter in to this place, with our clients.

---

27. Rambo, *Spirit and Trauma*, 6.
28. Janoff-Bulman, *Shattered Assumptions*; Jones, *Trauma and Grace*, 12–15.
29. Rambo, "Trauma and Faith," 239.
30. Rambo, *Spirit and Trauma*, 45–80.
31. Janoff-Bulman, *Shattered Assumptions*.

BEARING WITNESS

In light of this incarnational theology of trauma, anthropology, and hope, I am invited to pay attention to how I engage in work with people who have experienced trauma. The work of Weingarten[32] around "witnessing" has been extremely influential in how I undertake, and make sense of, this kind of counseling work. It is an important part of my work generally, but even more particularly when working with people who have experienced trauma. In the act of witnessing, all that was before the event, all that was lost, and what now remains is acknowledged.[33] In this space both death and what remains of living can be held compassionately. Rambo uses the example of the biblical story of the hemorrhaging woman and describes Jesus' encounter with her as an act of witness. As the woman touches his garments he witnesses the space where both trauma and healing exist, the place where hope lives. In this space, understanding is not the critical part of the story, but a stepping in to the "unknown" of the trauma experience is where the act of witness takes place. It is in the witnessing of what is, that the hope of life can be imagined.[34]

As I bear witness to the trauma stories of people's lives I step in to the place where both death and "living on"[35] may happen. In this way I bring a relational connection in to a space where trauma has fractured relationship. Witnessing moves in to a space beyond language, and brings the possibility of healing. As I have been saying, working with hope in this way challenges triumphalist hope and offers a more accessible hope for those living in the aftermath of trauma. Witnessing my clients and the stories they bring can, therefore, be seen as engaging in practices of "active suffering," reflecting the depth of love God has for his creation.[36]

In the in-between space a question emerges of how we acknowledge the presence of both death and life in our witnessing of our client and their story. Is it possible to remain with death (in a metaphorical or literal sense) while we engage in acts of living? For the counselor who holds tightly to values of hope and life this can challenge some fundamental beliefs about his or her work. While I am not suggesting that hope is forsaken, I am proposing that the central challenge is around how we can hold hope in this work, without making invisible the death present in the story.

32. Weingarten, *Common Shock*, 157–224; Weingarten, "Reasonable Hope"; Weingarten, "Sorrow"; Weingarten, "Witnessing, Wonder, and Hope."
33. Rambo, "Trauma and Faith."
34. Ibid.
35. Derrida, "Living On," 76.
36. Moltmann and Moltmann-Wendel, *Passion for God*.

RELATIONAL COUNSELING PRACTICES IN RESPONSE TO TRAUMA

I now want to suggest a very particular manner in which hope can be enacted in counseling without rendering death invisible, and this is in the relational encounter between counselor and client. As I said in the introduction there is an extensive field of research and writing in the area of trauma[37] which present many different ways to engage in counseling work with trauma survivors. It is beyond the scope of this chapter to present all of these, but in light of the theological anthropology which shapes my whole engagement with counseling practice, there are some practices which move to the foreground. These practices are ones which hold compassionate relationality as central, and value preferred identity stories that are *more* than the trauma story they are also living.

Much of my experience in the trauma field is from working with survivors of sexual violence, firstly as a counselor and then as a coordinator of clinical crisis responses in a sexual abuse help center. The following vignette is not based on a particular client, but is a collaboration of stories, and common experiences, from the women who I have joined with in this work. Some of the responses to trauma noticed in this story are more general to trauma experience, and others more particular to experiences of sexual violence. Drawing on the story, I will pay attention to the counseling practices I would engage with which reflect the incarnational and relational commitments I hold in the work.

Amy[38] is a twenty-one-year-old university student who, after a night out with friends, was sexually assaulted by a taxi driver as she tried to make her way home. Initially Amy told no one about this event, hopeful that "getting on with life" would help the memories and the impact of this traumatic experience disappear. Six months later Amy is experiencing flashbacks, increased anxiety, particularly while out in public, and also depression. She had been engaged in an online dating website but since the assault has felt too afraid to meet new people, and feels she has been disconnecting from her friends as she feels unable to talk about what has been happening to her. Her employer has issued her with a verbal warning due to the number of days she has had off over the last few months. She wishes she could just forget the whole experience, and feels guilty for getting so drunk that night that she was unable to stop what

---

37. Briere and Scott, *Principles of Trauma Therapy*; Ogden and Fisher, *Sensorimotor Psychotherapy*; Rothschild, *Body Remembers*.

38. Amy is a composite client based on work with a variety of clients in different contexts and in different times.

happened. Amy has come to counseling wanting to get everything back on track, and to stop the assault defining everything in her life.

As I introduced earlier, trinitarian theology invites us to understand ourselves as relational beings, created in and for relationship. It is in relationship that we are shaped and become known.[39] In the counseling context this positions me with a strong awareness that the relationship I establish with my client will become a site where we will both experience ourselves and each other, and will be shaped in this. I also hold the understanding that my client will have been formed through the other relationships in her life, and that the experience of trauma will likely, but not solely, play a significant role in this. These ideas position me in particular ways when I first engage with Amy. I meet Amy with the understanding that she is more than her stories of trauma,[40] and that, most importantly, my role is to act as witness, participating in the "active suffering" of Christ.[41]

In witnessing Amy, and the stories she brings, I want her to feel that I am present with her in the conversation, and that I can hold what she is sharing. While I might be listening for aspects of hope and life in the stories, I also want to bear witness to the unspeakable, that which might "fracture language,"[42] on behalf of a theology which asks me to be prepared to be touched and changed by others.[43] So in Amy's story I will be witnessing the isolation that has arisen from the silence of not being able to speak of the event, the depression and anxiety that have entered her life, the guilt from the night of the assault, and perhaps even guilt from the idea that despite her best attempts to "get everything back on track" she has found herself with a counselor. I am also likely to be witnessing the effects this assault has had on her sense safety, on her identity, on her body and on her relationships.

In some way these stories represent the place where death exists for a survivor of trauma. As a counselor I also hold that hope will also be present in the story.[44] So while witnessing this place of death I'm also listening for hope. In witnessing I am offering an experience of "being-with" which counters the isolation trauma brings. In this place hope can emerge. Weingarten[45] suggests working with reasonable hope which exists in the

---

39. Balswick et al., *Reciprocating Self*.
40. White, "Working with People," 55.
41. Moltmann and Moltmann-Wendel, *Passion for God*, 74.
42. Weingarten, "Witnessing, Wonder and Hope," 179. Weingarten suggests that as trauma fractures language, witnessing also moves in to an experience of the trauma which language cannot describe.
43. Moltmann and Moltmann-Wendel, *Passion for God*.
44. Carey et al., "Absent but Implicit," 321.
45. Weingarten, "Reasonable Hope."

present, notices what possibility exists right now, and acts out of that possibility towards a preferred future, in whatever circumstances a person might find themselves in. It is a hope that "flourishes in relationship" and makes space for uncertainty, doubt, and despair.[46] In the counseling relationship reasonable hope is enacted even as the death that trauma can bring remains present.

Wade[47] also invites us to witness in a particular way by listening for *responses* to trauma, that is, those actions, thoughts, and feelings which the survivor has in response to the trauma experience. Focusing on responses by the survivor, rather than effects, infers a level of action or agency in the experience that might not be as present if we were to focus on the effects of trauma. These can be the most invisible of activities, or the most explicit. Even in the face of circumstances within which we feel totally powerless we will be responding in some way. Michael White, Allan Wade and others have written about our responses to hardship/pain as being resistance, that in even the smallest responses there is a resistance to the unfairness, or painfulness, or "not-okay-ness" of what has happened.[48] Our resistance then directs us to what we are valuing, or what is important to us.[49]

Paying attention to the steps that have been taken which led up to your client meeting with you can, even at the beginning of your conversation together, bring in to awareness what he/she is valuing in his/her life. While trauma can have a far-reaching impact on individuals' lives and their relationships, many survivors that I encountered expressed a desire to forget it ever happened and move on. In my experience, however, this was seldom managed. We see this reflected in Amy's story above. Trauma challenges a basic assumption that life, and its participants, are good.[50] This common initial response to trauma could be seen as a way of endeavoring to hold on to this belief; through forgetting practices. Amy's efforts to "get on with life" may direct us towards some values and hopes she holds for herself. These may prove to be acts of living on.

In my work with young women who experienced sexual assault it was significant to notice even the smallest ways in which they had resisted the assault. Amy may tell some stories about the assault which reveal the ways in which she resisted and protested against what was happening to her. It

---

46. Ibid., 8.
47. Wade, "Despair, Resistance, Hope."
48. Wade, "Despair, Resistance, Hope"; Wade, "Small Acts of Living," 24–26; White, "Working with People," 28–30.
49. White, "Working with People," 28–30.
50. Janoff-Bulman, *Shattered Assumptions*.

might have been the thought that what was happening was "not ok!" It might have been a physical struggle with the offender. Both are forms of resistance which direct us towards what Amy values. Even in the vignette above we can see some places of protest and resistance for Amy. Amy wanted to forget that the assault happened. She did not want to give it space and attention in her life. Her decision to undertake counseling might also connect with this protest. Amy does not want her life to be defined by this trauma experience. She is claiming herself to be more than this moment in her life. By connecting to the responses people have to traumatic events and making connections to the values they hold and the hopes they have for themselves we are participating in an identity project.[51] This identity project notices the trauma, but also notices who the person is in response to the trauma. This (re)discovering of self can hold both the grief of what the self was, and the possibility of what remains, and what may emerge.

My point is that when I meet with Amy for the first time I hold an understanding that I am talking with a person who already knows something about how, and is acting in some ways, to resist the events life is throwing at her. I am going to be curious to know what it is that Amy is resisting, and what she is claiming as important in that resistance. As we start to explore what it is that is causing such distress for Amy we will be directed towards what she is hoping for.[52]

COMMUNITY PRACTICES WHICH STAND AGAINST TRAUMA

Ethical responses to trauma, I think, encompass more than the work done in the counseling room with clients and possibly their families. We live in a social domain which, either directly or indirectly, has contributed to the traumatic experience. What responsibilities do we have, as counseling practitioners, to act into the social worlds of our clients? Working with survivors of sexual violence I found myself being invited to respond to trauma in ways which took me outside my counseling room. This ranged from client advocacy with legal and social services, to participating in marches highlighting the risks women experience in their world, to training community groups on appropriate responses to victims. Taking up the invitation to respond more broadly to the experiences of my clients created an awareness of social issues which supported sexual violence, and perpetuated its effects. As I look back on my experiences in this work I believe that the broader

---

51. White, "Working with People," 26–8.
52. Reynolds, "Resisting Burnout."

responses I had to this particular kind of trauma made it possible for me to more fully witness the experience of my clients and also acted as a resistance to the isolation that trauma stories can bring.

Responding to trauma in the broader social context also makes available to counselors, and clients, the support and solidarity of others engaged in similar action.[53] While survivors of sexual violence may choose not to engage in social action, there are other practices which can invite connection for survivors. Narrative therapy engages in practices which intentionally work to create connection between clients and others, either those they are already in relationship with, or through practices of "communities of concern,"[54] creating connections with others who have similar stories. An example of this is the "Archive of Resistance,"[55] an online anti-anorexia archive which collects individual stories, on behalf of supporting a sense of community for clients. In these and other ways, the counselor and the client can engage in practices which step outside the counseling room and in to their social worlds, countering the isolation and separation which experiences of trauma often invite. In this space we can again see the transformative power of relationship. Social action in response to trauma is an act of resistance, perhaps on behalf of justice. Reynolds[56] suggests this is participation of a revolutionary love which invites community and solidarity, and can be expressed even in the most difficult of circumstances.

In this chapter I explored a theology which asks that I allow myself to become vulnerable to, and to be changed by, the "active suffering"[57] of witnessing and encountering the truly heart breaking stories of trauma my clients bring with them. I understand this to be an ethical position, a way of being in the work which reflects that which I value. I have also identified some counseling practices which enact this kind of engagement. Part of my experience of integrating theology and counseling practice is that, in the process, theology and counseling shape each other. As I have engaged in the work of counseling, I have endeavored to witness stories of trauma in ways that invite some experience of hope, and then explore responses to trauma which direct us towards that which the client holds dear. These are practices which remind me of the depth of God's love, that He might experience our suffering more fully than I could ever do. When I work with clients to bring forward people and relationships which are meaningful and counter the

53. Ibid.
54. Madigan and Epston, "From Spy-chiatric Gaze."
55. "Archive of Resistance."
56. Reynolds, "Resisting Burnout."
57. Moltmann and Moltmann-Wendel, *Passion for God.*

experience of isolation trauma brings I am reminded that we are created in God's image as relational beings, to be in deep, reciprocal relationship with each other. In these ways my counseling practice speaks in to the theology I engage with, continuing this integrative relationship.

References

"The Archive of Resistance: Anti-Anorexia/Anti-Bulimia." http://www.narrativeapproaches.com/?page_id=42

Balswick, Jack, et al. *The Reciprocating Self: Human Development in Theological Perspective*. Downers Grove, IL: InterVarsity Press, 2005.

Bondi, Roberta C. *Memories of God: Theological Reflections on a Life*. Nashville: Abingdon, 1995.

Boyd, Gregory A. *Is God to Blame?: Moving beyond Pat Answers to the Problem of Evil*. Downers Grove, IL: InterVarsity Press, 2003.

Briere, John. *Child Abuse Trauma: Theory and Treatment of the Lasting Effects*. Newbury Park, CA: Sage, 1992.

Briere, John, and Catherine Scott. *Principles of Trauma Therapy: A Guide to Symptoms, Evaluation, and Treatment*. Thousand Oaks, CA: Sage, 2006.

Carey, Maggie, et al. "The Absent but Implicit: A Map to Support Therapeutic Enquiry." *Family Process* 48 no. 3 (2009) 319–31.

Derrida, Jacques. "Living On." In *Deconstruction and Criticism*, edited by Harold Bloom, et al., 75–176. New York: Seabury, 1979.

Grenz, Stanley J. *The Social God and the Relational Self: A Trinitarian Theology of the Imago Dei*. Louisville, KY: Westminster John Knox, 2001.

Herman, Judith Lewis. *Trauma and Recovery*. New York, NY: Basic, 1992.

Janoff-Bulman, Ronnie. *Shattered Assumptions: Towards a New Psychology of Trauma*. New York: Simon and Schuster, 2002.

Jones, Serene. *Trauma and Grace: Theology in a Ruptured World*. Louisville, KY: Westminster John Knox, 2009.

Madigan, Stephen, and David Epston. "From "Spy-chiatric Gaze" to Communities of Concern: From Professional Monologue to Dialogue." In *The Reflecting Team in Action: Collaborative Practice in Family Therapy*, edited by Steven Friedman, 257–76. New York: Guilford, 1995.

Moltmann, Jürgen, and Elisabeth Moltmann-Wendel. *Passion for God: Theology in Two Voices*. Louisville, KY: Westminster John Knox, 2003.

Neimeyer, Robert A., et al. "Grief Therapy and the Reconstruction of Meaning: From Principles to Practice." *Journal of Contemporary Psychotherapy* 40 no. 2 (2010) 73–83.

Ogden, Pat, and Janina Fisher. *Sensorimotor Psychotherapy: Interventions for Trauma and Attachment*. New York: W. W. Norton, 2015.

Olthuis, James H. *The Beautiful Risk: A New Psychology of Loving and Being Loved.* Eugene, OR: Wipf & Stock, 2006.

Pearlman, Laurie A., and Karen W. Saakvitne. *Trauma and the Therapist: Countertransference and Vicarious Traumatization in Psychotherapy with Incest Survivors.* New York: Norton, 1995.

Rambo, Shelly. *Spirit and Trauma: A Theology of Remaining.* Louisville, KY: Westminster John Knox, 2010.

———. "Trauma and Faith: Reading the Narrative of the Hemorrhaging Woman." *International Journal of Practical Theology* 13 no. 2 (2010) 233–57.

Reynolds, Vikki. "Resisting Burnout with Justice-doing." *The International Journal of Narrative Therapy and Community Work* no. 4 (2011) 27–45.

Rothschild, Babette. *The Body Remembers: The Psychophysiology of Trauma and Trauma Treatment.* New York: Norton, 2000.

Tanner, Kathryn. "Incarnation, Cross, and Sacrifice: A Feminist-inspired Reappraisal." *Anglican Theological Review* 86 no. 1 (2004) 35–56.

Wade, Allan. "Despair, Resistance, Hope." In *Hope and Despair in Narrative and Family Therapy: Adversity, Forgiveness and Reconciliation*, edited by Carmel Flaskas, Imelda McCarthy, and Jim Sheehan, 63–74. London: Routledge, 2007.

———. "Small Acts of Living: Everyday Resistance to Violence and Other Forms of Oppression." *Contemporary Family Therapy* 19 no. 1 (1997) 23–39.

Weingarten, Kathy. *Common Shock: Witnessing Violence Every Day.* New York: Dutton, 2003.

———. "Reasonable Hope: Construct, Clinical Applications, and Supports." *Family Process* 49 no. 1 (2010) 5–25.

———. "Sorrow: A Therapist's Reflection on the Inevitable and the Unknowable." *Family Process* 51 no. 4 (2012) 440–55.

———. "Witnessing, Wonder, and Hope." *Family Process* 39 no. 4 (2000) 389–402.

White, Michael. "Working with People Who Are Suffering the Consequences of Multiple Trauma: A Narrative Perspective." In *Trauma: Narrative Responses to Traumatic Experience*, edited by David Denborough, 25–86. Adelaide, South Australia: Dulwich Centre, 2006.

8

Boys in Trouble at School
"I Am Becoming" Stories to Live in

Dr. Donald McMenamin

In this chapter I discuss how a community-based re-writing of young people's troublesome identity stories can make a significant difference to how they enact themselves at school. I also discuss how, for me as a narrative therapist, these practices which view identity as a social achievement are themselves one expression of a theology which sees people as made in the image of a relational God.

TWO KEY PERSPECTIVES

As a narrative therapist and teacher of thirty years of experience with young people in schools I come to this topic—boys in trouble at school—from two key perspectives. The first is to think of young people's actions (troubling or otherwise) as flowing from their identity stories. Here I am drawing on Epston and White's[1] understanding of story as a series of events across time, according to a theme or plot. I understand that a young person's stories about "who I am" guides his sense of "how I ought to act" in any given place and time.[2] Further, people's identity stories are shaped by the stories available within their communities.[3] That is to say, young people and others do not simply make up their identity stories—they piece them together from the stories available and acceptable within their world of influence. In

---

1. White, *Maps of Narrative Practice*; White and Epston, *Narrative Means*.
2. Ibid.
3. Freedman and Combs, *Narrative Therapy*.

that sense you could say that young people enact their own versions of the stories made available to them within their communities.[4]

The second perspective that shapes my approach to identity-storying is that different identity accounts have different effects. Some identity accounts focus on what young people care about, and what they might be trying to achieve and become in their sometimes misdirected actions. I call these *"I Am Becoming"* stories, such as I am becoming compassionate or hopeful, because they describe young people in terms of their often just emerging purposes and hopes for life. Identity stories such as these are often preferred by the people so described. Alternatively, some identity accounts highlight the misdirected steps taken by young people, and can produce identity descriptions such as "She is a thief," or "He is violent." While such descriptions often intend to help with behaviour change, they risk producing what I think of as *"I Am Not"* identity stories through bringing together a series of events across time highlighting a plot of a young person acting wrongly. In *I Am Not* identity stories the plot or focus is on linking transgressions rather than a person's intentions as highlighted in *I Am Becoming* stories. If, as above, young people enact the identity stories they live in, then the accounts people make of young people's actions are significant in helping to shape their subsequent behaviours. My experience of thirty years working with young people is that they most often prefer *I Am Becoming* versions of themselves, and the actions which flow from such identity stories are very likely to be less troubling for the young person and for those around them.

INTRODUCING JACK

As an example, let me introduce Jack: Jack[5] is a 14 year old young man who has a reputation for trouble at school and at home. The *I Am Not* stories around Jack draw on plots of continuous trouble maker at school, and non-cooperative and argumentative at home. Jack's actions, which both produce and follow these identity accounts, have Jack as a candidate for suspension from school, and have his mother bringing him to counseling in an effort to change things at home. In our counseling conversations Jack tells me *I Am Not* stories about trouble at school and home, plotting for example times he has been removed from classes and from school as well as times of trouble at home. While providing Jack a welcoming relational space to speak about his experience, I am listening carefully for echoes of any *I Am Becoming* stories as he speaks. Amongst the stories of trouble, I also hear that Jack has been

---

4. Shotter and Gergen, *Texts of Identity*.
5. "Jack" is a pseudonym and a composite client story.

watching other people in his class and noticing that they succeed at times when he does not—succeed in getting work done, in achieving grades, in avoiding too much conflict in class. I also hear that Jack notices the way conflict at home hurts his mother, and that he does not like that, and has, at times, taken steps to avoid hurting his mother. I also hear that Jack has some hopes for his future, and wants to succeed at school in order to get the job he is hoping for. As I listen, my aim is to explore with Jack these *I Am Becoming* accounts—stories of Jack as someone who notices how things could be different, and as someone who has hopes that things could be different for him and those he cares about. My hope is that, as we develop *I Am Becoming* accounts together, Jack's actions will begin to reflect those identity claims more closely. This hope is based on the idea that as these descriptions of him become available for Jack to consider, he will be able to decide whether he prefers them for himself or not. When I later invite Jack to take a position on whether these ways of describing him fit with his hopes for himself and those he cares about, Jack is enabled to further develop and potentially live into these alternative descriptions.

After our second conversation I wrote Jack this letter:

Dear Jack,

Thanks for the chance to speak again today.

Throughout our conversations one thread keeps returning: that you are someone with hopes for both now and for the future.

You told me that since Year Seven you have been observing how others succeed in class and you have been thinking about your future. You described your hopes for yourself as we spoke—hopes that include:

- That in daily life you can concentrate on work leading to a successful career;
- That every time you are in school you are able to focus on what you need—you called that a work ethic;
- That you see the big picture—you called that important;
- That you get what people have been saying: not talking, listening, doing what you are told—these basics lead from A to B;
- That you learn to do it even if you like it or not;
- That you be able to set your priorities at school, and avoid doing what causes unnecessary frustration, and anger at home;
- That you be more long-term oriented, mindful of your life goals;

- That you recognise what you need to improve yourself;
- That it is more about looking after your relationships than making a point in the short term.

When I asked you if you could do all that, you replied, "Yes, I've got what it takes."

I see your hopes for these things as really important. And also as something that can take as long as it takes. To my mind, moving towards these things is something for you to do, and also something for those who care for you to support you in doing. Am I right in thinking that your grandmother, your parents, and your brother are all keen to help with that? I wonder if any teachers might be keen next year too?

Again, thanks for the chance to talk—I enjoy that.

Warmly,

Mr Mac

In this letter I have reported back to Jack some of the things he has described which contradict stories about him as someone who does wrong. This is the beginning of a process of inviting Jack to consider if those ways of describing him fit with his hopes for himself and those he cares about. If Jack decides these descriptions do fit for him, our work together will be to co-write identity stories which highlight other times and places he has acted in these ways (or hoped to) in order to link a series of events across time according to Jack's preferred plot.

For Jack, as for all of us, *I Am Becoming* descriptions such as those in this letter co-exist alongside *I Am Not* identity stories. In my own experience it takes energy to choose to live in *I Am Becoming* stories; it seems that, unless I put deliberate effort into not doing so, I can readily default into available *I Am Not* identity stories. And this raises an important point for me as a counselor: Given that I am interested in helping young people and others to develop and live into their *I Am Becoming* identity stories, what practices help to keep these more nourishing identity accounts available and influential in a person's life?

THICKENING IDENTITY STORIES

In order to develop the emerging (and hopefully preferred) identity claims above, such as: "I have a work ethic" and "I can learn," *I Am Becoming* identity claims need to be richly researched and developed. That is, counselors and others need to support young people to re-engage with their history[6] in order to identify what and who it is that they care about, and highlight the actions they have taken towards achieving what they care about. For Jack, his noticing of others, his hopes for himself, and the efforts he has taken towards his goals, are stories which can be highlighted and developed in order that they become available to shape his actions at school and at home. Such stories, when more fully told, can develop a sense of self in keeping with Jack's own hopes in life as opposed to accounts of Jack's failings which he says later that he wants to move away from. And these hope-oriented stories, when told and retold, can go on to shape Jack's future actions.

One metaphor I use for preferred identity stories as they develop is that they are like the gravity attraction of planets in space: my understanding is that the more fully a preferred identity story is developed and enriched with other times and places the person has acted in keeping with their new identity claims, the more gravity that story has to attract and hold in orbit a young person's sense of self and their actions which flow from that sense of self. Specifically, if we can develop them as fully as possible, Jack's *I Am Becoming* accounts may well make a difference to how he acts at home and at school. Consistent with social constructionist thinking, to further develop their influence, *I Am Becoming* identity stories need to be told and retold to and with the significant figures in a young person's life.[7] The more that preferred identity stories are heard by, added to and supported by significant others, the more gravitational pull and influence they have. In Jack's story, we discussed who might know, or not be surprised to hear, that he was hoping to make a difference in his life and relationships. Jack reported that his grandmother, his parents and his older brother would all be interested in knowing and supporting his hopes. Jack and I discussed showing the letter above to these key people in order to recruit their support for his efforts.

AUDIENCE

One way of talking about the significance of others in the development of preferred identity stories is in terms of "audience." As a narrative therapist I hold that identity stories are a social construction, a social achievement.[8] I'm thinking of two points here. Firstly the idea that the stories through which young people make sense of themselves and others, and which shape their

---

6. White, *Reflections on Narrative Practice*.
7. White, *Reflections on Narrative*.
8. Gergen, *Social Construction*; Shotter and Gergen, *Texts of Identity*; White and Epston, *Narrative Means*.

actions, are pieced together from the ways of speaking that are available and influential within their communities.[9] If a young person is interested in making sense of themselves differently, they will draw on the ways they hear life being described around them as well as the ways they are spoken to and about by significant people such as peers and teachers. One implication of this is that working with young people to explore alternative and preferred identity stories must, wherever possible, include working with their support communities to clarify and thicken preferred identity stories—including what it is that the community values and is working for. This approach leads to working with a young person both as an individual and as a community member—as a person-in-relation. In this light it is important that both counselors and support communities help create alternative ways of making sense of life available to young people.

Secondly, and equally important to the successful development of preferred identity accounts, is the point that new stories cannot thrive without the support of these significant community-others. For example, if a counselor works with a young person to develop preferred identity stories, and his peers, teachers and family continue to relate to him in terms of his previous identity stories the new possibilities, however desirable, are unlikely to thrive. Therefore it is important that significant figures in the young person's life be invited to hear, add to and support new and preferred identity claims through times of telling and retelling of preferred stories.[10] An example of this can be imagined where Jack shows his grandmother, parents, and brother the letter above; their responses will play a large part in the new story's potential influence. The more they agree with and support the version of Jack described in the letter, the more it is likely to influence his future actions, and vice versa.

SOCIAL GOD, RELATIONAL SELVES

Although I come to these practices through training as a narrative therapist, one attraction for me is their resonance with my faith stance. When narrative therapy refers to identity as a relational achievement, a key relationship I have in mind is that with God—Father, Son, and Holy Spirit—a community of persons so lovingly relational that Christians speak of them as Three-in-One. In this light, to be the person Father is to be forever in

---

9. Burr, *Social Constructionism*.
10. White, *Reflections on Narrative Practice*.

relationship with the person, Son—that is each person of the Trinity exists in relationship.[11]

Balswick et al refer to a relational understanding of being made in the image of God on behalf of a project of human development. I take this to mean that we reflect God as Trinity in as much as we participate in social relationships according to the ethics of love and, in so doing, flourish as human beings. I draw here on a similar relational understanding to support a therapeutic approach—that to increasingly participate in God's shared life of love is to move towards wellness through "mutual love, mutual self-giving, mutual testifying, and mutual glorifying."[12] As Entwistle and Moroney[13] write "Jesus himself taught that we most completely fulfil our human calling when we love God and others with our whole selves."[14] By this understanding "the indwelling Spirit shapes the fellowship of Christ's followers after the pattern of the love that pre-exists in the triune life [producing] a visual, human coming-to-representation of the mutual indwelling of the persons of the Trinity."[15] In keeping with this theologically inspired example of becoming—one shaped around participation in love—I want to suggest that all *I Am Becoming* stories that have the potential to offer people experiences of wellbeing are actually reflections of God's way of becoming. I am not suggesting that any one choice to stand apart from a troubled reputation and develop a preferred identity story could be ever considered full participation in God's life of love, but I do mean to suggest that developing preferred identity accounts, *I Am Becoming* stories, can be considered in this light, however partial. Grenz argues that "although they present the anticipated fullness of community as a future reality, the early Christians were convinced that a partial, yet genuine foretaste of the eschatological fullness may be enjoyed prior to the eschaton."[16] It is this partial foretaste of the dynamic ontology of persons-in-relationship or persons-in-community that is highlighted and hoped for in the therapeutic practices described in this chapter. If, as I hold, we are made in the image of this relational God and invited to participate in a social project with a restoration *telos* (a vision of wellbeing), our personhood is also something which arises out of relationship. This initially and eternally with God, and then, modelled on

11. Balswick et al., *Reciprocating Self*.
12. Grenz, *Social God*.
13. Entwistle and Moroney, *Integrative Perspectives*.
14. See Matt 22:37–40, NIV.
15. Grenz, *Social God*, 336.
16. Ibid., 281.

Father, Son, and Spirit's love relationships, with those around us.[17] It follows therefore, that if being a person is to be in certain sorts of relationship, helpful therapeutic practices ought to pay attention to the relationships within which personhood exists. As McFadyen[18] offers, as soon as we acknowledge that personhood is a social achievement, we must immediately recognise that ethical and political questions need to be answered about the "best" form of relating. It is here that I find the language of social construction of identity helpful.[19]

Narrative therapy holds that people know themselves through the stories they tell about themselves, and the stories that others tell about them—what trinitarian thinkers such as Gunton[20] and Torrance[21] describe as persons-in-relation. What I highlight here is that identity stories are fundamentally relational. I claim this because the language from which identity stories are made is the socially available language of particular times and places. Further, the values that shape which identity stories are highlighted and which are not highlighted are the values of particular relationships in time and place. The acceptance or otherwise of a person's storied identity claims is not random, but depends on what is valued within the relationships between the persons involved. By this understanding relationship shapes the vocabulary, the selection of content, and the on-going valuing of people's identity claims.[22] Here I am saying that the project for narrative therapists is to help young people and their communities to research and develop the vocabularies, stories and audiences which highlight *I Am Becoming* accounts of a person's life. In as much as these accounts draw on a person's desire for loving relationships I maintain they echo the *imago Dei* stories of a person's life and identity.

When the Jewish and Christian scriptures write of Father, Son, and Spirit describing each other and their relationships, they say things like: "You are My Son, My Beloved! In You I am well pleased and find delight!"[23] And "That all of them may be one, Father, just as you are in me and I am in you."[24] In ways like these the three Persons of God speak each other's

---

17. Ware, *Holy Trinity*.
18. McFadyen, *Call to Personhood*
19. Burr, *Social Constructionism*.
20. Gunton, *The One, the Three and the Many*
21. Torrance, *Christian Doctrine of God*.
22. Gergen, *Social Construction*; Gergen, *Social Construction in Context*.
23. Luke 3:22, AMPC.
24. John 17:21, NIV.

identities into being—through words of love and inclusion.[25] In choosing to speak languages of love and inclusion, each divine Person offers and is offered a life-giving place to belong within—as Father, as Son, as beloved Spirit. Similarly, we as individuals-in-community are shaped in the image of God to the extent we speak in accord with love. The language and the stories we choose to speak to and about ourselves and others shape who we are and can be.

If, as I believe, people are created by a loving God and are invited to participate in God's shared life through Jesus and in the power of the Spirit, then we can say that people are invited to know themselves as beloved. This is the ultimate *I Am Becoming* story by which I can make sense of my own life and hope. How any one person will respond to that invitation is unknown. However it is my experience that young people respond warmly to projects which research the hopes and intentions implicit in their actions, and that those hopes and intentions can often be described as ethical. Where such ethical hopes and intentions can be developed into preferred identity accounts through connection with related intentions and actions, behaviour will often come to reflect that, and even dimly, to reflect *imago Dei*.

Here I ask: what effects might "knowing himself as beloved" have for Jack? When the people to whom he shows his letter respond (and let's assume here that they respond with support and appreciation—and because they are invited to read the letter on the prediction that they will do so it is a fair assumption) what responses will they offer? What words and actions of appreciation and support might they offer Jack? In my work I have often seen teachers taking up and offering new ways of relating and responding to young people, parents expressing heartfelt appreciation of the efforts of their children, peers making the kind of subtle affirmations which are so important to their friends—and equally I have seen significant changes of behaviour in young people like Jack as they respond with beloved-ness to these affirmations and supports. In this way *I Am Becoming* stories are produced as completely as possible, together with being told and retold as much as practicable to and with the significant figures in a young person's life.

RE-AUTHORING AT SCHOOL

When applied in the context of young people in trouble at school, a practice of community re-authoring of a young person's *I Am Becoming* identity stories includes several elements which overlap and repeat as required. Broadly speaking, the school guidance counselor (or similar) initially offers

25. Volf, *Exclusion and Embrace*.

an invitation to explore alternative and preferred stories of identity to a young person whose actions have him in trouble. At best this offer is invitational: just as being God's beloved is offered as a gentle invitation, deciding to explore alternative identity stories is something young people are invited to. While in a school context this invitation is often backed by unattractive alternatives such as stand-downs or suspensions, as much as possible it is important that participation is something the young person opts for himself. Thus the initial relationship within which an identity story re-authoring project takes place is best characterised by willing collaboration.

If that invitation is accepted, and when the time is right to do so, together with appropriate others the young person can participate in a process of restorative responses for any harm which may have been done by his actions.[26] At times young people in trouble have caused harm to others or to things. Attending to the righting of relationships and repairing of harm done clears the way for stepping into new identity stories. Restorative responses involve gathering the connected parties and discussing what happened, what effects that may have had on all concerned, and what could be done to help make things right.[27] My experience is that when young people hear and understand of the effects of their actions in a no-blame restorative conversation, and when others see that a young person understands the effects of their actions, something akin to grace often appears and unexpected ways forward can emerge. Where, as much as possible, harm to relationship and things have been attended to, a project of re-authoring of identity stories can continue. I say continue, because taking up an invitation to participate in a restorative process is itself a powerful demonstration of new and preferred identity claims—a step towards love in action.

Next the young person and the school guidance counselor might begin to develop alternative descriptions of the young person through exploring what his actions say about what he cares for.[28] As alternative identity stories develop through an exploration of times and places where a young person has acted on behalf of his preferred intentions, these are enriched and further developed together with chosen support people including peers, teachers, family, and community members.[29] There are two main threads to the initial re-storying of identity. Firstly, the actions taken by a young person, however unacceptable, can be understood as misguided attempts to

---

26. Drewery et al., *Restorative Practices*; Thorsborne and Vinegrad, *Restorative Justice*.

27. Thorsborne and Vinegrad, *Restorative Justice*; Winslade and Williams, *Safe and Peaceful Schools*.

28. Carey et al, *Absent but Implicit*; Wade, *Honoring Resistance*.

29. White, *Re-authoring Lives*.

achieve something good.[30] Exploring young people's actions with an eye for any ethical intentions implicit within their actions can help clarify what it is that the young person values in life. These values often have a history to be explored, and a future to be wondered about.[31]

Secondly, the young people themselves, or others close to them, may know of times and places where their actions tell a different story to the troubled one.[32] As above, within these other action stories are hints of the values which shape the young person's hopes for himself and others. These values also have a history to be explored, and a future to be wondered about. By gathering up accounts of times and places where the young person has acted on behalf of preferred hopes and values, it is possible to develop quite substantial identity stories which contradict and can replace prevailing problem-saturated accounts.

Throughout this process of re-authoring identity stories opportunities for telling and re-telling new stories of identity are explored together with chosen support people. As above, the more emerging stories are told and retold, the more it becomes possible for people to step into those identity claims, and act accordingly.[33] Telling and retelling preferred identity stories is achieved in many ways. Some examples include sending letters, such as the letter above, and other documents which highlight preferred identity accounts.[34] Letters and documents can be sent to the young person and to those they nominate. Telling and retelling can also be achieved through gathering peers, teachers, family, and community members in groups small and large (Outsider Witnessing, Definitional Ceremonies)[35] to hear and affirm alternative identity claims. Such times of telling and retelling allow supporters to say in effect, I hear what you are now saying about yourself, and I agree with and support that.

As emphasised above, *I Am Becoming* stories often co-exist alongside *I Am Not* stories. Stepping into preferred *I Am Becoming* stories does not necessarily remove *I Am Not* stories, nor do all relationships in a young person's life necessarily support preferred alternative identity stories. For these reasons it is important that the community of care remain vigilant in their support for a young person's preferred identity accounts and continue to promote actions in keeping with these. How that support looks will vary

---

30. Jenkins, *Becoming Ethical*.
31. Epston and Roth, *Engaging Young Persons*; White, *Re-authoring Lives*.
32. Denborough, *Retelling the Stories*.
33. White, *Workshop Notes*.
34. Newman, *Rescuing the Said*; Speedy, *Using Poetic Documents*.
35. White, *Reflections on Narrative*.

according to the community involved, but on-going support is important. Often that support can take the form of working together to make a difference for others—for example becoming involved in anti-bullying groups, or finding ways to tell their stories to younger people as a support for others' preferred identity stories and so on.[36] In this way, taking action to help others can be yet another site for the demonstration of, the telling and retelling of, new identity claims—which at their best are themselves echoes of the *imago Dei* the Spirit is bringing to life within and between us.

CONCLUSION

In this chapter I have described how, for me, a narrative therapy project of re-authoring identity stories for young people within community resonates with the invitation Father, Son, and Holy Spirit eternally offer each other and to all people: "You are my beloved in whom I am well pleased." I have done this through establishing a link between a young person's hopes for himself and his relationships and God's invitation to participate in lives shaped by love towards a restoration *telos*. Through focusing on the *I Am Becoming* actions and stories of young people's lives it is possible to highlight young people's hopes and the actions and relationships which support those hopes. In this work I see counselors and community members cooperating with God's project, "who reconciled us to himself through Christ and gave us the ministry of reconciliation."[37]

36. Denborough, *Retelling the Stories*.
37. 2 Cor. 5:18, NIV.

References

Balswick, Jack et al. *The Reciprocating Self: Human Development in Theological Perspective*. Downers Grove: InterVarsity, 2005.
Burr, Vivien. *Social Constructionism*. London: Routledge, 2003.
Carey, Maggie et al. "The Absent but Implicit: A Map to Support Therapeutic Enquiry." *Family Process* 48 (2009) 319–331.
Denborough, David. *Retelling the Stories of Our Lives: Everyday Narrative Therapy to Draw Inspiration and Transform Experience*. Adelaide: Dulwich Centre, 2014.
Entwistle, David, and Stephen Moroney. "Integrative Perspectives on Human Flourishing: The Imago Dei and Positive Psychology." *Journal of Psychology and Theology* 39 no.4 (2011) 295–303.
Epston, David, and SallyAnne Roth. *Engaging Young Persons in Externalizing Conversations: Developing Abilities and Knowledge*. New York: Norton, 1995.
Freedman, Jill, and Gene Combs. *Narrative Therapy: The Social Construction of Preferred Realities*. New York: Norton, 1996.
Gergen, Kenneth. *An Invitation to Social Construction*. Thousand Oaks: Sage, 1999.
———. *Social Construction in Context*. London: Sage, 2001.
Grenz, Stanley. *The Social God and the Relational Self: A Trinitarian Theology of the Imago Dei*. Louisville: John Knox, 2001.
Gunton, Colin. *The One, the Three and the Many: God, Creation and the Culture of Modernity*. Cambridge: Cambridge University Press, 1993
Jenkins, Alan. *Becoming Ethical: A Parallel, Political Journey with Men Who Have Abused*. Dorset: Russell House, 2009.
McFadyen, Alistair. *The Call to Personhood: A Christian Theory of the Individual in Social Relationships*. Cambridge, England: Cambridge University Press, 1990.
Newman, David. "Rescuing the Said from the Saying of it: Living Documentation in Narrative Therapy." *The International Journal of Narrative Therapy and Community Work* 3 (2008) 24–34.
Shotter, John, and Kenneth Gergen. *Texts of Identity*. London: Sage, 1989.
Speedy, Jane. "Using Poetic Documents: An Exploration of Poststructuralist Ideas and Poetic Practices in Narrative Therapy." *British Journal of Guidance & Counseling* 33 no.3 (2005) 283–298.
Thorsborne, Margaret, and David Vinegrad. *Restorative Justice Pocketbook*. New York: Management Pocketbooks, 2014.

Torrance, Thomas. *The Christian Doctrine of God, One Being Three Persons.* Edinburgh: T&T Clark, 1996.

Volf, Miroslav. *Exclusion and Embrace: A Theological Exploration of Identity, Otherness, and Reconciliation.* Nashville: Abingdon, 1996.

Wade, Alan. *Honouring Resistance: A Response-based Approach to Counseling.* Vancouver: Stepping Stone, 2005.

Ware, Metropolitan Kallistos. "The Holy Trinity: Model for Personhood-in-relation." In *The Trinity and an Entangled World: Relationality in Physical Science and Theology,* edited by John Polkinghorne, 107–129. Grand Rapids: Eerdmans, 2010.

White, Michael. *Reflections on Narrative Practice: Essays and Interviews,* edited by 25–33. Adelaide: Dulwich Centre, 2000.

———. *Maps of Narrative Practice.* New York: Norton, 2007.

———. *Re-authoring Lives: Interviews and Essays.* Adelaide: Dulwich Centre, 1995.

———. *Reflections on Narrative Practice: Essays and Interviews.* Adelaide: Dulwich Centre, 2000.

———. "Workshop Notes." www.dulwichcentre.com.au/michael-white-workshop-notes.pdf.

White, Michael, and David Epston. (1990). *Narrative Means to Therapeutic Ends.* New York: Norton, 1990.

Winslade, John, and Michael Williams. *Safe and Peaceful Schools: Addressing Conflict and Eliminating Violence.* Thousand Oaks: Corwin, 2012.

9

The Undercover Anti-Bullying Team Approach

Using Relational Solutions to Address Relational Problems in the Classroom

MIKE WILLIAMS WITH LEX MCMILLAN

Within a high school context, the quality of relationships has a marked effect on the student's capacity to achieve educationally. In my work as the Head of the Guidance and Counseling Department in an Auckland high school, I am drawn to pay attention to the quality of relationships among students. This attraction has to do with both my personal and professional commitments, it also has to do with the contour of the school community. In the high school where I am based there are approximately seven hundred students of mixed ethnicities. The largest ethnic group is made up of students from Pacific Island nations. These are communal cultures where family relationships are fundamental to the way they view their world.

In this chapter, I discuss my work in seeking to eliminate bullying and relational violence in the light of this context. I also explore how my own Christian values of justice, mercy, and humility—expressed as a renunciation of a position of expertise and violence in all of its many forms—connect with and support the student's value base. All this sits comfortably for me within a Christian story, that I situate myself in, of God "in community" involved in the production of people and communities that reflect the relational life of God.[1] As Volf argues, this is a life expressed in things like

---

1. Torrance, *Worship*.

mutuality, respect, and working for justice.[2] I view my place of work primarily as a learning community, a site where I can practice with regard to what I know of God's relational character and a place where I am learning what it means to be responsible and participatory citizens in an uncertain world. I also view bullying behaviors as a threat to these hopes.

DEFINITION OF SCHOOL BULLYING

Before going on to describe my work with undercover teams, I will identify what I mean by bullying in the context of the school community. Olweus defines bullying in the school as when a student is "exposed, repeatedly over time, to negative actions on the part of one or more students."[3] These "negative actions" can encompass a range of behaviors from intentional physical injury to teasing, mocking, humiliating, and name-calling. Researchers have typically viewed bullying as aggressive actions located within a power imbalance between the target of the bullying and the perpetrator, to the extent that the target is unable/unwilling to defend themselves.[4] Similar definitions of bullying were sent out to all New Zealand schools by the Ministry of Education.[5] This comprehensive guide provides information and specific tools that schools can use to develop safe and positive school environments. It is also designed to help schools to develop policies and procedures to meet legal requirements.

While such definitions are the most common ones, other researchers have challenged these definitions, and have instead described bullying in terms of a relational process of power relations. Here "bullying often involves students imposing behavioral norms on their peers or policing those norms once they are established."[6] Consistent with this view, Davies and her colleagues have suggested that bullying is better understood in relational ways and have resisted the labelling and pathologizing of bullies.[7] Jennifer Jeffrey, a researcher at Victoria University in Wellington, New Zealand, interviewed high school students in four schools and found participants did not place as much emphasis on need or intent in instances of bullying, nor noticed differences in power as traditional analysis suggests they might.[8]

2. Volf, "Social Program."
3. Olweus, *Bullying at School*, 9.
4. Carrera, "Comprehensive Understanding."
5. Bullying Prevention Advisory Group, "Bullying Prevention and Response."
6. Winslade, "Policing of the Normal," 1.
7. Bansel, et al., "Bullies, Bullying and Power."
8. Jeffrey, "Contextual Influences."

Many of the student stories she studied disagreed that the repetitive element was significant or that bullying necessarily demonstrates harm to the target of the bullying. Because these new definitions challenge how bullying is perceived, particularly by students, I have also been interested in approaching the problem of bullying from a different perspective. Rather than seeing both the bully and the victim of bullying as the focus of change, I prefer to locate the problem in the social context of relational exchanges. As such any effective solutions must address the relationships that are affected and produced by acts of bullying and relational violence. Shifting the focus of the bullying problem from individuals to its social and relational context has led us to develop a response that has become known as "undercover anti bullying teams."

UNDERCOVER ANTI BULLYING TEAMS (UABTS)

Undercover Anti Bullying Teams[9] utilize a non-punitive and non-blaming approach to bullying. The purpose of these UABTs is to solve the problem of bullying and to re-define the relationships between the victim/target of the bullying, the perpetrators, and those who observe the bullying. When an individual, or as is more common, a group of students act in unison in practices of power and might, traditional responses to bullying that employ greater displays of power by school authorities can create exactly the opposite effect of eliminating the bullying and can simply shift it to other locations and other students. When students are punished by the school authorities for bullying, it is more likely that the perpetrators will seek revenge in some way, either by a direct act of aggression or what is more likely, some similar action done in such a way that it is difficult to trace its origins back to the offender.

The term "undercover teams" was coined by Bill Hubbard.[10] Hubbard's work, initially based on the *No Blame Approach* developed by Maines and Robinson[11] has since been considerably developed by myself and my colleague, Dr. John Winslade.[12] Our work includes conceptualizing bullying as a narrative performance where perpetrators, targets, and observers all play out their roles according to a predefined storyline with a fairly predictable plot trajectory. Rather radically, this stance suggests that bullying originates

9. See: Williams, "Undercover teams"; Williams and Winslade, "Using Undercover Teams"; Winslade and Williams, *Safe and peaceful schools*.
10. Hubbard, "'No-Blame' Bullying Response."
11. Maines and Robinson, *Crying for Help*.
12. Winslade and Williams, *Safe and Peaceful Schools*.

outside persons, in the social and discursive context, a term that one of the founders of narrative therapy, Michael White, has called externalizing.[13] The externalizing approach separates the person from the problem and claims that "the person is not the problem, the problem is the problem." Thus, the person doing the bullying and the students who remain silent in the presence of bullying are themselves not problematic, it is the act of bullying and the inaction by others that are the problems. This unique way of viewing the problem of bullying is at the heart of this approach and is based on the belief that problems are relationally and socially produced, consistent with White's view of discourses shaping action and life.

Externalizing the problem as "bullying," enables me to open spaces between individuals and their harmful actions. It allows for other identity positions to be taken up by students, ones that may have been overshadowed by narrow descriptions of a student or students as bullies, victims or bystanders. Identity positions, once assigned by others and internalized by oneself, can be difficult to shift and can further constrain any movement towards actions that stand contrary to acts of bullying or passive observance of such acts.[14]

An UABT is primarily an alliance of students I strategically form for the purpose of interrupting those identity positions, usurping the storyline of bullying, and co-authoring a new story of harmonious classroom relationships. I do not attempt to discover why the bullying is occurring because investigation and interrogation rarely gets to the bottom of the problem. To do so would invite speculation on the perpetrator's motives, a notion itself incompatible with the narrative view that the bullying itself has produced the actors in the story and not part of an essential aspect of the bully's "character."

My own commitment is to see my engagement in this work as participation in God's life of love as a social project shaped around the values of mercy, justice, and reconciliation. I strive to do this both through the design of the interventions I lead and more generally through the way I attempt to speak and act within my various professional roles. I observe that the relationship between justice and reconciliation is etched in the very heart of the Christian faith. This is to say that the narrative of divine action can inspire and shape responses to individual conflict situations, and it can shape broader cultural patterns and specific school community ones. The particular culture I seek to develop through my UABT work is one that bears the fruit of peace. Volf argues that the Christian tradition makes central claims

---

13. White, *Maps of Narrative Practice*.
14. Russell and Carey, "Narrative Therapy."

about a kind of peace that is characterized by justice and the embrace of others.[15] This kind of peace, which is characterized by the will to be at peace with those who commit offence, is a primary feature of the Christian tradition. This is to say that based on belief in a God of indiscriminate love, Christ followers are obliged to welcome—and to give themselves to—others. This kind of "embrace" of others precedes any determination about "truth," or any reading of a student's actions with respect to justice. Second, the Christian story invites that intention be given to justice so that genuine embrace can take place. Put another way, this implies that our UABT work is orientated towards more than merely ensuring everyone gets what they deserve, its telos is healed relationships and the formation of community.

One important practice implication of this stance is that it invites me to avoid ways of speaking and practicing that pathologize people. This is because pathologizing practices shut down possibilities for transformation for both individuals and their communities which, in my opinion, is unjust.[16] In contrast, I find the narrative therapeutic practice of "externalizing" preferable because it avoids speaking as if the people involved are the problem, and shifts the focus onto social relating as the root of the problem.[17] I believe speaking this way is an act of mercy and that it constitutes justice towards those who would otherwise be constrained without voice by pathologizing language.

It becomes apparent that each story of bullying is unique to that time, location, and setting. Therefore, as the counselor I assume the responsibility to lead and manage the process and to help the victim of bullying give voice to his or her unique experiences of anguish and torment. This is typically the first time that the "whole story" is told. I view the expression of compassion towards victims of bullying as the key to any successful intervention, and so I begin the process of uncovering the shame of the bullying. In doing so, I invite the person who has been bullied into a relational shift with the problem. This begins to free the person from its grip and its power.

Validating and honoring the storyteller is to me, a reciprocal act of God's mercy and once again, is an identification with the Gospel message of love and acceptance.[18]

15. For more on this see Volf "The Trinity is our Social Program" and "Forgiveness, Reconciliation, and Justice."

16. See, for example, Timm, "Deconstructing Pathology."

17. Strong, "Externalizing questions."

18. Olthuis posits: "Feeling accepted and affirmed, seen and heard for the individual he or she is, a child's self is formed and forms in rhythms of taking in and letting out, collecting and dispensing, connecting and disconnecting—being loved and loving" *Beautiful Risk*, 72.

THE UNDERCOVER TEAM'S FIVE STAGES

In the first stage, the counselor listens carefully to the story told by the target of the bullying, and explores the main points of the bullying incident. If the counselor decides that an UABT may be appropriate he/she discusses the approach with the student. As is often the case, the student may be unsure whether this approach would help. The counselor can then refer to archival records of successful previous UABTs and invite the student to at least consider this novel approach.

Once the approach is agreed to by the targeted student, the second stage begins where the target's story is carefully recorded using his/her own words on the forms developed for this purpose. The judicious use of words is core to the work and is based on a revisionist understanding of language;[19] that words do more than give a report of an activity, they actually create realities. The story and the exact words the young person uses are recorded, however colloquial or grammatically incorrect they might be, because this is the real voice of the young person, a voice that has never been recorded in this way before. When the Team is assembled, it will be exactly this raw and uncensored account that the Team will hear read to them by the counselor.

This stage is completed when the counselor and the student assemble the names of the students on the Team. The composition of the Team is important and must include two of the students who are doing the worst bullying along with 4 others (two males and two females) who have respect and status in the class. Including in the Team those who have been doing the actual bullying behavior is a key distinctive of this approach. This creative blend of people on the Team attempts to accurately reflect the make-up of the school community and beyond to the world we live in. It positions the Team as people who are willing to make a difference and who care enough about themselves and others to respond to the invitation to responsibility. It is an obvious and explicit recognizing and valuing of an individual's capacity for compassion.

Teachers are told by email that there is bullying in their class, and they are given a short description of the nature of the bullying. The names of all the students on the UABT are shared with them without identifying those students who are responsible for the bullying. This communication has the less obvious effect of expanding the Team to now include the teachers and to further expose the tactics of bullying. Teachers are usually surprised and somewhat dismayed that they have not themselves noticed any bullying but they invariably respond positively to any intervention that will help their

---

19. Burr, *Social Constructionism*.

classroom management and support their students. By this deliberate and strategic re-positioning of teachers, they step into new positions and become part of an alliance of people equally committed to anti-bullying.

In the third stage, the counselor meets the Team and reads out the target's story without identifying names, and then asks the students to join an alliance against the bullying. When they give their consent they are given the name of the student and this usually comes as no surprise. The Team and the counselor works together to devise a plan to eliminate the bullying and this is recorded on the recording forms as a "five point plan." The role of the counselor is particularly important here as they need to pay close attention to identifying specific actions that will make a difference for the target of the bullying. Suggestions can be offered by the counselor, such as giving a friendly greeting at the start of the school day.

The fourth stage of the process involves monitoring the progress of the plan as it unfolds in the life of the school over the following days. The comments of the Team and the target which speak to positive changes are carefully noted and read out to each other and the teachers are invited to comment on changes they have noticed. This reading out serves to enhance the new identities and positions of those in the Team, and strengthen the story of change. Any modifications to the plan are decided by the Team. As relationships in the class begin to shift and feedback from all parties becomes more positive, this to-and-fro process continues until the target of the bullying decides whether or not the bullying has ceased.

When bullying has stopped, the Team and the teachers are informed that the project has been successful and a date set for a final ceremony (stage five) where Team members are presented with a certificate signed by the school principal together with a small food voucher. Participants are asked to complete a brief survey and this data is used to evaluate the program.

I am constantly amazed at the effectiveness of these Teams. Many times I have wondered at the outset if this approach would work, given the intractability of the bullying and the seriousness of the harm done to the target of the bullying. More often than not, the perpetrators of the bullying are the first persons to begin the process of developing the plan and are the first to suggest ways to eliminate the bullying. Often confessions are expressed both by those bullying and by those who have not done anything to stop it. When this happens, I calmly acknowledge the confession and remind them that we are not looking for anyone to blame but that we have a problem to solve and they are the experts recruited by the target of the bullying to stop it. The strength of this UABT process and the unexpected offers of help offers me a great sense of satisfaction as a counselor and facilitator of these Teams because the UABT approach aligns with my values and what I stand for. Uncovering the discourses that produce bullying, exposing their destructive effects and seeing how young people respond to invitations to right actions, connects with my belief that identities and reputations are not fixed but produced through repetitive acts. I am no different to the young people who are still finding out about themselves and discovering how to negotiate their way in the world.

Beyond my own experience, research data also supports the effectiveness of the UABT approach. John Winslade synthesized the research of four Masters students from California who had each studied particular aspects of archival data gathered by myself from 35 Undercover Teams over a four-year period.[20] 90.5 percent of participants (including bullies and victims) rated the process as successful or very successful.[21] In a further study, Lambie, et al. showed how the establishment of UABTs were followed by a statistically significant effect on classroom climate and "a reduction in feelings of victimization (in the classroom) and an increase in students' perceptions of support from others."[22] Themes of "social support" and "inclusion" emerged from the analysis of quantitative data[23] and students said that they enjoyed being given the opportunity to develop interpersonal skills through support for the victim. Lilllard took a different approach and interviewed four practitioners from California and New Zealand to document the implementation process used regarding UABTs.[24] She found that including the perpetrators of the bullying in the intervention process enhanced the likelihood of success and that long term relational changes were more likely for the bully. She found that UABTs have the potential to end the bullying almost immediately which is different for other intervention methods.

I will now offer a case vignette that illustrates these ideas in practice.

A CASE VIGNETTE

A teacher approached me about a student who seemed unhappy and unusually withdrawn in class. He described this boy as new to the school and that he was from an African country. He had noticed that he had few friends and spent time walking around by himself. When asked how he was feeling, he told that the teacher that he was "all right."

20. Winslade, "Policing of the Normal."
21. Ibid., 29.
22. Lambie, et al., "Evaluation," 29.
23. Ibid.
24. Lillard, "Effectiveness," 160.

I called George (not his real name) out of class and after reassuring him that it was safe to talk to me, I asked what was happening. He began to tell me about teasing by students in his class. From his initial explanation I had an idea that an UABT might work in this instance and briefly explained what I had in mind.

After gaining his permission to record his story, using the forms devised for this purpose, I wrote down his account in his own words:

> *There has been some racism, name calling, sometimes pushing, shoving and that's basically it. Sometimes they take stuff out of my bag. They take my books, my pens, my lunchbox. They always make jokes about things that are black and they look sideways at me when they are talking. Today we were just playing and they mentioned something about black sh*t, they saw some dog sh*t and they looked at it and then at me and went "Oooo" and they all laughed.*

I asked what he thought that meant and he said:

> *I took that to mean that the dog sh*t was me. Most times they call me fat, they say something about what I eat, how I eat and they say stuff about my mum. They ask me if she is black and if she has white teeth. They ask if she is fat too. Sometimes I am walking down the stairs and they bump in to me on purpose.*

I asked George how all this made him feel different:

> *Well, mostly they just look at me. I hate that. I hate people staring. I have been made to feel different because of my skin color. Racist jokes and all that, saying that I'm from Jamaica, black Sambo, and I'm really from Kenya. I was in history class and I got this answer wrong and this kid said I was a dumb*** and he got his book and started hitting me on the head. It happened yesterday in science. He calls me names like "dumb***" and sometimes racist names and he says something about my mum's private parts. He said he "did" her last night. He hits my head with books.*

"How has this affected you George?" I asked:

> *I feel sad. It makes me feel sometimes angry. I have thought that no one wants me here. It's 'cause they always exclude me and stuff and on the weekends when things are going on, they don't tell me about it. I would like them to get to know me so we can become friends. I thought that when I came here that no one would really care about my skin color and that they would just look at me as if I was a normal person. This all started in my last school and it's just*

the same now. I've told my parents and they say, "just go to school do your work and ignore it."

I then asked George how it was affecting his school work:

It hasn't really affected me that much. But when we were in P.E. (Physical Education), sometimes they choose other people and leave me alone. I am all alone and it feels like I am an outsider. But yeah, it has affected some of my work. I stopped focusing in class and I couldn't do my work.

Then I asked George what the bullying has got him to do or think about doing.

It's got me thinking about what I should be doing, like school work. Sometimes I wish I could go to a different school. Heaps of Kenyans go to that other school and nobody gets bullied there, nobody really cares about who you are or where you come from. I wish I could change schools but it's too far away. I had thought about punching the kids who say rude things about my mum but I stopped because I know you shouldn't get angry. It will just make it worse. I sometimes would like to say things back but I'm not that good at making smart comments.

Finally, I asked him how he would ideally like things to be:

No racism, no name-calling. We'd all just be friends. We'd make jokes and laugh. I don't want the kids to be punished or stood down from school. I just want to be included by them. I'd like to be treated with respect, you know. Yeah, that they'd be nice to me.

Then using class photographs as our guide, I asked him to select 6 students from his class including the two students who were responsible for the worst acts of bullying. I explained that the students that he chose (apart from the ones doing the bullying) were to be students who other kids looked up to, ones that don't bully others and are respected by the class and teacher and that the other two students would not be exposed by me at any time.

After meeting the Team the next day and reading out George's story, a plan was formed by them. Those who had been doing the bullying were never identified and they were told that they were recruited for their leadership qualities. I explained that they had been personally selected and endorsed by their teachers as ones who had power and influence in the class.

There is usually an element of surprise when the Team is first assembled because the ones who bully would not normally co-operate with the other students in such a task, let alone be personally selected for it! This element of surprise is a component of its success I believe because the acts of bullying reported in the target's story have now been "opened up" for scrutiny to a select group with the expectation of positive action on their part.

They developed a typically simple plan that included sitting next to him, sticking up for him, checking to see if he was okay and "giving him positive thoughts." Everybody had ideas that would help and they were excited to get started.

At my next meeting with George, he told me that there had been a huge change and that things were completely different to how they had been. Everything he had mentioned in his story had been addressed by the Team.

As the to and fro process of meeting the target and the Team continues, a recovery of something that was previously swamped by relationally aggressive ways of being begins to form. This something may have been previously known in their lives—a compassion for others or a desire to make a difference for others—or it may be an emergence of new ethics for life, or some blend of these.

When the person who has been targeted for bullying agrees that the bullying is over, we have a celebration where stories of new learning are shared, news plans made to consolidate the changes are made and certificates of appreciation from the school principal are exchanged and canteen vouchers are given out.

Sometimes I ask the Team at the first meeting why they would like to take part in this task and they always reply that is because it is the right thing to do. I suspect that the "bullies" and the "observers" see the opportunity that the UABT offers to re-story themselves and to try out positive ways of relating to the target within the safety of the camaraderie of the Team. The relative anonymity of the Team provides space for them to show support for the person who had previously been bullied without them being identified as such. They tell me that they feel proud to do this work and because they are not exposed or labelled as "bullies" or "passive observers" they enjoy the opportunity to act in accord with their values and beliefs, values that may have been temporarily subverted by a story of bullying. These wonderful statements of transformation fit with my belief that reputations or statements of identity are not fixed and that we can change where we are given an invitation that we respond to and an environment where that change can be supported.

Another factor that I consider being central to the effectiveness of these Teams is the absence of blame associated with any persons caught up in the revelations of bullying. Presenting the problem as "bullying" and including all the Team members in its solution, allows those who would normally be repelled by the idea of bullying to recover their value position and show others what they would prefer to be known as standing for.

In George's case, teachers reported that the class was much happier and that George had changed a lot. The meetings continued for a couple more times until George said that the bullying had completely gone. He said he was much happier and now he didn't want to change schools anymore. He agreed that it was time for our celebration ceremony and he asked if he could personally present the certificates and the food vouchers to the Team.

After organizing the food vouchers and the certificates, we all met during a morning break and talked about the progress of the Team and what they had learned about themselves and about being ambassadors for peaceful relationships. The Team members said that they were thankful that they had been given the opportunity and enjoyed being on an UABT. George shook hands with the Team members and thanked them as he presented their certificates.

Their final task was to complete an evaluation form that gathers data to support future research.

DISCUSSION

While this example might seem remarkable, the story of this particular UABT is typical of the way that other Teams have functioned. The reporting and recording of the story is structured in such a way that each step is carefully mapped to elicit a rich understanding of the impact of the bullying. Every story typically begins with a description of the anguish of injustice and ends with a new understanding of relationship for all the participants in the story. This vision of communities characterized by justice, kindness, and humility, and of schools where students treat each other with respect and appreciation for their own gifts and differences are what lies at the heart of this approach. Furthermore, these are the things that resonate with the same values that I position my hope for the work within.

I see the most basic tenets of my work being the relational ethics that sit within the ancient story of God's hopes for mankind for the way that human social life might be arranged around wellbeing and living in harmony with creation. Micah 6:6–8 puts it most simply as being fair, kind, and compassionate. These are the explicit values that underpin the actions of UABTs and what I attempt to live my life by. In assisting students to identify and confront the injustice of their actions and be at peace with one another, I hope that I am joining in God's commitment to reestablish justice in the lives of individuals and their communities. This is a concrete example of the narrative of God's action at work, not only motivating and shaping the behavior of individuals in conflict situations, but also shaping the "the broader cultural habits and expectations that make peaceful solutions possible."[25]

The notion of "caring," i.e. of self, of others, of learning, and of the school community, is reflected in school policy and informs the way that teachers teach and students learn. These are the espoused values of my workplace and are explicit throughout the culture of the school. As the young people on the Teams, the teachers in the classroom, the counselor or facilitator of the UABT, and the target of the bullying themselves are touched by these ideas, something of the divine narrative takes shape. I like to think that together we participate in God's embodiment in the world and usher God's just and loving presence into the world. This is to say that the essence of God is the freedom to love, and to be free in love.[26] Furthermore, all people are invited to participate in God's liberating and life-giving pattern of fellowship as they go about their daily lives—and most significantly for me—in the classroom.

To put this another way, I see the classroom as a site where young people can learn what it means to be ethical citizens of the future and to develop an appreciation of the complexity of our world. Beyond the intimacy of the classroom, I also see the school as a microcosm of the wider local community and the diversity of the families that make up the classroom culture reflect the diversity of the world at large. My work sits alongside this as my participation in the social construction of a just and merciful society—as a counter movement to the destruction associated with experiencing bullying and all other forms of injustice.

The seeds of these values that inform my ethical hopes for my work were planted in my life primarily by my mother. She grew up in an impoverished family and even though she finished her schooling at the tender age of twelve, she left the small town she grew up in to study to be a nurse in a much larger metropolitan center. She overcame tremendous odds in order to register as a nurse and in doing so she modelled for me the idea of emancipation and liberation from her surroundings. She subsequently devoted her life to caring for others less fortunate than herself and she died as she lived, in acts of service. Her Methodist faith was uncomplicated and simple, and she instilled that compassion for others by the way she lived her life.

My work is shaped by her example. She gave her life to building communities of support and every UABT that I form in response to an injustice and in the hope of contributing to a more loving community, is a unique

---

25. Volf, "Forgiveness, Reconciliation, and Justice," 876.
26. See for example Moltmann, *God in Creation*.

expression of the way she lived her life. My role in the process of the life of each UABT, is driven by her example and although I have never experienced the extent of bullying that these students have, I certainly have experienced the value of a supportive network of friends and family.

At the successful completion of the process and the winding up of the Team, there are three significant relational shifts I am looking for. Firstly, the target of the bullying has his or her dignity restored by being treated as one who *is* respected and by being included back into the school community. Secondly, the perpetrator/s of the bullying have re-storied their reputation by stepping out of the mantle of "the oppressor;" and thirdly, the observers have had their dignity restored by enabling them to act in accordance with their values. With regard to this third shift, teachers are invited to respond to the new awareness that bullying is happening in their classroom, and based on this insight to pay closer attention to student relationships in the future. The school principal may also have had her community leadership position enhanced and validated by signing certificates of recognition of anti-bullying activities of a group of students. Others in the classroom, who are not part of the Team, may also get caught up—often unwittingly—in the rewriting of relationships, and become part of the wider community of change and restoration.

CONCLUSION

The story of George as told above is a story of redemption and transformation. Through participation on a Team dedicated to eliminating bullying and developing more just classroom communities, young people are invited to participate and contribute towards a process of liberation, both for the person who has been bullied and for themselves at the same time. As the Team is assembled for the first time and they hear the moving story, each member comes to understand that by their previous action or inaction they are complicit in the production and continuation of another's distress. It is these stories that provide each UABT with a call to action and an opportunity to change the direction of one of their peer's life.

This strategic intervention designed to address the damaging effects of bullying does not require the target of the bullying to change in any way. Neither does it call for apologies or require the Team to do anything to change in any way. They are simply invited to do what they know is right. Other students in the class are witness to unexpected actions that take place by a seemingly unusual combination of classmates and they typically come on board and support the actions of the UABT thus extending its impact.

In these ways, the Team provides members with genuine opportunities to try out positive ways of relating and a chance to re-define identities, both for themselves and for the victim. Thus the UABT approach is a targeted intervention that addresses an actual instance of bullying through mobilizing peer relationships in support of victims. A Team is simple to set up and manage but is profound in its impact. In over forty-four such Teams, I have had not had one that was not effective in eliminating bullying for that student at that time.

In my reading of program evaluations, students typically say that they have appreciated being on the Team. What is gratifying to me is that there is no distinction between those identified as "the bullies" and those who were observers of bullying when they expressed gratitude with their selection and were thankful to be given the opportunity to be on an UABT.

Reading of this change of heart, I conclude that reputations are not fixed and that just as young people can be caught up in acts of bullying, they can be released from them as well and with the right kind of intervention, they can just as easily grow a counter story of justice, peace, and harmony.

References

Bansel, Peter, et al. "Bullies, Bullying and Power in the Contexts of Schooling." *British Journal of Sociology of Education* 30 no. 1 (2009) 59–69.

Bullying Prevention Advisory Group. "Bullying Prevention and Response: A Guide for Schools." http://www.education.govt.nz/school/student-support/student-wellbeing/bullying-prevention-and-response/bullying-prevention-and-response-a-guide-for-schools/

Burr, Vivien. *An Introduction to Social Constructionism*. London: Routledge, 2006.

Carrera, Maria Victoria, et al. Toward a More Comprehensive Understanding of Bullying in School Settings. *Educational Psychology Review* 23 no. 4 (2011) 479–499.

Hubbard, Bill. "The "No-Blame" Bullying Response Approach: A Restorative Practice Contender?" Masters diss., Massey University, 2004.

Jeffrey, Jennifer. "Contextual Influences on the Perception of Bullying Behaviors for Youth in New Zealand." Masters diss., Victoria University of Wellington, 2015.

Lambie, Ian, et al. "The Evaluation of Undercover Anti-Bullying Teams." www.dulwichcentre.com.au/UABT-Final-Report.pdf

Lillard, Dory. "Effectiveness of Anti-Bullying Undercover Teams from Practitioners' Perspectives." Masters diss., California State University.

Maines, Barbara, and George Robinson. *Crying for Help: The NO Blame Approach to Bullying*. London: SAGE, 1997.

Moltmann, Jürgen. *God in Creation: A New Theology of Creation and the Spirit of God. The Gifford Lectures* 1984–85. Translated by Margaret Kohl. San Francisco: Harper Collins, 1985.

Olthuis, James. *The Beautiful Risk: A New Psychology of Loving and Being Loved*. Eugene, OR: Wipf&Stock, 2006.

Olweus, Dan. *Bullying at School: What We Know and What We Can Do*. Oxford, UK: Blackwell, 1993.

Russell, Shona, and Maggie Carey. Narrative Therapy: Responding to Your Questions. *The International Journal of Narrative Therapy and Community Work* 2 (2002) 67–91.

Strong, Tom. "Externalising Questions: A Micro-Analytic Look at their Use in Narrative Therapy." *The International Journal of Narrative Therapy and Community Work* 3 (2008) 59–71.

Timm, Maria. Deconstructing Pathology: A Narrative View of the Intake Process. *Journal of Constructivist Psychology* 28 no. 4 (2015) 316–328.

Torrance, James. *Worship, Community and the Triune God of Grace.* Downers Grove, IL: Intervarsity, 1996.

Volf, Miroslav. "The Trinity is Our Social Program": The Doctrine of the Trinity and the Shape of Social Engagement. *Modern Theology* 14 no.3 (1998) 404–421.

———. "Forgiveness, Reconciliation, and Justice: A Theological Contribution to a More Peaceful Social Environment." *Millennium: Journal of International Studies* 29 (2000) 861–877.

White, Michael, and David Epston. *Narrative Means to Therapeutic Ends.* New York: W.W. Norton & Co, 1990.

White, Michael. *Maps of Narrative Practice.* New York: Norton Professional, 2007.

Williams, Mike. "Undercover Teams: Redefining Reputations and Transforming Bullying Relationships in the School Community." *Explorations: An E-Journal of Narrative Practice* 1 (2010) 4–13.

Williams, Mike, and John Winslade. "Using Undercover Teams to Re-Story Bullying Relationships." *Journal of Systemic Therapies* 27 no.2 (2007) 1–16.

Winslade, John, and Mike Williams. *Safe and Peaceful Schools: Addressing Conflict and Eliminating Violence.* Thousand Oaks, CA: Corwin, 2012.

Winslade, John. Deconstructing the Policing of the Normal: An Examination of the Work Done by "Undercover Anti-Bullying Teams." *Narrative and Conflict* 1 no.1 (2013) 76–98.

10

The *Tree of Life*
A Narrative Therapy Approach to Healing Identity in Response to Trauma among West African Children

DEBORAH GILL

In 2010, my family and I moved to Nigeria for a two-year term where I worked as a counselor in a voluntary capacity, in an HIV/AIDs clinic. Soon after our arrival, I was approached to also work with a group of children who were described to me by others as "desperately needy." Here I will discuss my use of narrative therapy's *Tree of Life* and its role in unearthing preferred identity stories that more suited these young lives that I had the privilege to work alongside. I will connect my personal motivation for this work to my own childhood experiences, and consider this modality in light of a Kingdom of God mandate, showing how this approach gives my work expression for a relational theological anthropology.

MY STORY

My own motivation for this work has strong connections with a childhood encounter that I now like to describe as a Kingdom of God experience. Following the sudden death of my mother when I was six years old, our family were embraced by a loving community of people who supported us through this difficult period of our lives. In particular, my father's brother Ken, and his wife Jill, came to live alongside us to help my father care for me and my five siblings. They made sacrifices, moving away from their community,

Ken relocating his employment, and Jill resigning from her work to be our full-time "mother." She was just 24 years old, and she embraced us with a compassionate love that was practical and kind. While in my experience the reality of this grief has left a lonely space in my soul, my identity has been shaped by the attachment Jill facilitated, and the value she placed on my life as being worthy of her making these sacrifices. Her mostly unspoken yet consistent Christ-like ability to love was my pathway into an awareness of the presence of, and the nature of, God.

Years later, in 2010, as I was being introduced to children on the other side of the world, in a culture far from my own, Jill passed away from this life. My grief and my gratefulness combined to propel me into this rewarding, sometimes-messy work. My hope was that others—these children—would have their preferred identities shaped as I had—as a loved and valued person-in-relation, in community with others and a loving God. James Olthuis says "because we are gifted with connections that forge our identity, we are called to develop and sustain those connections as our way of becoming who God calls us to be."[1] Just as I was invited into a preferred sense of myself, and just as we all are invited into our preferred identities through relationship described in the Biblical narrative, so it is that I desire to invite others towards the same Kingdom of God invitation that sees our identities informed by love.

THE CHILDREN

The children were housed in a care center located in a small village on the outskirts of the city we were living in. As I worked individually with four of the 120 children onsite, initial therapeutic sessions felt frustratingly inefficient and culturally inappropriate to me. Within those early sessions however, with windows and doors crowded with wide-eyed faces watching in longing, some of the most striking stories of survival, resilience, and hope that I had ever heard were spoken. While each child had a story of experienced trauma that needed to be attended to, it was immediately clear that "desperate" and "needy" were incomplete descriptions of these young people.

Discourses—taken for granted cultural assumptions—within the cultures that supported the care center organizationally and financially allowed single-storied descriptions to be told both by the children and the wider community. It was assumed that orphaned children were "vulnerable," "hungry," "abused," and "abandoned." There were many stories that

1. Olthuis, *Beautiful Risk*, 48.

supported these narrow descriptions of them and what they knew about themselves, and in spite of my critique of these ideas, it was also these stories that inspired people to work in and support a safe environment for the children. The same discourses, however, had neglected other stories about them from being investigated, known, or heard. "Resilient," "vibrant," "clever," and "caring" were also valid descriptions and these too had supporting stories.

These descriptions better suited the ideas I have about humans as persons-in-relation who are created to participate in the triune life of a loving God. Uncomfortable with the description of "desperately needy," knowing that I was possibly the only one "hearing" these alternative stories, and that each of the other 116 children had stories to tell, I set about to find a more satisfactory and efficient way of working. This commitment fits with my desire to hear and tell multiple stories of these children's lives. My interest is in working with the rich fabric of stories that make up people's lives, and I wanted to hear and value all of the stories. Furthermore, I longed to invite everybody who knew of these children to hear their "new" stories of tenacity, cleverness, and deep resourcefulness, and to view them through new lenses as a result. My search for an alternative way of working led me to revisit my acquaintance with narrative therapy.[2]

Narrative therapy, and in particular the *Tree of Life* approach,[3] gave me a way of working with the children that allowed rich stories about their lives to emerge, and for them to choose the ones they preferred to represent them. It changed the way they talked about themselves, and how others viewed them.

TREE OF LIFE METHOD

Narrative therapists David Denborough from Australia, and Ncazelo Ncube from South Africa, collaborated to develop the *Tree of Life* methodology in response to their work with vulnerable children in Southern Africa who were living with the effects of HIV/AIDS.[4] The *Tree of Life* is designed to be used within a group setting, making it particularly attractive to cultures where interdependence is dominant, and naturally introducing "Outsider Witnesses,"[5] an important component to narrative therapy work. With the help of the care center staff, I divided the children into groups according to age and gender, and worked with two groups each week for three months. I

2. White and Epston, *Narrative Means*.
3. Denborough, *Collective Narrative Practice*, 71.
4. Ibid., 71–98.
5. White, *Reflections on Narrative Practice*.

was helped by "Uncle Bawa," a staff member who showed a natural affinity with the work of caring for the children on a therapeutic level. He was invaluable, particularly with his familiarity with each child and their culture. We were in a race against time to finish before the rains started making the road less accessible, before the national elections started, heightening the risk of "troubles," and to appease the children's impatience as a growing sense of excitement grew about their day off school to participate.

Using their own drawings of a tree, I invited the children to use different parts of the tree to metaphorically illustrate aspects of their lives. The roots of the tree represented their own roots. Their birth places, names of parents, grandparents, siblings, primary caregivers, languages, traditions, and childhood memories combined to speak to their short yet colorful histories.

The ground represented their present realities, and on the grass or dust names of friends, favorite things to do, and where they live and go to school were listed.

The trunk of the tree held lists of skills and abilities. Nothing was considered too insignificant, and as skills such as washing dishes, playing football, caring for younger children, smiling, and many more were written about, we encouraged the children to wonder about how it was that they came to be so good at these things. As we gradually elicited stories that connected with people on their roots or ground, we were able to see that it was sometimes hardship that had caused them to be able to do certain things. For many of the children, it seemed that this was the first time they had noticed what they are uniquely good at.

Hopes and dreams for their future, many of which had never been considered, were written along their branches. I noticed they often began by copying each other's ideas, until the concept caught on and they came to life, eyes sparkling, with ideas and desires of their own. This added further layers of connection to others, as we thought about how these dreams had come to be. As with any tree, some branches were strong and well established, while others were newly sprouting.

Leaves represented significant people, bringing to life again relationships that were no longer physically available to them, as well as honoring those that are still physically present. As the children spoke about their special people, it also gave us an opportunity to wonder about the reciprocating significance the children's lives have had on them.

Gifts and blessings the children had received were named, bringing colorful fruit to the trees. I asked the children to think about what the receiving of gifts suggests about them. How does a giver of gifts view the other, the receiver of gifts?

Together, different parts of each tree contributed to an organic picture of lives interwoven, each one uniquely designed and purposed. The finished trees offered physical evidence of connectedness, belonging, resourcefulness, experiences, and meaningful relationships, both past and present. Each story was told and listened to carefully. I was aware that "within the new stories, people live out new self-images, new possibilities for relationships and new futures."[6] I witnessed shy tears and wide smiles as the stories of others resonated with their own. Combined and hung alongside each other on the wall, the pictures created a forest, offering extra shade and support for each other. The children enjoyed being given time to contribute to each other's trees too. Flowers, birds, and kind words added to the trees saw them blossom.

I would then re-tell their stories, highlighting unique features of each tree, as well as drawing attention to themes that wound through the forest. From the perspective of narrative therapy, this reflective process of the re-telling allows each child to know that their story has been heard by another. In this way each story is honored as being individually unique while also sharing common ground, and as an important piece of the emerging forest.

The strength of the new-found stories rooted in relationships, standing alongside others with preferred identities woven throughout them, provided a psychologically and emotionally safe platform for revisiting some of the traumatic events that the children had experienced. To facilitate this I continued with the metaphor of a tree as a basis for discussing as a group some of the storms trees are vulnerable to. "Drought," "termites," and "people chopping them for firewood" were commonly mentioned by these African children. We then thought about the particular storms the children's lives had experienced. Just as any tree can be impacted by storms, so too these lives had experienced and survived difficult times.

I use the term "trauma" to describe any event whereby personal safety is threatened, and the survivor is unable to change the event. Judith Herman says "traumatic events overwhelm the ordinary systems of care that give people a sense of control, connection, and meaning."[7] For these children this included everything from unimaginable acts of cruelty and violence, to seeing a friend fall out of a tree, or getting dirt in their eyes. In this work, I was mindful, as White states, that "psychological and emotional safety in working with children who have been subject to trauma cannot be too strongly emphasized."[8] While we witnessed tears, honored sadness, and

---

6. Freedman and Combs, *Narrative Therapy*, 16.
7. Herman, *Trauma and Recovery*, 33.
8. White, *Trauma*, 145

noticed the place grief held in their young lives, there was no apparent evidence to suggest children were overwhelmed, much less re-traumatized by these discussions. The aim of attending to these things in conversation was to restore their sense of meaning, control, and connection. I loved that they could question, express anger, beam with pride, cry, and laugh in the shade of confidence their trees had given them.

Crucial to this narrative therapy approach is the unearthing of stories that speak to responses to trauma. It is thought that it is in the way people have responded to difficulties that we discover emerging skills and resources that contradict the problem stories told by the effects of traumatic experience. Often overlooked, these kinds of efforts to resist and responses to trauma hold keys to valuable information about survivors' skills and abilities, and to what they accord value.[9] White contends noticing children's responses to trauma is critically important to the restoration of their sense of personal agency, and agency is crucial to wellbeing. These noticings can be powerful antidotes to the discourses of victimhood that have become so influential in the construction of their identities.[10] "Running away," "finding the pastor's house," "doing what we were told," "crying," "praying," and "I said 'No!'" were all ways these children had responded to moments of terror. Together, we often noticed links between how a child had responded to, or resisted traumatic events, and the trees' histories and people, both of which reaffirmed their connectedness and relationality.

A quiet time of reflection was encouraged as the children were asked to write a letter to one of the people they had named on their tree. Letters expressing thankfulness, grief, apologies, and kind words were penned on letters—some of which were posted, some that were handed to friends and care givers, and others that I was asked to keep safe.

At the end of each day, the children participating were given a certificate to honor the work they had completed. Certificates formed an important part of the re-telling of the stories, as each certificate listed their skills and abilities, their hopes and dreams, as well as their special people. This approach fits within narrative therapy where "narrative counselors include as part of their methodology a search for . . . a 'nurturing third.'"[11] To that end, care center staff were instrumental in affirming and thickening the plot of the children's new storylines, as the certificates became tools for conversations long after I had left for the day. The caregivers were frequently astonished at the new stories they heard, seeing their children in new ways

9. White, *Children, Trauma and Recovery*.
10. Ibid., 14.
11. Pembroke, *Renewing Pastoral Practice*, 62.

for the first time, and they showed genuine pride and interest in them. One commented that "I had no idea my children had dreams like this. I am getting to know them for the first time!" and "There is more room for love now that we know each other." The staff were also quick to suggest that they too should have trees of their own!

A celebration of our forest of over 130 trees at the conclusion of three months also offered a wider opportunity to include Outsider Witnesses, and share the stories of the trees—stories that were fresh and exciting, stories that told of preferred identities, and that were proud to be told. Witnessing visitors included the local pastor, school teachers, care center executives, and expatriate and national staff. When we ran out of food we realized we also had several village children with us too!

Facilitating the writing and sharing of documents was another pathway to include third parties, and one that I found personally rewarding. Freedman and Combs refer to these kinds of activities as "spreading the news"[12] and David Newman writes "I understand that as language is central in shaping identity, the re-telling of those little gems via documents ... is crucial practice."[13] As I read the document pertaining to the children at our celebration and watched the faces of visiting witnesses brighten, I felt a strong sense of advocacy on behalf of these beautiful and resilient children.

Encouraged by the collective practices of narrative therapists around the world linking the stories of survival, skills, and knowledge between individuals and groups, we also read a document from a group of young people in Australia to our children. They too had experienced hard times, and wanted to share their stories and ideas with other young people. Denborough believes that this experience of sharing each other's stories " ... can be the catalyst to reduce the effects (or transform the nature) of the suffering in a person's life."[14] This collective practice offers another method of contradicting the sense of isolation trauma has invited into communities.

To conclude the process, we planted Flame trees within the sparse compound as permanent reminders of the preferred stories of the children's lives. Flame trees are particularly poignant in that they flourish, producing vivid orange flowers in the midst of the driest, most difficult season in Africa, and seemed an apt choice to represent our newly planted forest. Finally, a book of photographs and documents was printed for the children's school library.

---

12. Freedman and Combs, *Narrative Therapy*, 247.
13. Newman, "Rescuing the Said," 25.
14. Denborough, *Collective Practice*, 3.

TRAUMA HEALING AND THEOLOGICAL REFLECTIONS

For me, the heart of this work connects to the heart of my faith. My faith is centered on a God who shows us uniqueness, interconnectedness, and interdependency within the community of the trinitarian relationship. Reflecting on the *Tree of Life* process from this theological perspective has broadened my understanding of why the effects of traumatic experience cut to the core of who we are, why interacting dialogically with others is intrinsically healing for people, and why the language we use is so potent to the healing process.

Trinitarian theology has informed my understanding of personhood, and so I also turn to this to understand the effect traumatic events have on us as persons-in-relation. An anthropology based on trinitarian theology requires an understanding of the trinitarian relationship—one in which fully unique individuals are equally reliant upon, yet independent of each other. Theologian Alistair McFadyen[15] writes that our personhood, determined by the trinitarian God whose image we imitate, relies on us being people in relation. He says that this insight "will lead to a specific understanding of individuality as a sedimentation of interpersonal relations which is intrinsically open to others as to God."[16] Balswick et al. agree that "unity and uniqueness—in reciprocity—is at the heart of the triune God . . . Theological anthropology [therefore] would suggest that bearing the image of God means living as unique individuals in reciprocating relationships with others."[17] These things lead me to the conclusion that by observing the nature of our triune God, and in particular the trinitarian relationship, we can affirm that we best reflect our creator God, and our preferred identities flourish, within loving relationship with each other, creation, and God.

Psychological evidence also supports the idea that humans function best when in healthy relationships with others; that is people are "wired to thrive and survive as a social species."[18] Judith Herman says "the belief in a meaningful world is formed in relation to others and begins in earliest life."[19] Considering this, the suggestion that "a profound sense of isolation from others is routinely one of the most damaging effects of traumatic experience"[20] begins to make sense. As such, the effect of traumatic

---

15. McFadyen, *Call to Personhood*.
16. Ibid., 24.
17. Balswick et al., *Reciprocating Self,* 35–36.
18. Ziegler, *Traumatic Experience,* 19.
19. Herman, *Trauma and Recovery,* 54.
20. Denborough, *Collective Narrative Practice,* 27.

experience on the human brain can leave a sense of aloneness and isolation, contrasting this relational aspect of ourselves. Theologically, I understand this to mean that even though we are created to be in relationship, creation is marred by relational separation, so our relationships often do not reflect the fullness of the Trinity. Indeed "we are still related to God, and in God's image, but we are so in a distorted way. Consequently, we are also related to ourselves and to one another in a distorted way."[21] It is this distorted relationality and resulting sense of isolation that creates the damaging effect on our sense of ourselves, sometimes more so than the physical act of violence or oppression.

In such a communal and interdependent culture as the West African one that I engaged, the psychological isolation inflicted by traumatic events is sometimes masked by the communal living and sharing of day to day activities. In addition, physical isolation was a reality for the children I worked alongside, as attachment to parents and primary caregivers had been swept away for many of them. This further diminished their sense of who they were both as unique individuals, and as persons-in-relation.

As a Christian and a counselor, I see myself invited to participate in bringing others towards renewal and restoration in this life, as we await the fullness of God's Kingdom to be fully present again. Some ways that I might do this is to encourage them back into relationship, while still recognizing and treasuring their uniqueness. The *Tree of Life* process invited the children into an encounter with their preferred identities and others. It was a visual, spoken, and heard way of working, and proved to be an effective way to reverse their sense of isolation.

McFadyen's theological writings about personhood resonate with what I observed as I worked with the children, using the *Tree of Life* modality.[22] Each tree is individually unique, and beautiful in its own right. However it was as each tree, or life story, was spoken about and intertwined with others, that the new stories came alive. Speaking about, and hearing of others' traumatic experiences broke through the isolating sense of "I'm the only one" that had hindered preferred identities emerging. I agree with Herman's argument that "recovery can take place only within the context of relationships; it cannot occur in isolation."[23] A new "knowing" of themselves and each other enhanced the children's sense of belonging and connectedness, as well as their uniqueness. A person's uniqueness is no longer felt as lonely isolation, rather as a uniquely crafted piece of a relational connectedness.

21. McFadyen, *Call to Personhood*, 44.
22. McFadyen, *Call To Personhood*.
23. Herman, *Trauma and Recovery*, 133.

My personal experience of relational encounter overcoming the impact of traumatic experience also finds support in the writings of McFadyen: "the Persons are what they are only through their relations with the others, it must also be the case that their identities are formed through the others and the ways in which the others relate to them."[24] To this day I can recall the sting of shame, and the looks of pity that sometimes landed upon myself as a motherless child. Yet far outweighing this is the richness of my relationship with Jill, and the way she related to me—such a giving "other," whose ways of being were informed by love. This relationship, over time, restored my sense of who I believe I was created to be. As Jürgen Moltmann says " . . . nothing is so humanizing as love, and a conscious interest in the life of others, particularly in the life of the oppressed."[25] The hope I hold for my counseling work with these children was informed by my relationship with God whose primary way of knowing is love,[26] and by those who I have encountered that with.

TRAUMA AND LANGUAGE

As relational beings, it is language in its varied forms that enhances our sense of who we are intended to be. The centrality of language to our very being is demonstrated in the creation story of Genesis: "And God said . . . and it was so." Thus, "humanity is fully in the image of God only where it is a lived dialogical encounter."[27] The silencing impact of trauma—isolation—therefore directly contradicts how we have been designed to be and know ourselves as persons-in-relation, and language makes up an imperative part of the healing process when our sense of who we are has become distorted. Narrative therapy has a strong focus on language as being a constructing and powerful relational activity between persons. Freedman and Combs say that change involves a change in language, with new language creating new possibilities, because "languages are essentially shared activities . . . every time we speak, we bring forth a reality."[28] The *Tree of Life* model uses different types of language—each with the purpose of defining and enhancing a preferred identity story. The drawing of and writing on the trees, the telling and the re-telling of the new stories, the production and presentation of

---

24. McFadyen, *Call To Personhood*, 27.
25. Moltmann, *Crucified God*, 62.
26. 1 John 4:8, NIV.
27. McFadyen, *Call to Personhood*, 32.
28. Freedman and Combs, *Narrative Therapy*, 29.

certificates and documents, and the singing of celebratory songs all contribute to this language-based methodology.

Given this understanding of language as a creating activity, the way we speak and enquire about trauma with survivors matters. Traditionally, survivors of trauma have known about themselves through the language of effects. Changing from a language of effects to a language of responses has significant impact on the stories we hear. When we enquire about the responses to trauma we hear hope-filled language, indicating a preferred identity story. Cathy Richardson and Vikki Reynolds, narrative therapists renowned for their strong orientation to social justice-based community work, speak of "honoring resistance."[29] They hold that resistance has a strong link to repairing dignity when people's lives and identities are under attack. Indeed "resistance may not stop violence or social cruelty, but it does connect us with our sense of human and collective dignity."[30] This understanding was a key link in the *Tree of Life* process. Uncovering a person's response to trauma, as we did when we had conversations about storms and how the children had responded to them, connects them with what it is they accord value to in life, and begins to reverse their sense of isolation.

Therapist Alan Wade says that noticing resistance to either the acts or the effects of the violence and/or trauma, is important in "helping persons recognize their already existing strength and resourcefulness."[31] White points out that while the experience of trauma will never be mitigated by these noticings, drawing attention to the significance of responses to trauma emphasizes the fact that the negative consequences of trauma do not represent the whole story of a child's life and identity.[32] Using the language of responses places the survivor in a more robust place where they can address the consequences of trauma whilst developing a preferred sense of themselves in the process. For many of my young participants, the simplicity of their acts of resistance to traumatic events belied their importance and effectiveness. "I ran away," "I said 'No,'" were enough to allow them to survive and opened up space for further responses, eventually resulting in their safety in the care center. Realizing the significance of their responses brought smiles to young faces.

When we investigated the origins and histories of these acts of resistance and responses to trauma, connections to others were re-membered. This was another pathway to enhancing connection, and eliminating

29. Richardson and Reynolds, "Amazingly Alive," 8.
30. Ibid., 8.
31. Wade, *Small Acts*, 35.
32. White, *Trauma and Recovery*, 12.

isolation. Grandparents, siblings, parents, pastors, and teachers were attributed to teaching the children these things. Telling those stories rekindled those lost relationships. As well, hearing about each other's responses (including other children from across the globe via collective document sharing), invited the children to feel as if they are a part of a wider group of people who have similar knowledge and skills. It gave me a glimpse of a global, dialogical interconnectedness.

CONCLUSION

In this small village in Nigeria, the dominant stories held about the children had been traumatic tales of abandonment, loss, poverty, and abuse. As a Christian, a daughter, mother, a counselor, and as someone who has had her identity adequately forged by the love of others, it was not acceptable to me that these stories had the loudest voice. Nor was it acceptable that alternative stories had not yet been considered. Dan Allender says "every person alive has legions of stories of heartache and shame, loneliness and betrayal. But every human being also has at least one story of redemption that is full of surprise and delight."[33] The *Tree of Life* approach to working with vulnerable children enabled me to bring to light the stories that surprised and delighted, contradicting the pervading problem-saturated themes that were known too well. In so doing, I was able to share the experience of love and relationality that has largely forged my own identity.

Theologically, the "call to personhood"[34] is an invitation to participate in dialogical interconnectedness in a manner that reflects the trinitarian relationship of the Father, Son, and Holy Spirit. Traumatic events draw people away from this—isolating and silencing them, causing their identity as persons to be "less than," or seem flawed. Restoring relationship with dialogical encounter sees preferred identities, identities that reflect more of the original intent of our creator God, re-emerge as noticeably made in His image. While traumatic experience invites isolation and undermines relationship, language, and the way we use it, can reverse that isolation. A re-creation of preferred—love-orientated—identities is possible, simulating our being languaged into life in the original creation narrative.

The process of developing the new, preferred identity stories via the *Tree of Life* gave a tangible picture of relationality mirroring the triune relationship. The ebbing and flowing of drawing introspectively followed by sharing their story with each other—the quiet reflection as well as the

---

33. Allender, *Healing Path*, 121.
34. McFadyen, *Call to Personhood*.

joyful contributing to each other's trees, the laughing as well as the crying—and the movement of uniqueness and relationality worked together to allow growth. The subtle yet damaging, quiet sense of isolation lifted as the children shared their own stories and contributed to others.

As I went on to use the *Tree of Life* with over forty different people groups in West Africa, I witnessed as within each one new and deepened relationships broke down barriers ranging from shyness to sectarian tension. Many alternative stories were brought forward that I believe deserve to be heard because being heard is pivotal in the process of healing trauma. Perhaps it is appropriate to allow the voice of a young, once marginalized girl to finish, with her emerging, preferred identity story: "I thought I had an ugly and useless life, but now I can see I have a story."

References

Allender, Dan. *The Healing Path: How The Hurts In Your Past Can Lead You To A More Abundant Life.* Colorado Springs: WaterBrook, 1999.

Balswick, Jack, et al. *The Reciprocating Self: Human Development in Theological Perspective.* Downers Grove, IL: InterVarsity, 2005.

Denborough, David. *Collective Narrative Practice: Responding to Individuals, Groups, and Communities who have Experienced Trauma.* Adelaide, South Australia: Dulwich Centre, 2008.

Freedman, Jill, and Gene Combs. *Narrative Therapy: The Social Construction of Preferred Realities.* New York: W.W. Norton & Co, 1996.

Herman, Judith. *Trauma and Recovery: The Aftermath Violence—From Domestic Abuse to Political Terror.* New York, NY: Basic, 1997.

McFadyen, Alistair. *The Call to Personhood: A Christian Theory of the Individual in Social Relationships.* Cambridge, New York: Cambridge University Press, 1990.

Moltmann, Jürgen. *The Crucified God.* Translated by R. A. Wilson and John Bowden. Tottenham Road, London: SCM, 1974.

Newman, David. "Rescuing the Said from the Saying of It": Living Documentation in Narrative Therapy. *The International Journal of Narrative Therapy and Community Work* 3 (2008) 24–34.

Olthuis, James H. *The Beautiful Risk: A New Psychology of Loving and Being Loved.* Eugene, OR: Wipf & Stock, 2006.

Pembroke, N. *Renewing Pastoral Practice: Trinitarian Perspectives on Pastoral Care and Counseling.* Aldershot, England: Ashgate, 2006.

Richardson, Cathy, and Vikki Reynolds. "Here We Are, Amazingly Alive": Holding Ourselves Together with an Ethic of Social Justice in Community Work. *International Journal of Child, Youth and Family Studies* 1 (2012) 1–19.

Wade, Allan. "Small Acts of Living: Everyday Resistance to Violence and other Forms of Oppression." *Contemporary Family Therapy* 19 no.1 (1997) 23–39.

White, Michael. *Reflections on Narrative Practice: Essays and Interviews.* Adelaide, Australia: Dulwich Centre Publications, 2000.

———. "Children, Trauma and Subordinate Storyline Development." In *Trauma: Narrative Responses to Traumatic Experience,* edited by David Denborough 143–165. Adelaide, South Australia: Dulwich Centre, 2006.

———. Children, Trauma and Recovery: From Political Terror to Domestic Violence. *The International Journal of Narrative Therapy and Community Work* 3&4 (2005) 10–21.

———. Working with People who are Suffering the Consequences of Multiple Trauma: A Narrative Perspective. *The International Journal of Narrative Therapy and Community Work* 1 (2004) 44–75.

Ziegler, Dave. *Traumatic Experience and the Brain: A Handbook for Understanding and Treating Those Traumatized as Children.* Gilbert, Arizona: Acacia, 2011.

SECTION THREE

Stories of Counselor Education

11

Welcoming the Stranger
Teaching in a Context of Cultural Diversity

WATIRI MAINA

Counseling across cultures is important, and particularly so in *Aotearoa* New Zealand due to the founding bicultural commitments of this nation. As *Aotearoa* New Zealand continues to grow upon this basis as a culturally-diverse society, I argue that counselors need to broaden their ability to practice within a context of cultural diversity. My view of diversity moves beyond ethnic definitions to include gender, race, ability, age, socioeconomic, and other types of difference. Counseling educators who are Christians are potentially well positioned in this "new milieu" for counseling, as trinitarian theology specifically invites participation in practices of relational engagement with "strangers"—others who are different—through the offering of hospitality.

As a Christian counseling educator, I hope to facilitate a learning environment that creates a climate of acceptance and invites students to engage in positions and practices that offer hospitality to the stranger. This hope grew throughout my varied life as I sought to engage people on behalf of the Gospel example of love. My journey began in Kenya where I grew up valuing community and came to value unity and uniqueness in diversity. My education as a counseling therapist, work with African refugees in Nairobi, educating homeless children, travels, and many cross cultural experiences as a professional shaped my deep commitment to finding ways to encounter difference with grace.

I have come to believe that we are not only strangers to each other; we are also sometimes strangers to ourselves, in need of an encounter with gracious and generous hospitality from another to develop intrapersonal and interpersonal integration. This is one way that the interactions we have with each other in the classroom are significant for developing the hospitable positions and practices necessary for the bicultural and multicultural context of *Aotearoa* New Zealand. As a counseling educator, I hope to meet each student and their culture with deep interest and curiosity that makes room for them to be known as individuals-in-community. This experience of meaningful engagement can act as a model for the environment counseling students in turn create when working with each other and with people in their communities.

My aim in this chapter is to identify points of intersection between my pedagogical practices and trinitarian theology. I explore both the practice of teaching counseling as an act of hospitality, and the purposes and values that shape my practices as a counseling educator.

MY EXPERIENCE OF INHOSPITALITY AND HOSPITALITY

Many years ago, as a Kenyan living in South Africa, I stood in line with a Canadian friend waiting to buy food. When I got to the cashier, all those behind me were invited to buy their lunch but I kept being overlooked. I did not immediately make sense of this experience of exclusion. I asked again for some food but I was continually ignored as if invisible. I was treated as if I had no presence and no voice. Ultimately my friend bought me what I needed. At that moment I was aware of my confusion, the sense of violation, and the disruption of my inner peace. The world seemed to suddenly change around me. Previously I had not noticed that I was the only darker-skinned African in that queue. I felt upset, invisible, and robbed of something that was precious to me—equality.

A decade later, I was buying food again at a small stall in a Nairobi market. As I waited for my food, the discussion and tone of conversation changed. The woman selling food began talking about the Kikuyus (my tribe), explaining how the coming general and presidential elections would see their defeat from power. This was not just casual Kenyan tribal talk or banter; instead I heard an uncomfortable edge in her voice. Her language was forceful and the dialogue with the other customer intimidated me. I found myself unable to shake off a sense of dread. A few months later the post-election intertribal violence took many lives, many were horrifically maimed and scores were left homeless, living as refugees in their own country. My grandmother, cousins, and aunty lived to tell stories of pain, trauma, and suffering. This was the third time that tribal clashes left my family homeless and traumatized.

These events jarred me as they were opposed to the African hospitality that I had grown up knowing and enjoying, where "whenever there is food to be taken, everyone present is invited to participate... it would be a height of incredible bad manners for one to eat anything however small, without sharing it with anyone else present."[1] In summary, these experiences jarred with my value of *ubuntu*:

> Africans believe in something that is difficult to render in English. We call it *ubuntu, botho*. It means the essence of being human. You know when it is there and when it is absent. It speaks about humaneness, gentleness, and hospitality, putting yourself on behalf of others, being vulnerable. It embraces compassion and toughness. It recognizes that my humanity is bound up in yours, for we can only be human together.[2]

As a result of my experiences in both food queues, I came to realize what it felt like to become a victim of racial prejudice and to know its impact on my identity. As I reflected on the dissonance between these experiences and my cherished association with *ubuntu*, I began to appreciate why people retaliate. I found myself needing to make a choice to take a different route in dealing with the injustice, to not harm others, but "reach out, touch and be touched, bridge or promote difference."[3] I now see that, in both situations, the choice between embracing diversity and shunning otherness was mine to make.

I wanted to gain self-agency, the ability to feel, think, choose, and behave in liberating ways that welcomed new possibilities. I was aware that it was important to reflect on my experiences so as to foster resilience and diminish the possibility of repeating the painful past.[4] I therefore found myself faced with the choice of becoming a "compassionate witness" of my experiences and the experiences of others as I recognized our shared humanity. This restored my sense of common humanity when it faltered, and blocked the dehumanizing of others.[5]

The ideas of sharing a common humanity and living in a diverse community were a familiar part of my upbringing. African hospitality to strangers was a central cultural value that was instilled formally and informally as I grew up. Differences were celebrated and visitors were seen as a blessing, bringing

1. Okafor, "Africa at Crossroads," 21.
2. Tutu and Tutu, *Desmond Tutu*, 69.
3. Weingarten, "Compassionate Witnessing," 16.
4. Anderson, *Conversation, Language, Possibilities*, 231.
5. Weingarten, "Compassionate Witnessing," 2.

richness, and never an inconvenience. Each person was seen as created by God and worthy of honor, and we were expected to treat everyone with respect and in a dignified manner. I carried with me these things as an inner knowing that we are all interdependent with each other, with the environment and with God. I therefore chose to become a compassionate witness in an ethnically diverse African community which included multiple people groups, and joined those who sought to foster unity in diversity. Looking back, this was a key part of shaping my ideas of relationality, welcoming strangers, and becoming a community in the midst, and in spite, of our differences.

Christianity and Experiences of Inhospitality and Hospitality

Another key part of shaping my commitment to diversity was my family's exposure to a version of the Christian religion. Like many in the community, my grandfather had two wives. However, when my grandparents first encountered Christianity in the 1930s, my second grandmother and my grandfather were excluded from the church because of what was considered to be the polygamous nature of their relationship. As the voice of the church became dominant they responded by shutting out second wives and their children. As a result, families became estranged from each other. Children were all at once left fatherless and sentenced to lives of poverty. People lost their identity and the values of community care were upset. Understandably, religion was seen as dividing and excluding, bringing disturbance to the social structures that supported the life and wellbeing of individuals and of the community. I struggled with these excluding ways. I was confused, upset, and conflicted when people were treated unequally and marginalized by others.

In recent years I have been fortunate to encounter an alternative way of understanding the Christian story that does not associate with exclusion and the destructive forms of legalism. This has come through searching for answers to puzzling questions such as: Who are human beings? Why is the world full of pain and suffering? Where is God in the midst of pain and suffering? I sought for answers by immersing myself in scripture reading, prayer, psychology, and theology. My personal encounter with the crucified and resurrected Christ also brought me deep hope in justice and equality. Jesus chose to come and dwell among us with a relational ethic that brought reversals—the weakest became the strongest, the least became the greatest, the crucified became the saviour. Jesus' story and his connection to the Father and the Holy Spirit—a loving unity in diversity that is drawn from the otherness-in-relation[6]—captivated my imagination and shifted my view of the gospel to one of hope and generous hospitality of the Triune God.

6. Gunton, *One, Three, Many*.

HOSPITALITY UNPACKED

A few years ago I was powerfully encountered by the triune God through Andrei Rublev's *Trinity*, a classic painting of the three angels who visited Abraham and Sarah in Mamre, subtly depicted as the Father, Son, and Holy Spirit (see figure one).

Figure one: *The icon of the Holy Trinity by St Andrei Rublev (1425)*

Within the icon, I was drawn to meditate on the space in the front of the three "strangers." It felt welcoming, moving, and loving. As I gazed on the image, I felt embraced in a community of love, a community that included me just as I was. I then realized that being in such communion could not be enjoyed without others around me, nor could I remain closed to and from others. I wanted to extend the same welcome to all. I wanted others to know, find, and experience this deep and embracing hospitality that had profoundly and tangibly transformed me.

Theologically, I understand my practice of counseling and counselor education as a commitment to share Christ's welcome with clients, students, and others around me. I seek to share God's desire for restoration, recovery, and reconciliation for all and of everything, and to be an agent of God's transformation. Just as God has welcomed me, I can welcome others. Like Russell, I am "continuing the search for new ways of understanding difference as a gift, and practicing hospitality as an act of justice."[7] Hospitality in this paper is seen as "the practice of God's welcome, embodied in our actions as we reach across difference to participate with God in bringing justice and healing to our world."[8] This type of hospitality is seen throughout the Bible.

Biblical Hospitality

Throughout the Old Testament the people of God were called to offer hospitality to the aliens, orphans, and widows among them. For example, Abraham and Sarah are represented as offering generous hospitality to three strangers under the Oaks of Mamre and entertained God (Father, Son, and Holy Spirit) unaware.[9] Within one year they are blessed with a son of promise. Through liturgy and ritual, the people of Israel are also urged to remember that they were once aliens in need of hospitality and so extend the same hospitality to those different from them. The stranger always has room in God's economy: "when a stranger sojourns with you in your land, you shall not do him wrong. You shall treat the stranger who sojourns with you as the native among you, you shall love him as yourself; for you were strangers in the land of Egypt: I am the Lord your God."[10] Hospitality is an expression of God's character, the nature of a Holy God[11] who desired that his people lived a holy life too, a life depicting God's gracious love to all including the strangers among them.

We can also see this grace-filled form of hospitality illustrated in the New Testament in examples such as when the risen Christ walks with the two disciples to Emmaus. Here, the men respond with awe and wonder when they recognize him as he breaks the bread and their hope is restored.[12] Not only does welcoming strangers have the possibility of bringing benefit and enrichment as echoed in Hebrews 13:2, scripture also reminds me that I too have been a stranger and was welcomed by God/the triune community. This same community of love now invites me to participate in their life as I offer hospitality to all, especially the least of his brothers and sisters.[13] This solidarity with the marginalized is, as Russell so beautifully puts it: a

---

7. Ibid.
8. Ibid., 2&53.
9. Gen 18:1–15, ESV.
10. Lev 19:33–34, ESV.
11. Lev 19:2, ESV.
12. Russell, "Outsiders Within," 70.
13. Matt 25:31–46, ESV.

"mutual relationship of care and trust in which we share in the struggle for empowerment, dignity and fullness of life."[14]

Hospitality is, then, mutual and reciprocal. In the Greek New Testament, the word for hospitality is *philoxenia*, love of the stranger. The opposite word is *xenophobia*, hatred of the stranger or unreasonable fear towards strangers. *Xenos* simultaneously denotes a guest, a host or a stranger, showing how fluid this relational encounter can be. It is an encounter of reciprocity and reversal. At a given moment one can be a host and in the next moment a guest in the same relational engagement. Koenig aptly notes that *philoxenia* "refers literally not to a love of strangers per se but to a delight in the whole guest-host relationship, in the mysterious reversals and gains for all parties which may take place."[15]

To summarize, for me biblical hospitality is about welcoming the stranger. Out of the overflow of our encounter with the Triune God's generous love, we are called to extend this gracious hospitality to others through the mutual welcome of the other as God's image bearer, by advocating for the marginalized, and seeking to create a community of welcome. As a result many times there is an experience of unexpected divine presence.[16] As Yong clearly states, "For Christians, the practices of hospitality . . . embody the trinitarian character of God's economy of redemption. In the economy of God, the unconditional gifts of God in Christ and the Holy Spirit mean that there is never any lack of hospitality to be offered and received."[17]

I am suggesting that the stranger can be understood as anyone who is different, whether that difference be cultural, ethnic, racial, social, sexual, gender, economic, age, able-ness, or any other difference. Relationally, God can be a stranger to us or we can be estranged from God. Psychologically we can even be strangers to ourselves, unaware of our different selves or identities. Furthermore, there is a vital—relational—link between awareness of others and awareness of ourselves. Prominent American psychologist Kenneth Frank posits that as there is a limit to self-understanding, we need others to help us know ourselves: "the self develops not by way of solitary introspection but by seeing oneself through others' eyes."[18] Now that I have outlined my position on hospitality that has been shaped by my cultural heritage and social/relational trinitarian theology, I will now consider my work as a counseling

---

14. Russell, *Just Hospitality*, 20.
15. Koenig, *New Testament Hospitality*, 8.
16. Deut 1:6–17, ESV; Pohl, *Making Room*; Russell, *Just Hospitality*.
17. Yong, *Hospitality and the Other*, location 3370–3372.
18. Frank, "Strangers to Ourselves," 316.

educator and the ways in which hospitality informs my pedagogical and clinical practices, using the metaphor of "welcoming the stranger."

PRACTICING HOSPITALITY IN COUNSELOR EDUCATION

Counselor educators and counselors are constantly challenged to review their philosophy of practice. I suggest this legitimately includes their perceptions of those who are different from them, who would be considered strangers. This call to review one's philosophy of practice has two particularly important challenges for counselors in New Zealand, due to the bicultural foundation[19] and increasing multicultural nature of this country.[20]

The first is the challenge to embrace biculturalism,[21] that is, become engaged in the spirit of the Treaty of Waitangi guided by its principles of partnership, participation, and protection, which are expressions of hospitality. Crocket[22] suggests that counselors respond personally to the meaning of the Treaty—their response is shaped by their "unique cultural identity" and how that identity arises from or relates to the Treaty. Given that each client will have a unique perspective of their own and the counselor's cultural identity, determining safe biculturally appropriate practices takes place in effective dialogue between the counselor and the client.

The second challenge is to rethink the ways in which counselors face the present multicultural zeitgeist, appreciating and making room for difference within a bicultural context. Counselors have an obligation to be reflective and reflexive of their experiences of diversity, becoming more socially self-aware and self-knowledgeable and developing interpathy (intercultural empathy).[23] These are important cultural safety considerations. Interpathy, coined by David Augsburger, extends the concept of empathy. It is experiencing a separate other without one's assumptions, values, and views being imposed on their

---

19. This bicultural foundation is based upon the Treaty of Waitangi, the founding document of *Aotearoa* New Zealand, signed in 1840 by many *Māori* tribal leaders. In it the British crown, under Queen Victoria, guaranteed to defend the property rights of the indigenous *Māori* people after increasing land encroachment by European settlers. See: Consedine and Consedine, *Healing Our History*; King, *Penguin History*.

20. Statistics New Zealand, "Migration"; Weir and Harris "NZ Migration Boom."

21. Crocket, "Biculturalism indicates both that *iwi* and the Crown represent valid interests and that individuals might be able to relate effectively in the terms of two cultures" *Exploring the Meaning*, 61.

22. Ibid., 62.

23. Rakoczy, "Responding to Difference."

perspective and meaning-making. It is embracing of what is truly other.[24] I suggest that interpathy offers an important place to begin when teaching and practicing counseling-as-hospitality in a context of diversity.

Competencies and standards for multicultural counseling competence involve three areas. First is the area of beliefs and attitudes; second, knowledge and learning; and third, skills development. In my teaching, hospitality invites me to touch on all three of these areas through theoretical and experiential learning. Like Stratman "if my pedagogy concerning . . . hospitality solely revolves around reading and thinking, then I am still engaged in a narrow understanding of how my students (or any of us) come to know something."[25] I therefore use the metaphor of hospitality as it stirs me to facilitate connections between my students, strange ideas, and the "other," both in and out of the classroom.

My hope is that hospitality is extended both to strangers and to strange or new ideas. When students come to train as counselors, they are often surprised, unsettled, or uncomfortable as they face themselves and new ideas. Palmer describes hospitality in academia as, "receiving each other, our struggles, our new born ideas with openness and care. It means creating an ethos in which the community of truth can form, and pain of truth's transformation be borne." He powerfully contends "to be inhospitable to strangers or strange ideas, however unsettling they may be, is to be hostile to the possibility of truth."[26]

TEACHING COUNSELING AS A PRACTICE OF HOSPITALITY

Hospitality as Holy Ground

Both teaching and practicing counseling can be regarded as practices of hospitality in partnership with strangers.

I believe that to offer hospitality is to enter into a holy space. By this I mean that hospitality is the space where the moral and the spiritual dimensions intersect in an embodied encounter. The moral dimension is evident because it is born out of our value, respect, and honor of the stranger as another human being with dignity. It is also spiritual because in the space between persons, the relational encounter impacts each and potentially brings transformation as each opens up to the other. Neither is left untouched or

---

24. Augsburger, "Interpathy Re-envisioned."
25. Stratman, "Pedagogy of Hospitality," 34.
26. Palmer, *Know As We Are Known*, 73–74.

unmoved by the encounter. There is an unexpected divine presence in those moments where love is enacted. This transforming experience of hospitality can be contrasted with the example given above where I was excluded on the basis of racist judgment.

In my teaching of counseling, the aim of forming hospitable attitudes and beliefs is grounded on a trinitarian anthropology. This perspective of human beings plays a key role in enabling students to understand that they are created by a relational God to be relational beings of value and dignity, bearing God's image.[27] We talk about the loving mutual and interpenetrating relationship of God: the Father, the Son, and the Holy Spirit. All three persons are distinct but they are all one; they exist in a dance of unity in diversity founded on love. One way this is enacted is as a place of hospitality that makes room for the other.[28] This image of a loving, triune, relational community of God is the conceptual framework I work in with my students. The Trinity gives us a mirror to reflect on when seeking to be image bearers and also seeking to be present in the world around us. The Trinity invites us to be both guest and host, sometimes simultaneously.

In class, I endeavor to invite my students to form into one big group and also small process groups of different individuals seeking to become a community where unity in diversity is embraced and hospitality is extended. They engage relationally through sharing personal story exercises in small groups, dyads, and triads. As they do so, the hope is that they encounter themselves, each other, and God, on the basis that they are "brothers and sisters created by the same God and living as mutual guests in the same house provided by the same divine host."[29] My hope is that the class setting becomes an experiential group, helping students develop their ability to welcome difference through engaging with each other's ideas and experiences. Through person-centered therapy, or practices of encounter and relational depth, the students learn to suspend their ideas, thoughts, and judgments about the strangers and new ideas facing them, and enter into another's frame of reference, namely their client's phenomenological world. Overall, I view this as an incarnational process. Just as God enters our world and dwells with us, trainee counselors begin to enter into another's world through empathic listening and mutually participate in partnership with a stranger other.[30]

---

27. I acknowledge that this position leans towards theologians like Zizioulas, Grenz, and Torrance, among others, and that there are alternative understandings of God's image that sit outside this relational, Trinity-based nature of humanity.

28. Zizioulas, *Being as Communion*; Grenz, *Rediscovering the Triune*.

29. Oden, *You Welcomed Me*, 52.

30. Koenig, *New Testament Hospitality*.

Students are also invited to extend hospitality beyond the classroom setting. An assignment on "Engaging with Otherness" requires the students to enter the wider community and choose a people group that represents significant otherness from their own positioning. They organise a visit within the semester to safely engage this group in some meaningful way. Some students choose a Christian church from a different tradition than their own, or another religious group such as Buddhist, Muslim, or Hindu communities. Some choose to connect with people living in poverty, with disabilities or with severe illnesses like Parkinson's disease, with the gay or lesbian community, elderly or adolescent people, or attend a *tangi*[31] or Alcoholics Anonymous group, to mention a few. This assignment invites students to discuss and evaluate their personal experience, considering the historical and contemporary factors that have affected this group and their view of the group, and how they would engage an individual from that group as a counseling client. As students take a hospitality approach to these encounters, the hope is that they will be challenged to discover their own biases, prejudices, and assumptions that foster disconnection. It is also hoped they begin to renegotiate their positions towards others and redirect their imaginations towards inclusion rather than exclusion.[32]

Hospitality as Personal Confrontation

Hospitality is often confronting in that it challenges ourselves in the face of the stranger, both within and without. Our fears, our sense of inadequacy and imperfections are very often brought to the fore. In these moments we are faced with the choice of either embracing or rejecting others, and we risk the very same rejection of ourselves. When we make the choice to embrace the other we are not only choosing to step into vulnerability and the risk of being changed by the other but we are simultaneously challenged to let go and make room for the stranger and the gifts they bring. These gifts are not always visible, but they are nonetheless significant. When we reject the impact of the relational encounter, we deny both the other *and* ourselves the possibility of enriched deep relational engagement. My hope is that students are quickly confronted with the reality that strangers can make us uncomfortable. My view is that these experiences of uncomfortableness are often associated with the challenge to extend hospitality to parts of our own lives that we would rather deny or suppress, because of the fear of vulnerability or

---

31. *Māori* funeral custom.
32. Ogletree, *Hospitality to the Stranger*, 3.

rejection if they were more fully known. Thus, encountering strangers can be personally confronting and therefore uncomfortable.

My overall hope here is that through reflective and reflexive practices, my students learn to be self-aware and self-compassionate, and recognize with time that they are both a guest and a host of themselves.

Another way I seek to bring about these developments is through an exercise in class where I use "pictures of alterity," seeking to create an environment of connection with the "other." Sometimes I use a picture of an anonymous boy sitting outside the door of a shack, and have each student write a story about the picture. These stories are then shared in the group. I hope that these things become learning moments about difference, perceptions, and assumptions and the impact they have on the other. I am particularly interested in challenging the use of labels because in my view the labels and names we use have a significant impact on the "other." In class we therefore talk about what hospitality looks like, what it is like when we are misnamed or judged, and how we can avoid misnaming others and so divest ourselves of powerful positions of certainty making room for curiosity, wonder, and creative healing possibilities and encounters.

Hospitality and the Stranger Within

Both my thinking and experience suggest that the ability to offer hospitality to a stranger is enhanced as we welcome the stranger within. The experience of grace mediated by another leads us to welcome the stranger within and enlarges the capacity for compassion and welcoming of others. My personal experiences of exclusion lead to fear, feelings of invisibility, loss of voice, dissonance, and anger. In contrast, through experiences of God's hospitality mediated through my friend, through other hospitable Africans who embraced me in my pain, and encounters with God through prayer and Scripture, I learnt to be a compassionate witness of the actions of passive violence. I began to notice how I and others made meaning of ourselves and our experiences, the names and labels we gave ourselves and others, and that the spaces that we made or did not make for our humanity were either life-giving or life-limiting. Coming face-to-face with another who intentionally or unintentionally brings an experience of encounter that is life-limiting can be nullified by an encounter with another who embraces the stranger, giving him or her an opportunity to see life as hopeful.

To illustrate this, I offer an example of a simple class activity in which an "other" can offer a redemptive experience of encounter by being a compassionate witness who gives empathic attentiveness and genuine feedback. On a piece of paper each student writes a story of an encounter that has impacted them lately. The unnamed papers are passed around and each student seeks to empathically respond to the story of the other. The story teller finally receives his/her own paper back and shares how the responses of the others connected to his/her frame of reference and impacted him/her. We then reflect together on this exercise. This exercise has elicited positive responses from students who experience empathic connection with the class and sometimes find themselves moved to tears because someone has heard their pain, their story. I notice too that the class feels connected to each other's stories, value each other more, and psychologically seem closer. Strangers become neighbors and they enter into mutual partnerships through the journey of counselor training. The students find that their private space is suddenly expanded, open, and free. When ideas and stories are received by hospitable other, new meaning and fresh perspective emerge.[33] Further to this, the students are invited to use reflective and reflexive journaling to process any emotional upsets and the edges of self-awareness arising from their encounters with alterity that trigger cognitive and emotional incongruence. They learn that welcoming strangers within can make room for alterity, which is an act of courageous hospitality. Hospitality is therefore a vulnerable, humbling, reciprocating space of giving and receiving.

Hospitality as an Act of Grace

Hospitality can also be seen as an act of grace. Grace-filled relational encounters facilitate therapeutic change. Person-centered counseling, founded by Carl Rogers, proposes six necessary and sufficient conditions[34] for facilitating an engagement of relational depth.[35] Relational depth is "a state of profound contact and engagement between two people, in which each person is fully real with the Other, and able to understand and value the Other's experiences at a high level."[36] This deeply impacting, intersubjective connection goes beyond procedural knowing and operates from the implicit knowing of the counselor. It demands that the counselor be fully present. Mearns and Cooper liken relational depth to Rogers' notion of "presence": moments in which the therapist's "inner spirit" seems to reach out and touch the inner spirit of the other, and she or he is closest to his or her "inner, intuitive self."[37]

33. Palmer, *Know As We Are Known*.
34. Rogers, "Necessary and Sufficient."
35. Mearns and Cooper, *Relational Depth*.
36. Ibid., xii.
37. Baldwin, "An Interview with Carl Rogers."

Furthermore, "therapeutic presence involves therapists using their whole self to be both fully engaged and receptively attuned in the moment, with and for the client, to promote effective therapy."[38] In order to prepare the ground for presence, Geller and Greenberg propose that counselors prepare before the session by having an intention for presence, clearing a space in their inner world for the other, through putting aside self-concerns, bracketing or containing (theories, preconceptions, and therapy plans) and having an attitude of openness, acceptance, interest, and non-judgment. This preparation is a way of life too that includes holding a philosophical commitment to presence, personal growth, practicing presence in their own life, engaging in meditation, and ongoing care for their own needs.[39]

Research suggests that therapeutic alliance is a significant predictor of therapeutic change.[40] The client can be viewed as a stranger to the counselor because it is their first time of meeting, the client may reveal to the counselor new information about him or herself, or may bring new ideas that are strange to the counselor. When the client and all that the client brings is received by a counselor who genuinely seeks to care, and desires to understand the client and his or her inner world, the client's experience of being truly heard and known by another can be described as an experience of grace incognito.[41] My hope is that unconditional positive regard, empathy, and congruence[42] working together create an environment that makes room for authentic engagement with the other, enhancing the relational depth that facilitates change.

The ability to welcome well and extend hospitality courageously invites the counselor to host the client as he or she is and at the same time become a guest in the client's inner world. By doing so the counselor's attitude of warmth and acceptance becomes akin to "making room." Indeed, this may be the main place the client finds psychological rest as another joins him in his pain, hosts his hurt, celebrates his joys, and enters into deep communion with him. This attitude of grace values the whole person including their failings in an open authentic way that honors and accepts humanness. The counselor becomes the person that offers hope. The other (client) finds that even in one's darkest moments, a gracious space of welcome, acceptance and understanding is extended, as the counselor offers conditions that facilitate transformational shifts and foster possible changes in the client's life: in their thinking, feeling and behaving. As the counselor offers hospitality to

38. Geller and Porges, "Therapeutic Presence."
39. Geller and Greenberg, "Therapeutic Presence."
40. Lambert and Barley, "Research Summary."
41. Cooper, *Sin, Pride, Self-Acceptance.*
42. Rogers, "Necessary and Sufficient."

the client, so too is the counsellor a guest in the client's inner world: "I am the novice, she the expert. I can only sit at her feet to learn. That the stranger and I enjoy an equal dignity emerges concretely only as our interactions unfold over time.[43] I hope my students find this same dignity through their counselor formation journey.

Teaching counseling-as-hospitality in a diversity context invites embracing of self and other, sameness and difference, with grace and honor. This is expressed by staying grounded and open in one's beliefs without being rigid, but having a desire to understand, be curious, let go of assumptions and seek connection with otherness.

CONCLUSION

It is my hope that the counselor in training grows in his or her capacity to offer hospitality to others in class and the community by engaging in encounters that facilitate opportunities for interpathic understanding of another's phenomenological world. This entering into the frame of reference of the other, withholding judgment and without losing one's own frame, is a challenging learning and growth process. It can be likened to the trinitarian dance: *perichoresis*, where in the context of perfect love each member of the Trinity interpenetrates the other. Yet within this unity, the uniqueness of each is distinct; unity-in-diversity, mutuality, equality, and reciprocity are valued in a community of love—a space of generous hospitality. As a counselor informed by trinitarian theology, both the inner life and external salvic work[44] of God challenge my personal and professional life as an educator and counselor. One cannot be an effective counselor without having inner character and integrity embodied in empathic/interpathic understanding of the other, positive regard, and congruent living that facilitate relational depth in the work of the counselor. As students experience personal awareness and growth and professional competency within the hospitable training context, slowly a paradigm shift beings take place. It is a continuing growth curve that *accelerates* when they then go out on placement and truly meet the stranger in the community away from the safety of the classroom.

Thus, the metaphor of hospitality offers a way forward for counselors in our multicultural world.[45] As a counseling educator and counselor, I am aware that I am a mediator of God's hospitality to my students and clients, and my hope is that my students will be the same.

43. Ogletree, *Hospitality to the Strange*, 4.
44. 42 Tam, *Trinitarian Dance*, 43–48.
45. Russell, *Just Hospitality*, 82.

References

Anderson, Harlene. *Conversations, Language and Possibilities*. New York: Basic, 1997.

Augsburger, David. "Interpathy Re-envisioned: Reflecting on Observed Practice of Mutuality by Counselors who Muddle along Cultural Boundaries or are Thrown into a Wholly Strange Location." *Cross-Culturality in Formation and Supervision* 34 (2014) 11–22.

Baldwin, Michele. "Interview with Carl Rogers on the Use of the Self in Therapy." *Journal of Psychotherapy & the Family* 3 no.1 (1987) 45–52.

Consedine, Robert, and Joanna Consedine. *Healing Our History: The Challenge of the Treaty of Waitangi*. Auckland: Penguin, 2001.

Cooper, Terry D. *Sin, Pride and Self-Acceptance: The Problem of Identity in Theology and Psychology*. Downers Grove, IL: Intervarsity, 2003.

Crocket, Alistair. "Exploring the Meaning of the Treaty of Waitangi for Counseling." *New Zealand Journal of Counseling* 33 no.1 (2013) 54–67.

Flintoff, Vivianne J., and Shirley Rivers. "A Reshaping of Counseling Curriculum: Responding to the Changing (Bi)cultural Context." *British Journal of Guidance & Counseling* 40 no.3 (2012) 235–246.

Frank, Kenneth A. "Strangers to Ourselves: Exploring the Limits and Potentials of the Analyst's Self Awareness in Self-and Mutual Analysis." *Psychoanalytic Dialogues* 22 no.3 (2012) 311–327.

Geller, Shari M., and Leslie S. Greenberg. "Therapeutic Presence: Therapists' Experience of Presence in the Psychotherapy Encounter." *Person-Centered and Experiential Psychotherapies* 1 no. 1&2 (2011) 71–86.

Geller, Shari M., and Stephen W. Porges. "Therapeutic Presence: Neurophysiological Mechanisms Mediating Feeling Safe in Therapeutic Relationships." *Journal of Psychotherapy Integration* 24 no.3 (2014) 178–192.

Grenz, Stanley. *Rediscovering the Triune God: The Trinity in Contemporary Theology*. Minneapolis: Augsberg Fortress, 2004.

Gunton, Colin. *The One, the Three and the Many: God, Creation and the Culture of Modernity. The 1992 Bampton Lectures*. Cambridge, England: Cambridge University Press, 1993.

King, Michael. *The Penguin History of New Zealand*. Auckland: Penguin, 2003.

Koenig, John. *New Testament Hospitality: Partnership with Strangers as Promise and Mission*. Eugene, OR: Wipf&Stock, 2001.

Lambert, Michael J., and Dean E. Barley. "Research Summary on the Therapeutic Relationship and Psychotherapy Outcome." *Psychotherapy: Theory, Research, Practice, Training* 38 no.4 (2001) 357–361.

Mearns, Dave, and Mick Cooper. *Working at Relational Depth in Counseling and Psychotherapy*. London: Sage, 2005.

Oden, Amy. *And You Welcomed Me: A Sourcebook on Hospitality in Early Christianity*. Nashville: Abingdon, 2001.

Ogletree, Thomas. *Hospitality to the Stranger: Dimensions of Moral Understanding*. Louisville, KY: Westminster John Knox, 2003.

Okafor, Festus Chukwudi. *Africa at the Crossroads: Philosophical Approach to Education*. New York: Vantage, 1974.

Palmer, Parker. *To Know as we are Known: A Spirituality of Education*. San Francisco: Harper and Row, 1983.

Pohl, Christine. D. *Making Room: Recovering Hospitality as a Christian Tradition*. Grand Rapids, MI: Eerdmans, 1999.

Rakoczy, S. "Responding to Difference: Challenges for Contemporary Spiritual Directors." *Forming Religious Leaders in and For a Diverse World* 29 (2009) 97–104.

Rogers, Carl. "The Necessary and Sufficient Conditions of Therapeutic Personality Change." *The Journal of Consulting Psychology* 21 (1957) 95–103.

Russell, Letty M. *Just Hospitality: God's Welcome in a World of Difference*, edited by J. Shannon Clarkson and Kate M. Ott. Louisville: Westminster John Knox, 2009.

———. "Outsiders within." *Church & Society* 96, no. 3 (2006) 64–72.

Statistics New Zealand. "Migration." http://stats.govt.nz/browse_for_stats/population/Migration.aspx

Stratman, Jake. "Toward a Pedagogy of Hospitality: Empathy, Literature, and Community Engagement." *Journal of Education and Christian Belief* 17 no.1 (2013) 25–59.

Tam, Sharon. *The Trinitarian Dance: How the Triune God Develops Transformational Leaders*. Eugene, OR: Wipf & Stock, 2015.

Tutu, Desmond, and Naomi Tutu. *The Words of Desmond Tutu*. New York: Newmarket, 1989.

Weingarten, Kaethe. "Compassionate Witnessing and the Transformation of Societal Violence: How Individuals Can Make a Difference." http://www.humiliationstudies.org/documents/WeingartenCompassionateWitnessing.pdf

Weir, James, and Catherine Harris. "NZ Migration Boom Nears 60,000 a Year, as Indians and Returning Kiwis Flood In." *Stuff* (August 21, 2015). http://www.stuff.co.nz/business/industries/71329261/NZ-migration-boom-nears-60-000-a-year-as-Indians-and-returning-Kiwis-flood-in

Yong, Amos. *Hospitality and the Other: Pentecost, Christian Practices, and the Neighbor (Faith Meets Faith)*. Kindle ed. Maryknoll, NY: Orbis, 2008.

Zizioulas, John. *Being as Communion: Studies in Personhood and the Church*. London: Darton, Longman & Todd, 1985.

12

Doing Justice and Holding Care
Conceptualizing the Aims of Teacher-Student Engagement in Counselor Education

SARAH PENWARDEN

As a counselor educator, I draw on two philosophical streams in how I position myself in relation to students: my desire to offer spaces of dialogue, paying attention to power and positioning within a narrative therapy framework, and also my Christian faith commitments. These commitments lead towards both noticing power relations and taking up a position of humility, through the influence of Jesus' pattern of self-giving love.

Within my life story, many factors have influenced my attraction to narrative therapy, a poststructuralist-inspired therapy originating in New Zealand and Australia.[1] I strongly resonated with the sense of people living storied lives; co-creating overarching narrative structures through which daily life gains coherence and meaning. I was also drawn to the lens narrative therapy offers with which to view the operation of power relations. When I "met" narrative therapy, in 2001 in my Masters of Counseling degree at Waikato University, New Zealand, I found in this therapy a fit with my own implicit values about offering power and voice to others in conversations about their lives. A poststructuralist perspective on power suggests that while we are always living within relations of power,[2] power may be managed so that relational benefit, rather than harm, is produced.

Indeed, I observe that when power is managed in line with the wellbeing of others, growth-producing relationships can result. Over the course of

1. White & Epston, *Narrative Means*.
2. Foucault, *Power/Knowledge*.

my work as a narrative therapist, for ten years in high school contexts, I held strongly to the value of noticing and seeking to moderate my own power as an adult and a counselor. I located myself within narrative therapy's stance of the client being the expert in his or her life, with the therapist taking up a "decentered but influential"[3] position in the conversation. This stance meant that the client had "primary authorship status" in the life/life stories, and the therapist was "influential not in imposing an agenda . . . in the sense of building a scaffold through questions and reflections."

When I later became a counselor educator, part of the role required stepping into a more centered position, where I graded and assessed students' practice. Unlike the de-centered therapist positioning, this teaching role involves taking positions and articulating these clearly, whether it is in a classroom or via marking, by commenting on the quality of a student's counseling work. It was and is a role saturated with power. My quest is to find a way to educate and train counselors that allies both with narrative therapeutic values of noticing power and positioning, and with my Christian faith commitments; in particular, my choosing to live with the story of Jesus, who described himself as "gentle and humble in heart."[4]

In this chapter I reflect on the pattern of Christ in Philippians 2:5–7, and his taking up of a stance of humility. I focus on Jesus' relationship to power, and how Jesus chose not to grasp equality with God in becoming human, but took on the nature of a humble servant. I argue thus that humility is an ethical response to power relations that are present within teacher-student relationships in counselor education.

POWER AND HUMILITY

Power is "the capacity to direct or influence the behavior of others."[5] According to French poststructuralist scholar Foucault, rather than being thought of as a possession, power is more like a field of force that acts on subjects.[6] Power happens within the macro field of social systems and the micro field of relationships, including education and therapy. We all take part in power relations all the time. Power is *productive* in the sense that it works on people to effect action. Yet power can oppress others, particularly if power relations are fixed in rigid power-over positions. I argue that an ethical managing of power sees power flowing between people, rather than

3. White, "Workshop Notes," 9.
4. Matt 11:29, NRSV.
5. Oxford English Dictionary, "Power."
6. Foucault, *History of Sexuality*.

power pooling within one role. I suggest that relational practices of opening space for dialogue rather than monologue, and situating oneself in positions of humility, create a bidirectional rather than unidirectional flow of power. This, I argue, is a relational, ethical response to managing the flow of power when in positions such as counselor or educator.

I will now offer a reflection of the ethical positioning I aim to take up as a counselor educator, which is influenced by the pattern of Christ, before moving onto exploring how this position may be taken up in two of the key tasks of counselor education—to hold care for the student and a concern for justice for future clients. I offer a reflection here on an aspect of Christ's relational positioning in the world—that of self-giving love—through one biblical text, Philippians 2:5–7.

THEOLOGICAL ETHICS OF HUMILITY

Philippians 2:5–7 reads as follows:

> Let the same mind be in you
> that was in Christ Jesus,
> who, though he was in the form of God,
> did not regard equality with God
> as something to be exploited,
> but emptied himself,
> taking the form of a slave,
> being born in human likeness[7]

These verses drawn from the Christian scriptures, which have been referred to as the Christ hymn, speak of the mystery of the "incarnation." Taken together these verses form a hymn in which we see a "coming into 'union' (however construed) of the divine Logos and humanity."[8] This hymn/passage, and the notion of Christ's *kenosis* (emptying), has been the subject of much scholarly debate. Debate has focused particularly on Christ being fully human and fully divine *and* the notion of emptying himself through the incarnation.[9]

My particular interest in this scriptural passage is to offer a reading of it which is in tune with taking up an ethical relational position of humility in counseling/counseling education relationships. I read the Son of God

---

7. Phil 2:5–7, NSRV.
8. Coakley, "Kenosis," 261.
9. Evans, *Exploring Kenotic Theology*.

taking form in the person of Jesus as an act of self-giving for others. In this act "divine equality meant sacrificial self-giving. Accordingly, the hymn reveals not only what Jesus is truly like but also what it means to be God."[10] In my reading, I focus on two particular aspects: how Jesus chose not to grasp equality with God in becoming human, and how Jesus took on the nature of a humble servant. I am also interested in the Christ-pattern of self-giving love, taking into account a critique by feminist theologians. I will conclude this section by reflecting on what this passage and this commentary offers counselors/counselor educators who wish to live within the Christ story.

In becoming human, Jesus did "not regard equality with God as something to be exploited" (NRSV), or "something to be grasped" (ESV). I am interested here in Jesus choosing not to *take* power, not stealing it or using it by force.[11] Paul uses the noun *harpagmos* to denote "grasping," meaning "to seize, steal, snatch, take away."[12] Paul sees that Christ, who is the image of God, does not exploit this equality for his own benefit. Unlike a king who may seize power for personal ambition, glory or to inflate his status, Christ gives himself for and to others. This is the attitude of Christ. Jesus taking up the form of a servant *(doulos),* a position of extreme humility. Looking at Jesus' giving up power/taking up humility, I am taken by the suggestion that becoming a servant "is how divine love manifests itself in its most characteristic and profuse expression."[13]

If one identifies with Christ and his life, death, and mission in the world, a response to this gift may be to live towards offering self-giving love to others. Yet, there has been significant critique among feminist theologians of the potential effects of embodying this pattern. There has been some concern expressed around how the pattern of self-giving love may position women within gender roles which require the surrender of the self onto the altar of others' needs.[14] Such a concern is highly relevant to Christian women training to be counselors, who may come from contexts in which self-renunciation is a relational pattern into which they are often invited. Indeed, as Groenhout articulates, the dilemma remains whether kenotic theology actually reinforces an unhealthy self-self relationship. She wonders whether "this theology holds up for us the example of a self-sacrificing saviour whom we are to emulate by giving up our claims to power

---

10. O'Brien, *Epistle to the Philippians*, 216.
11. Keown, "Christ-Pattern," 94.
12. Fee, *Philippians*, 94.
13. Ibid., 95.
14. Valerie Saiving Goldstein, "Human Situation."

and authority, and by sacrificing ourselves for the sake of others."[15] Such a pattern of surrender may arc towards self-negation, and may invite abuse. As such, this is the antithesis of the aim of counselor training—to form an emotionally present, grounded counselor who works *from* and *with* herself, rather than negating herself. Indeed, as Yalom comments, in therapy "there is that most elegant and complex instrument of all . . . the therapist's own self."[16]

In considering how one may enact self-giving love as a response to Christ's love in a way that does not lead to self-renunciation, I focus on the work of systematic theologian Tanner.[17] For Tanner, gift-giving is actually part of God's nature: "an incarnation-centred Christology emphasizes the fact that God does not so much require something of us as wants to give something *to* us."[18] For Tanner, our giving in response, as "ministers of divine benefit should be as wide as God's gift-giving purview."[19] Yet in writing about gift-giving, she describes a human "community of mutual fulfilment," where giving does not result in "impoverishing ourselves."[20] "Giving away," she writes, "should not be at odds with one's continuing to have."[21]

Here we find an echo between giving in a way that does not impoverish oneself, and a counselor's giving within the bounds of a professional, caring relationship *while* paying attention to her own needs, so she is not ultimately impoverished. A counselor gives within the hour of the therapeutic relationship and, outside of this relationship, takes steps to nurture herself. A counselor uses her self as an instrument,[22] to encounter another person, to be present, to offer dialogue. The therapist's self is to be cared for, through her own supervision and personal counseling perhaps, so that she can sustain herself in the work, and avoid burnout. Therapists have an ethical responsibility to care for themselves in the work, so that they can "be fully present with clients, keep their suffering at the center, and bring hope to the work."[23]

My argument here is that while the counseling relationship involves the counselor's self-giving, this giving does not involve a renunciation or

---

15. Groenhout, "Kenosis and Feminist Theory," 291.
16. Yalom, "Gift of Therapy," 51.
17. Tanner, *Jesus, Humanity and the Trinity*.
18. Ibid., 69.
19. Ibid., 89.
20. Ibid., 95.
21. Ibid., 95.
22. Baldwin, *Use of Self in Therapy*.
23. Reynolds, "Resisting Burnout," 29.

negation of the self, but rather involves a living encounter between the selves of the client and counselor. The counselor takes responsibility to care for herself, so she is nourished and well-watered. It is from this well-watered self that the therapist can be become a servant to the client, through relational practices such as using the client's language. As Gau says: "out of compassion, the therapist becomes poor so that the client might become rich."[24]

In becoming human, Jesus did not grasp for power or exploit his privileges. He demonstrated, not invulnerable power, but "power-in-vulnerability."[25] Within counselor education, I suggest that such an ethic of humility, of self-giving, could invite the counselor educator to relinquish practices through which power pools around them, such as monological forms of conversation. A counter-practice might be to take up positions of hospitality to the other, with generous space for dialogue. I will now move into exploring in greater detail what an ethical, relational response to power relations within counselor education might involve. In this, I draw on both narrative therapy's attunement to power relations, and pattern of Christ as explored here.

POWER WITHIN THE TEACHER-STUDENT ENGAGEMENT

I now wish to show how the ethical positioning outlined above can be maintained in the two tasks of counselor education: to *care* for students, and to hold *justice* for future clients. I see care for students as involving a noticing of how power is operating in the teacher-student relationship. I may then make an ethical response to the role power I am situated in by offering positions of genuine dialogue to students. The second task is to hold a commitment to *justice* for the students' future clients, which necessitates a strong commitment to professional codes of ethics, and to assessing students' practice in line with these.

Counselor education is a microcosm of power relations. Students' growth journeys into professional counselors is suffused with educator power to grade, critique, and dis/approve.

Within a Foucauldian understanding, schools and training institutions, along with prisons, are sites which seek to conform people to social norms.[26] Through their power/knowledge, educators surveil students, observing their practice in the classroom, in tapes and transcripts, and process

---

24. Gau, "Gestalt of Emptiness/Receptivity," 407.
25. Coakley, *Powers and Submissions*.
26. Besley, "Foucauldian Influences."

groups. Indeed, the New Zealand Association of Counselors—along with similar bodies around the world—go to considerable lengths to specify what an appropriately shaped counselor identity looks like. Given this, it should not be surprising that students become subjectified, eventually learning to gaze on and police themselves with regard to counseling norms. The benignity of counselor education (or any education) may mask the way in which a student is governed to become a particular kind of person. While students consent to this governing so they can become a professional counselor, it is important to notice how power relations are an intrinsic part of the education contract.[27]

Given this, it may be inevitable that in the classroom and in one-to-one conversations, power pools more on the side of the educator. Yet, as has been previously argued, power is potentially bidirectional. Educator power can be moderated; it can shift as students position themselves as speaking about their own lives/development, and through deliberate practices of educators. Educators have some choice about how they take hold of the "relational, circulating energy" of power within the classroom.[28] They can act monologically, allowing space only for their voice, or dialogically, where generous positions in dialogue are offered to counselors-in-training. They can critique their own power through collaborative conversations with colleagues, through supervision, or moderation of assignments. I argue that while the teacher-student hierarchy cannot be erased,[29] educators can work in ways that invite the student into a position in the conversation as a thoughtful, ethical other.

For example, New Zealand counselor educators Gremillion, Cheshire and Lewis, if called into taking an "expert" position on a piece of student work, attempt to make their "positions available for examination and critique" by students so that "any and every performance of expertise, including our grading, is up for review."[30] These educators see their position with students as shifting over time, from taking up "instructor" positions to more like "witnessing" positions of students' work.[31] The educators thus may move across a range of positions in response to students moving to position themselves differently. While power relations will never be equalized, what is significant here is that we can see the flow of power, bidirectionally, as educators' taking up different positions invite students to also do so.

27. Lewis and Cheshire, "Te Whakaakona."
28. Speedy, "Issues of Power," 37.
29. Gremillion, et al., "Scaffolding a Community."
30. Ibid., 52.
31. Ibid., 51.

Thus power may flow bidirectionally as students take up speaking positions and educators make clear the notions behind their performance of expertise. This bidirectional flow of power supports counseling trainees, who are often mature students with voice and responsibility in their own lives, to speak about their own journey into becoming a counselor. It also enables students to witness their educators modelling the taking up/offering back of speaking positions. Students can thus gain a sense of the coherence between a counselor educator's therapeutic modality and how he or she engages with students relationally. Thus I argue that care for students, the creation of growth-producing climates for learning, involves making space for genuine dialogue between student and educator.

While care for students is important as they navigate these identity shifts and the "baptism of fire" of beginning practicum,[32] rigor is also important. I observe that one aspect of the educator-student relationship which can produce growth is the educator's offering of caringly rigorous feedback to students where practice ethical issues have been overlooked.

Rigor is directly connected to wider ethical requirements of the professional community in which students will enter and find their place after graduating. Counseling can be extremely delicate work, requiring high levels of skill and self-awareness to nurture trusting relationships and "do no harm."[33] Each year, a significant number of counselors are subject to complaints to New Zealand Association of Counselors by clients who are unhappy, or feel harmed by the service they received, or who felt their counselor breached counseling ethics. Counselor educators play a key role in introducing counseling students to professional ethics and facilitating the development of the reflexive thinking required for safe practice.[34]

As part of the learning process, educators may raise concerns with students about their "ongoing unavailability for reflection about power relationships, or a continued imposition of strongly held ideas."[35] They might challenge students if they are "enacting gender entitlement, heterosexism, or taking for granted ethno-cultural privilege."[36] Thus educators hold a concern that clients might be heard, respected, and their trust maintained. Counselor educators are thus gate-keepers of the profession, and they take up this responsibility by raising concerns with a student where aspects of

---

32. Folkes-Skinner, et al., "Baptism of Fire."
33. New Zealand Association of Counselors [NZAC], "Code of Ethics."
34. Winslade and White, "Ethics Complaints."
35. Gremillion, et al., "Scaffolding a Community," 52.
36. Crocket, et al., "Reflections on Shaping Ethics," 31.

their work have not reached the necessary ethical standards. Educators thus hold dual loyalties to *both* the student and the profession.

POWER WITHIN THE CLIENT-THERAPIST ENGAGEMENT

The impetus for counselor educators to take up and use their power to train students on behalf of professional ethics is seen in the nature of the counseling relationship, a relationship often characterized by intimacy and trust, *and* by therapist power. Within therapy, power may pool towards the therapist in three ways.[37] Firstly, through role power, and the structuring of the relationship where the therapist is the expert and the client, the consulter. As the therapeutic relationship is constructed through a particular set of discourses, or prevailing social ideas,[38] even if the therapist attempts to give the power away, power returns to the therapist because it is supported by therapeutic discourses within which the therapist is the expert and the client is the one soliciting help.

Secondly, societal power may be skewed towards the therapist in situations where there are distinctions of age, gender, or culture (or conversely skewed away from the therapist when such factors are in play).[39] Thirdly, power may work through the particular historic discursive environments both clients and therapists bring with them into the room, namely their personal histories.[40] People come to therapy often bringing with them experiences of being marginalized. They may have experienced some kind of social injustice or discrimination based on ethnicity, gender, or belief.[41] They may have had varying historical experiences of being silenced or abused physically, sexually, or emotionally, and these experiences and scripts can also play out in therapy. Therapists also come to the counseling relationship with their own relationships to power/powerlessness. These are some of the ways in which power pools on the side of the therapist.

As argued above, I suggest that power relations may be experienced as oppressive when rigid hierarchies of dominant and subordinate positions are maintained; when power is unidirectional. I propose that a therapist has choices around whether to see power at work, and the ways in which she might choose to manage it. These choices connect with overarching values

37. Proctor, *Dynamics of Power*.
38. Burr, *Social Constructionism*.
39. Gillian Proctor, *Dynamics of Power*.
40. Ibid.
41. Boff and Boff, *Introducing Liberation Theology*.

that therapists take up, with regard to the relational ethics of their practice. In my practice, I am aware of the subtle potentials to step into *autho*rity[42] in clients' lives. A concern for justice for clients, who may have experienced oppression and marginalization, invites me to offer spaces for dialogue *and* to continue to critique the way power is flowing around me.

In this, Foucault's analysis of power is useful, in that he reminds us that power is not a possession, but a "field of force relations."[43] These relations can shift in response to practices within therapy. Using a liquid metaphor, power pools on the therapist's side of the relationship, yet power is bidirectional. A flow towards the client might occur when she takes up a powerful speaking of her knowledge about her own life, or when she evaluates therapy, or when the therapist practices self-disclosure and/or collaborative actions. It is thus the practices within therapy which contribute to how power flows;[44] "an ethical counselor cannot remove the operation of power from the relationship and create some kind of ideal power-free zone . . . but the counselor can conceive of the counseling conversation as an exchange in power relation and seek to ensure that the flow of power is closer to mutual rather than unidirectional."[45] This conceptualization of the power relations within counseling can be one aspect of the work of counselor education.

HOW COUNSELOR EDUCATION CAN SHAPE A STUDENT'S RELATIONS TO POWER

Counselor education, by aiming to develop student counselors' ethical thinking, seeks to create ripples of learning between the student's emerging counselor identity and her previously held commitments. I characterise this engagement as the student enacting justice within her embodied interior life by being prepared to notice and critique her own power as a therapist. At Laidlaw College, we invite students into articulating the positions they are taking up in the conversation with clients, so that they can notice how monological or dialogical their conversations are. We also invite them to notice when they are stepping into a more authoritarian stance, and to be able to reposition themselves to work more collaboratively. Indeed, we invite student therapists to take up "curious inquirer" positions with clients,[46]

---

42. Davies, *Concept of Agency*.
43. Foucault, *History of Sexuality*, 101.
44. Monk, et al., *New Horizons*.
45. Ibid., 186.
46. Monk, et al., *Narrative Therapy in Practice*.

rather than a "problem-solver" position. The hope is that such positioning invites clients to see themselves as the expert in their own lives.

It is important that student counselors are invited to notice role power in therapy, and how to facilitate dialogical flows of power, rather than accepting invitations to become the special, wise other in the client's life. At Laidlaw College, we also require students to engage in their own personal therapy, to give them the opportunity to take into account the historical discursive environments in which they have "become" themselves, so that they can notice when their own stories enter the counseling room. There are strong ethical calls towards noticing one's own power as a therapist, which are echoed in the Code of Ethics of the New Zealand Association of Christian Counselors, which suggests counselors should "recognise the power differential implicit within every therapeutic relationship, and seek to minimise the potential negative impact of that differential."[47] Curiously, the more pluralistic New Zealand Association of Counselors' Code of Ethics does not mention the use of counselor power, but does talk about the importance of advocating for social justice and supporting "empowerment" of clients.[48]

As previously mentioned, one aim of counselor education is to create a ripple effect in the student's own reflexivity, so she can be able and prepared to notice her own power, to acknowledge her own needs, while not taking up positions of expertise in the client's life. Thus this care for the client, in their vulnerability, needs more than unconditional positive regard; it needs a willingness to notice and address our own capacity for power-over. A willingness to notice how power is being managed can be modelled by a counselor educator attuned to her own usage of power, her own taking up or relinquishing of positions of expertise in students' lives.

OFFERING DIALOGUE TO KARIN

With this background of the importance of a counselor offering a quality of humility in relationships with others explored, I now give an example of how I work to invite the development of reflexivity in students, through a gentle *and* rigorous relational engagement. This relational engagement is one in which I seek to draw on both narrative therapy's dialogism and the theological ethics of humility as explored above.

I present an example of my counselor education practice as I dialogue with a student around an ethical issue that arose in her practice. In this example, which draws on a composite of students I have worked with, my hope is

47. New Zealand Christian Counselors Association, "Code of Ethics."
48. NZAC, "Code of Ethics."

to show an engagement with counselor-power-as-responsibility, which brings to the relationship both care and rigor on behalf of justice. I see this holding of both care and rigor as a values framework which keeps me accountable both to the student and the wider community and counseling profession.

While I do not work within a holistic indigenous New Zealand *Māori* framework, my integrity framework has echoes with the approach taken by two social workers educators in Auckland. Appleton and Adamson use a *tikanga Māori* framework to engage students who are experiencing marginalization or failure.[49] They also draw on an "integrity framework" which echoes *Māori whānu* (family) values of *tika, pono,* and *aroha*. These values can be understood whereby *tika* equates with justice or doing what is correct or proper; *pono* means integrity or honesty, and *aroha* means care or love.[50] I refer to this framework here as it is similar to the ethical stance I am taking with regard to care and rigor.

When I met Karin,[51] who is *Pākehā* (New Zealand European) and in her thirties, she was just starting her first counseling placement in a low decile multi-cultural high school. While teaching in class, when the students were updating the class on how their practicum placements were progressing, Karin talked about how she was enjoying working in the high school setting. She also talked of how she had counseled one young woman, Grace,[52] who had a very difficult situation at home. While Grace was physically safe, she felt silenced at home, marginalized within the larger family unit. Karin grew impassioned when talking about the frustrations around Grace's life. Karin acknowledged she was finding it very difficult to hear Grace's story. Karin felt quite strongly that she wanted to intervene and ring Grace's mother to talk about the situation, although Grace was adamant she did not want this. I silently noted the strength of feeling for Karin and wondered if she had noticed herself that she was the subject of strong impulses towards intervening directly in her client's life.

A few days later, there was a knock on my door. Karin came in to talk. I asked Karin if she was open to me raising an issue with her. I directly and gently shared my wondering about the passion in her desire to intervene in Grace's life. I wondered out loud about whether she too had noticed this strong desire. She said she had. Using externalizing language,[53] I described

49. Appleton and Adamson, "Concept of Integrity."

50. Tate, "Unseen World."

51. Karin is a composite of several students I have engaged with over a number of years.

52. In the classroom context, we use pseudonyms if discussing client work, in line with the NZAC Code of Ethics about researching clients.

53. White, "Deconstruction and Therapy."

the "pull to help". Grace as the focus of our conversation. Was she aware of this pull? When did it first turn up for her? How did she make sense of the "pull to help" Grace? Were there other ethical values that were pulling her in other directions too, such as to empower Grace to help herself?

I was implicitly inviting Karin into speaking about her own life, through the respectful externalizing of the "pull to help" her clients. I also positioned Karin as being subject to other ethical pulls, such as desiring to empower Grace rather than do it for her. Through these invitations to dialogue, Karin began to talk about the interactions with Grace from the position of her own life. Karin spoke about while as she was working with Grace, she had become angrier about the injustices of Grace's life, particularly around a sense of marginalization within the family. There was a long pause. Karin then spoke, in a quiet voice, of how she had very recently become aware of her own experience within her family of origin where she had felt marginalized in certain family gatherings, feeling that her parents had strongly preferred her brother.

One way of thinking about my practice is in the terms of Doucet's "gossamer walls." I conceptualize Karin at this point as seeing behind the "gossamer walls" of her own life history; namely the counselor's (or as I like to think of it, researcher's) past history which exists as a gossamer wall in counseling conversations, both "fragile and tenuous."[54]

As we talked further, Karin made links between the anger she had experienced when growing up and her current engagement with Grace. She came to see this anger as separate from Grace's emotions about the situation, which were more about sadness and some resignation and acceptance. Karin could then notice the powerful position she *could* have taken up by intervening in Grace's life against her wishes, without this being warranted because of safety concerns. She decided to talk more about this situation in supervision, and possibly in her own personal counseling. My hope was that doing so would help enhance her reflexivity, to be able to notice her own stories as intertwining with her client's stories.

In working with Karin in this manner I sought to communicate care rather than judgment. I did this through inviting Karin into a dialogue about a moment in her professional and personal development as a counselor. Through offering a broad space for the other, Karin took up a position of speaking about her own life, on her own terms. I did not take up a position of judging her, disciplining her, or requiring her to act in a particular way. However, though all of this I did still hold a concern for her ethical decision-making around her feeling for Grace. The dialogical stance of the conversation

---

54. Doucet, "Gossamer Wall(s)."

resulted in Karin being able to make connections between her life history and her practice, which strengthened her counselor identity characterized by the ability to reflect on herself and become an insightful, ethical practitioner.

In summary, through conversation with Karin, I held a concern for Karin's personal wellbeing and development; to grow her fledging sense of counselor self into confidence. I also held as a concern for justice for her current and future clients, which led towards me offering rigorous and genuine feedback. I sought to develop her ability to tune into clients' needs in the moment, without the cloudiness of her own story intervening. Thus, I was aiming to join with her journey as she wrestled with her intentions and humanness, in her ethical becoming as a counselor.

In Karin's wrestling, I also experienced a personal wrestling with how power works through me at such meeting places with students. I desire to model a relationship with counselor educational power that opens space for dialogue and mutual learning, which models humility and openness. For students, engaging in counselor education asks for a great deal of humility and openness to learning. It is these qualities that I seek to model myself, drawing on the pattern of Christ.

CONCLUSION

Counseling is an engagement where care, power, and ethics are intertwined. Amongst other goals, counselor education seeks to sharpen the students' awareness of how power is at work in this engagement, so that they can enact justice by offering positions of collaboration with clients. Yet as I teach about power relations, I am also part of them. As a counselor educator, power pools around my role; it flows towards me in the classroom and one-to-one interactions. An ethic of humility would invite me to relinquish practices which solidify hierarchical power relations. A counter-practice might involve taking up positions of hospitality to others, with generous spaces for dialogue. It may involve shifting positions from instructing a trainee, to witnessing her growth and respecting her as a peer. Such offering of dialogical positions to students also fits within a wider concern for justice for their future clients. This relational ethic of humility in my counselor education is one I will never fully attain, but I am walking toward it. It is an ethic of humility that seeks to follow Christ, who is "the unique intersection of vulnerable, 'non-grasping' humanity and authentic divine power, itself 'made perfect in weakness.'"[55]

55. Coakley, *Powers and Submissions*, 38.

References

Appleton, Cherie, and Carol Adamson. "The Concept of Integrity in Relation to Failing and Marginal Students." In *Practice Placement in Social Work: Innovative Approaches for Effective Teaching and Learning*, edited by Avril Bellringer and Deirdre Ford, 181–202. Bristol, United Kingdom: Policy Press.

Baldwin, Michele. *The Use of Self in Therapy*. New York, NY: Haworth, 2000.

Besley, Tina. "Foucauldian Influences in Narrative Therapy: An Approach for Schools." *Journal of Educational Enquiry*, 30 (2002) 125–143.

Boff, Leonardo, and Clodovis Boff. *Introducing Liberation Theology*. Maryknoll, New York: Orbis, 1988.

Burr, Vivian. *Social Constructionism*. 2nd ed. London, United Kingdom: Routledge, 2003.

Coakley, Sarah. "Does Kenosis Rest on a Mistake? Three Kenotic Models in Patristic Exegesis." In *Exploring Kenotic Christology*, edited by C. Stephen Evans, 246–264. Oxford, United Kingdom: Oxford University Press.

———. *Powers and Submissions: Spirituality, Philosophy and Gender*. Malden, MA: Blackwell, 2002.

Crocket, Kathie, et al. "Reflections on Shaping the Ethics of our Teaching Practices." *Journal of Systemic Therapies* 26 (2007), 29–42.

Davies, Bronwyn. "The Concept of Agency: A Feminist Poststructuralist Analysis". *Feminist Critical Theorising* 30 (1991) 42–53.

Doucet, Andrea. "From Her Side of the Gossamer Wall(s): Reflexivity and Relational Knowing." *Qualitative Sociology* 31 (2008) 73–87.

Evans, Stephen C, ed. *Exploring Kenotic Theology*, Oxford, United Kingdom: Oxford University Press, 2006.

Fee, Gordon. *Philippians*. Downers Grove, IL: InterVarsity, 1999.

Folkes-Skinner, Julie, et al. "'A Baptism of Fire': A Qualitative Investigation of a Trainee Counselor's Experience at the Start of Training." *Counseling and Psychotherapy Research* 10 (2010) 83–92.

Foucault, Michel. *The History of Sexuality, Volume One: An Introduction*. New York, NY: Pantheon, 1978.

Foucault, Michel and Colin Gordon. *Power/knowledge: Selected Interviews and Other Writings: 1972–1977*. New York, NY: Pantheon Books, 1980.

Gau, James. "The Gestalt of Emptiness/Receptivity: Christian Spirituality and Psychotherapy." *Journal of Pastoral Care* 54 (2000) 403–409.

Goldstein, Valerie Saiving. "The Human Situation: A Feminine View." *The Journal of Religion* 40 (1960) 100–112.

Gremillion, Helen, et al. "Scaffolding a Community of Competent Practitioners: Positioning and Agency in a Training Program for Narrative Counseling." *Family Process* 51 (2012) 43–55.

Groenhout, Ruth. "Kenosis and Feminist Theory." In *Exploring Kenotic Christology*, edited by C. Stephen Evans, 219–312. Oxford, United Kingdom: Oxford University Press.

Keown, Mark. "The Christ-Pattern for Social Relationships: Jesus as Exemplar in Philippians and Other Pauline Epistles." In *Paul and His Social Relations*, edited by Stanley Porter and Christopher Land, 301–331. Leiden, Netherlands: Brill.

Lewis, Dorothea, and Aileen Cheshire. "Te Whakaakona: Teaching and Learning as One." *Journal of Systemic Therapies*, 26 (2007) 43–56.

Monk, Gerald, et al. *New Horizons in Multicultural Counseling.* Thousand Oaks, CA: Sage, 2008.

Monk, Gerald, et al., eds. *Narrative Therapy in Practice: The Archaeology of Hope.* San Francisco, CA: Jossey-Bass, 1997.

New Zealand Association of Counselors. "Code of Ethics." http://www.nzac.org.nz

New Zealand Christian Counselors Association. "Code of Ethics." http://www/nzcca.org.nz.

O'Brien, Peter. *The Epistle to the Philippians.* Grand Rapids, MI: William B Eerdmans, 1991.

Proctor, Gillian. *The Dynamics of Power in Counseling and Psychotherapy: Ethics, Politics and Practice.* Ross-on-Wye, United Kingdom: PCCS, 2002.

Reynolds, Vikki. "Resisting Burnout with Justice-Doing." *The International Journal of Narrative Therapy & Community Work* 4 (2011) 39.

Speedy, Jane. "Issues of Power for Women Counseling Educators." In *Balancing Acts: Studies in Counseling Training*, edited by Hazel Johns, 96–109. London, United Kingdom: Routledge.

Tanner, Kathryn. *Jesus, Humanity and the Trinity.* Minneapolis, MN: Fortress, 2001.

White, Michael. "Deconstruction and Therapy." In *Experience, Contradiction, Narrative and Imagination: Selected Papers of David Epston & Michael White, 1989–1991,* edited by David Epston & Michael White, 100–151. Adelaide, South Australia: Dulwich Centre Publications.

———. "Michael White Workshop notes." http://www.dulwichcentre.com.au.

White, Michael, and David Epston. *Narrative Means to Therapeutic Ends.* New York, NY: W.W. Norton & Co, 1990.

Winslade, John, and Carol White. "An Analysis of Ethics Complaints to NZAC: 1991–2000." *New Zealand Journal of Counseling* 23 (2002) 1–13.

Winslade, John. "Utilising Discursive Positioning in Counseling." *British Journal of Guidance & Counseling* 33 (2005) 351–364.

Yalom, I. *The Gift of Therapy.* New York, NY: Harper Perennial, 2002.

13

Psalm 23 as a Site of Integration
Telling a Story of Professional Counselor Identity Formation

HANNAH FORDE

The process of integration and developing a professional counselor identity is something that counseling students are engaged in from the moment they decide to begin their counseling education, whether they are aware of it or not. This chapter is an outline of how I, as a recently graduated counseling student, understand the process I went through to story my own identity as a counselor. Much of what follows is adapted from an assignment that I wrote in my final year of study which specifically addressed the concept of storying one's professional counselor identity.[1] At the time, I struggled to plot a storyline that made sense of my lived experience of counseling work and my ideas about the purpose and process of counseling. I found that I needed to hold " . . . the constructionist understanding that it is in the articulation of a practice that a practice develops"[2] firmly in mind as I wrestled with language to make sense of who I was in the work. I have had to return to this understanding again as I have attempted to re-articulate the development of my counselor identity here.

The idea of "faithful improvisation" has also guided me in this re-articulation process. Walsh and Middleton argue that, as Christians, "we need to indwell the [biblical] story, to so live inside it that it becomes *our* story;"[3] and that as we do this, our individual and communal narratives

---

1. Winslade, *Storying Professional Identity*, 35.
2. Ibid., 36.
3. Walsh and Middleton, *Truth is Stranger*, 183&174.

can become creative improvisations that remain faithful to the biblical narrative. With this in mind, this chapter can also be seen as an exercise in describing what "faithful improvisation" looks like for me as a counselor. While the overarching narrative of the Bible frames my understanding of this, it is a particular piece of Scripture—Psalm 23—which I "indwelt" in a very personal way that became a guiding analogy as I storied my professional counseling identity. It is both the content of this analogy and the story of how it came to be that is my place to stand as a counselor. The remainder of this chapter outlines the narrative of my counseling identity development and explains the way in which Psalm 23 has been formative for me in the process of integration, engaging in particular with the theological themes of narrative and participation.

The final year of my counseling degree was a difficult one. I started the year still dealing with grief from a miscarriage in the previous year, suffered another in the same week the previous pregnancy would have come full term, and again another as I was finishing the academic year. These losses were not kept private, and I was supported by those around me in various ways. Despite this, the grief of losing these pregnancies was still a private and isolating experience, something which many women (and men) who miscarry report.[4] Sometime after the second miscarriage, I began a practice of meditation on Psalm 23 as a way of inviting God into my grief. For me, meditating on this psalm simply meant repeating the words either out loud or silently, but slowly, and with the intention of feeling them and letting them impact my experience of grief. I have reproduced Psalm 23 here for the convenience of the reader:

> The Lord is my shepherd, I shall not be in want.
>
> He makes me lie down in green pastures, he leads me beside quiet waters, he restores my soul.
>
> He guides me in paths of righteousness for his name's sake.
>
> Even though I walk through the valley of the shadow of death, I will fear no evil, for you are with me; your rod and your staff, they comfort me.
>
> You prepare a table for me in the presence of my enemies.
>
> You anoint my head with oil; my cup overflows.
>
> Surely goodness and love will follow me all the days of my life, and I will dwell in the house of the Lord forever.[5]

The meditation process became a kind of "indwelling" of the psalm, and through this I had several distinct experiences of God's presence with

---

4. Frost, et al., "Loss of Possibility," 1019.
5. Ps 23, NIV.

me as I deeply felt the loss of those babies, my dreams and hopes, and sense of control. At the time, my conscious articulation of the experience could have been distilled down to a deep and trusting sense of God being with me in my grief, and this being a source of hope. As I negotiated study, family life, and the grieving process, I returned to this psalm again and again to be sustained; and as I did so it became a narrative that shaped my sense of personal identity. Against the backdrop of this personal process, my professional identity was also being invited forth by the content and requirements of my studies.

The main focus of the final year of the counseling degree at Laidlaw College is integration—integration particularly of counseling with theology, and of the two modalities we study (person-centered and narrative therapy). Our lectures, readings, assignments, and process groups[6] provided space for learning and reflection on where we saw ourselves in the process of integration. Participating in these contexts challenged me to become more knowledgeable and articulate about how my personal experiences, values, ideas, and skills as an individual counselor were contributing to the development of my professional counseling identity. This structure reflects Winslade's view that counselor education can be a process of "co-authoring (students and counselor educators together) a story of professional identity development[;] . . . identities that are constantly formed in relationship."[7] And indeed, the process by which Psalm 23 shifted from being personally meaningful to being something that guided and supported me in my sense of counselor identity was a social and relational one.

My consciousness of something shifting in my counseling identity began with an Outsider Witness conversation that took place in my process group. Outsider Witness conversations are a narrative therapy practice that aim to assist a development of rich descriptions of people's identities.[8] The conversations in the second semester of group process invited us to bring a story of practice from placement that we saw as contributing to our growing awareness of ourselves as counselors. As we witnessed these conversations between other group members, we were asked to reflect on four areas. First, noticing what expressions, words, or phrases we were drawn to. Second, discussing images, metaphors, or awareness of values that come to mind as we reflect on these expressions. Third, identifying what personal resonance these expressions had for us. And fourth, articulating what we were

---

6. Laidlaw's process groups are focused on developing both personally (awareness of self and self in relationship to others) and professionally (counseling knowledge and skills).

7. Winslade, *Storying Professional Identity*, 35.

8. White, *Maps of Narrative Practice*, 166.

moved to do in response to what we had become aware of by witnessing the conversation. This structure is designed specifically to invite acknowledgement that is personal and outside many of the traditional and common ways of responding to others' stories.[9] During the first group of the second semester, I was impacted by a conversation between two other group process members in which a peer described how a supportive relationship with her onsite supervisor enabled her to trust her own instincts more and feel a sense of freedom in her counseling work. The personal resonance I felt with my peer's words "trusting my instinct and that being okay—it set me free" led to an awareness of a desire to trust myself in the counseling process more.

I carried that awareness with me as I met with a client in the community agency where I had my internship later that day; a client that I had felt somewhat out of my depth with. My client, Mary,[10] was a *Māori*[11] woman who was feeling overwhelmed at work and at home as she managed a business and parented her children, one of whom had a physical disability. Being a student, younger, and *Pākehā*,[12] I had felt a sense of doubt in my ability to meet her needs for counseling. However, that day I found myself more present, confident, and relaxed in the counseling process than in earlier sessions. This experience of increased presence led to me taking a risk in offering what I felt to be a "depth reflection."[13] My offering was not taken up by Mary, but as we continued to dialogue, we were able to clarify and explore an important value for Mary, and we experienced a mutual appreciation within the counseling relationship.

Later that week I met with my external supervisor and described my experience of how group process had impacted the outcome of the session with Mary. Working from a collaborative position,[14] my supervisor helped me to reflect on and investigate this experience in order to develop more awareness around it. She asked me questions which focused on expanding the conscious knowledge I had about the interaction between myself and Mary, in the hope that it could become something I valued and could therefore incorporate into my counseling identity and use as a resource for future sessions and clients. During this conversation, my supervisor offered a metaphor for the counselor's role as being to "lay a table" for clients. When

9. White, *Maps of Narrative Practice*, 165.
10. Client names and details have been changed to protect client confidentiality.
11. The indigenous people of New Zealand.
12. New Zealander of European descent.
13. Mearns and Cooper, *Relational Depth*, 71.
14. Wosket, *Integration and Eclecticism*, 283.

she said this, verse 5 of Psalm 23 came to mind: "You prepare a table before me in the presence of my enemies." As we continued the conversation, I made connections between the personal meaning those words had for me and ideas I held about the counseling relationship. This dialogue with my supervisor was the starting point of my analogy for the counseling encounter and contributed something foundational to my integration process. I remember wishing I had recorded the conversation, because I sensed that it was helping to shape and give voice to my understanding of my counseling identity.

Back on campus and in my process group the following week, I volunteered to be the subject in the Outsider Witness conversation. As another group member interviewed me I was able to retell the events of the previous week; how the previous group process conversation had impacted my counseling session, and my understanding of counseling that emerged during supervision. Through the responses of the group members as witnesses, various layers of the developing story of my counselor identity were enriched. I was moved as one member described an image of Captain Cook[15] poring over maps, charting territory alone in his cabin late at night. The verbalizing of this image left me with a sense of being seen and acknowledged in my counseling work. This was further strengthened by another member's reflection that the conversation felt to her a kind of sacred moment. This fits with White's understanding of how Outsider Witness conversations work, that they create opportunities for "resonance that contributes significantly to rich story development, to a stronger familiarity with what one accords value to in life."[16] Through the resonance that my group members experienced in this conversation, I realized that I was moving toward a valuing of myself in the process of counseling. This valuing was further strengthened during this conversation as I became more aware that I believed (and had experienced) that what I did and who I was as a counselor mattered; that I was contributing to God's work in the world, and that God valued *me* in the work I was doing. It was a sacred and moving experience which allowed me to situate myself and my counseling work in the context of God's purposes in more meaningful ways.

Not long after these conversations, I began working on an assignment that required me to articulate my understanding of my developing identity as a counselor. The relational forming of my counseling identity continued as I dialogued with counseling theory and practice, theology, and also with

---

15. Captain James Cook was a British navigator, one of the earliest Europeans to "discover" New Zealand in 1769.

16. White, *Maps of Narrative Practice*, 189.

myself and God as I struggled to put words to who I was becoming as a counselor. The analogy of "preparing a table"[17] for clients was a starting point, but when I submitted the finished assignment, it was the whole of Psalm 23 that had become something that helped me to comprehend and articulate " . . . who I am as a counselor and . . . what I'm trying to do in the world."[18] The psalm had become a place where I felt empowered and connected—the site of integration between the personal, the theological, and the professional, both in counseling theory and practice.[19]

My personal indwelling of Psalm 23 established for me a deeper sense of trust in God, and brought me comfort and hope in an emotionally and spiritually difficult time. The comfort was a deep sense of his caring and loving presence as I grieved my loss. Verses 1, 4, and 6 all told me that his presence was more ultimate than my circumstances, and this made my reality—a background sense of grief and aloneness—seem less threatening. Verses 3 and 4 told me that he walked with me in the daily reminders of my loss, and verse 5 invited me to sit with him and face my "enemies": death, grief, and isolation. Because he was the host of this encounter, I felt less fearful of acknowledging and exploring my pain. This experience reflects, in part, Brueggemann's commentary on Psalm 23:

> It is God's companionship that transforms every situation. It does not mean there are no deathly valleys, no enemies. But they are not capable of hurt, and so the powerful loyalty and solidarity of Yahweh *comfort*, precisely in situations of threat . . . Psalm 23 knows that evil is present in the world, but it is not feared.[20]

While my feelings did not align completely with the psalmist's assertion "I will fear no evil"—I *was* afraid, afraid of the pain of loss—there was comfort in the knowledge that the psalmist could declare this so confidently because it gave me hope that I might eventually do the same. As I indwelt Psalm 23, God provided me with comfort through his presence and relationship, and hope through a story that I could live from. This impacted my sense of self and invited me to view myself as both loved and purposeful, even in the midst of grief and loss. This personal experience highlights the

---

17. Ps 23:5, NIV.

18. Winslade, *Storying Professional Identity*, 35.

19. My explanation here of how Psalm 23 incorporates all these aspects is largely drawn from the assignment I wrote, though in writing this chapter I have been able to reflect further and therefore expand on the analogy in ways that I was unable to in its initial development.

20. Brueggemann, *Message of the Psalms*, 156.

main theological themes that this chapter seeks to engage with: narrative and participation, within a trinitarian theological framework.

As I worked on developing the analogy from Psalm 23, I found elements of the psalm connecting with my understanding of the over-arching Biblical narrative. The beginning verses of the psalm describe God as a shepherd who provides safety, peace, and rest. This connected to my understanding of God's good and loving purposes in creating the world. In particular, verse 5a "you prepare a table for me" spoke to me of the hospitable invitation that the three divine persons of the Trinity extend to humanity: to fulfil our purpose as human beings by sitting at their table and participating in their life and communion of loving relationship, relating with God and others.[21] In this encounter between God and humanity, God is both the host and servant, and we are honored guests: "you anoint my head with oil, my cup overflows."[22]

However, the presence of sin, brokenness, and evil in this world is acknowledged in this invitation to encounter, as it is made "in the presence of my enemies." Here the psalm reflects the biblical narrative's "radical sensitivity to suffering,"[23] in that God does not ignore the existence of our enemies and let us leave the table to face them alone: "even though I walk through the valley of the shadow of death, I will fear no evil, for you are with me, your rod and your staff comfort me."[24] Furthermore, God is not threatened by or afraid of our "enemies," and we are invited to sit down with him in safety and experience his love and blessing—"my cup overflows."[25] The images in these verses connect with what I understand of God's action in and purposes for this world: that Jesus' suffering with and on behalf of humanity was the means by which evil and death was defeated, that this was the inauguration of God's kingdom, and that one day all creation will be reunited with its Creator and the earth will be filled with his love and presence: "I will dwell in the house of the Lord forever."[26],[27]

Seeing the larger Biblical narrative paralleled by Psalm 23 drew me into a deeper understanding of my identity and role within this story. This narrative forming of my identity, both professional and personal, invited me to consider myself as called and valued by God—"as one-who-is-loved

---

21. Torrance, *Triune God of Grace*, 38.
22. Ps 23:5b, NIV.
23. Walsh and Middleton, *Truth Is Stranger*, 88.
24. Ps 23:4, NIV
25. Ps 23:5b, NIV
26. Ps 23:6, NIV
27. Wright, *Surprised by Hope*, 87, 97, 101.

within the larger narrative plot of God's loving purposes for the world, for society, and for the self."[28] As I worked on developing the analogy from Psalm 23 for my assignment, I experienced what I have come to understand as a kind of "felt experience" of participation in the relational life of God. A theological understanding of participation is that, through salvation, we are "in Christ"; and in him and by the Spirit we are drawn "to participate both in [Jesus'] life of worship and communion with the Father and his mission from the Father to the world."[29] As I worked on the assignment describing my developing counselor identity, I realized that I was beginning to believe that by doing what I loved, and was good at—counseling—I was offering worship to God and contributing to his developing kingdom; I was experiencing the Psalmist's declaration "he leads me in paths of righteousness for his name's sake."[30] During the writing process I often felt moved, amazed, and grateful that my identity as a person and a counselor was being shaped to serve God's purposes. Plantinga's words on vocation in the kingdom of God seemed to express what I felt was happening as I articulated my sense of counseling identity:

> In her best moods she longs not just for happiness, but for joy; not just for joy, but for God; not just for God, but also for the kingdom of God. Because of her enthusiasm for the kingdom, she doesn't merely endorse justice in the world; she hungers and works for it. She doesn't merely reject cruelty; she hates and fights it. She wants God to make things right in the world, and she wants to enroll in God's project as if it were her own. She "strives first for the kingdom" in order to act on her passion.[31]

Psalm 23 also offers parallels for the counseling encounter. Just as "you prepare a table for me" speaks of the generous welcome that the Trinity offers humanity, it also speaks of the primacy of invitation to a relational encounter in a counseling relationship; the notion that we need to "make space for others in ourselves and invite them in."[32] In this picture of preparing a table the counselor is positioned as the host, holding power to influence the encounter with the guest, the client. As a counselor, this view of myself as a host strengthened my desire and commitment to be self-aware and authentic; "a solid and grounded 'Otherness' with which the client can interact."[33] This is

---

28. Thiselton, as cited in Grenz, *Social God*, 330.
29. Torrance, *Triune God of Grace*, 30–31.
30. Ps 23:3b, NIV.
31. Plantinga, *Engaging God's World*, 108.
32. Volf, *Exclusion and Embrace*, 329.
33. Mearns and Cooper, *Relational Depth*, 39.

particularly connected to a dialogical (two-)person-centered model of counseling which emphasizes that it is the interpersonal process, the interaction of client and counselor both being real that is at the core of what brings healing and change.[34] This view of counselor as host also reflects the position taken in narrative therapy that there is a power differential between counselor and client, and on behalf of safety and ethics, counselors must do what they can to equalize power dynamics through a number of practices, including a curious "not-knowing" stance.[35] Just as God gives the Psalmist a place of honor at the table and serves him, so a counselor's role is to honor and serve the client with her full presence and a genuine curiosity about his or her life.

And just as God walked with us in "the valley of the shadow of death" through Jesus' entering into human life, to "prepare a table . . . in the presence of . . . enemies" means there must also be a willingness to acknowledge and explore the painful and difficult things that clients bring to counseling. These "enemies" may be relational wounds or difficult relational situations, traumatic memories, grief, problem stories, or oppressive societal discourses. Sitting together, the client and I may "get things out on the table" to get some perspective and make meaning of these difficult things. As a counselor positioned in the narrative metaphor, using externalizing language and deconstructive questions are ways to create safety for clients who are in the presence of such "enemies." But in another sense, just as I invite my client to the table, an invitation may be extended to the "enemies" also, knowing that God invites his enemies to encounter too—the result of which is the cross.[36] Thus to make space for my clients is to make space for their "enemies"; to enter into their suffering and vulnerability. It is this "tough, disciplined, and personally costly love"[37] that should characterize what a counselor offers her client.

This analogy from Psalm 23, "you prepare a table for me in the presence of my enemies," is now part of what I bring to the counseling encounter. The analogy incorporates personal identity, a theological narrative that supports my professional identity, and a concept of counseling that integrates person-centered and narrative therapy theory with theology. In my practice as a counseling student, I was conscious of developing my integration of person-centered and narrative therapy skills, and was hopeful that my theology was an influential underpinning of my work. Aspects of my work with various clients throughout the final year of my degree illustrate more concretely how

---

34. Ibid., 9.
35. Morgan, *What is Narrative Therapy?*, 4.
36. Volf, *Exclusion and Embrace*, 129.
37. Benner, *Incarnation as Analogy*, 292.

the "prepare a table" analogy was influencing my identity as a counselor and being outworked in my skills as a person-centered and narrative therapist.

My work with Mary, referred to earlier, is part of what led to the development of the "prepare a table" analogy in the subsequent supervision session and is worth expanding upon as it provides an example of the type of counseling relationship I hope to offer and participate in with all my clients. In my second session with Mary, I had come with the intention of staying present to my own process and trusting my own sensing, while providing a safe space for her to be heard. As she described the challenges she was facing, I felt a sense of grief over opportunities lost in her life. I offered what I felt to be an empathic "depth reflection"[38] which invited Mary to explore this. She did not like the idea of grief, so I held to my intention to make space for her, knowing also that a client is the expert on her own life.[39] In this I was hoping to use the power associated with my position as the "host" of the encounter in an ethical and loving way. So I asked a narrative enquiring question—"What is it about this idea of grief that feels unhelpful or threatening?"—in an attempt to invite the "absent but implicit" values behind this response, hoping to elicit what was important and preferred for her.[40] In response, Mary identified a precious value "keeping on moving," and she felt that this new awareness of what she valued would support her in making sense of the challenges she faced. This conversation was influenced by my ongoing process of integration between person-centered and narrative therapy as well as my internal dialogue around what it meant for me to be a counselor. The result was a collaboration which in a small way, reflected the mutually loving dynamic within the Trinity. It seemed that these dialogues allowed us to "honor[s] difference, even disagreement, as an opportunity for rather than an obstacle to shared life."[41]

My efforts as the host of the counseling relationship to make space for Mary also led to a consistent experience of empathy; "a process of *being with* the client."[42] At times this was experienced as "embodied empathy," where, like Mary, I physically and emotionally felt a sense of being overwhelmed and confused by her difficult life circumstances.[43] I also conveyed empathy by regularly offering reflective statements and summaries, distilling Mary's experiences into the themes I heard to communicate my presence with her

---

38. Mearns and Thorne, *Person-Centred Counseling*, 71.
39. Morgan, *What is Narrative Therapy?*, 4.
40. Carey, et al., *Absent but Implicit*, 320–321.
41. Lamborn, *Beyond Co-Existence*, 520.
42. Mearns and Thorne, *Person-Centred Counseling*, 68.
43. Mearns and Cooper, *Relational Depth*, 38.

and to invite more self-awareness.[44] I offered such a noticing during one session, contrasting her current perspective of God, "be still and know that I am God," with one that Mary had voiced in a previous session "he would want me to get on with the job and stay strong."[45] Mary was moved to tears, as was I, as she came to realize that God was with her in her difficulty, saying "he's for me, he's got me." I noticed that that phrase was particularly impacting for her, so I asked an open reflective question: "what difference does it make to know—and experience—that God is 'for you; has got you'?" This question invited more tears, and she expressed how amazing and relieving it was to know and experience God in this way. This conversation was deeply satisfying—it felt as if my role had been simply to communicate God's invitation to Mary to sit at his table, and to witness and enjoy her experience and acceptance of that.

My work with another client in my final year, Jessie, also shows aspects of the "prepare a table" analogy. Jessie was in her early twenties and sought counseling due to experiences of anxiety and episodes of depression. As a client she was very engaged in the counseling process, and the dynamic we established was largely focused on "getting things out on the table," to use my supervisor's words. This meant I employed my narrative knowledge and skills to externalize problem stories and invite deconstruction of discourses that were hindering her efforts to live well and be freer of depression and anxiety. I also researched particular narrative-based therapeutic conversations so I was able to develop lines of questioning to help Jessie make more sense of her struggles.[46] These ways of "preparing a table" made it more possible for Jessie and I to consider her "enemies" from new angles, allowing her greater freedom to engage with them safely and on her terms. One such "enemy" was the storyline of "getting on with it," or, "responsibility," and the impact this had on Jessie. "Responsibility" had helped Jessie to become a reliable and mature person, but it had also kept her from knowing her own needs, looking after herself, and invited her to feel guilty when she did. Jessie had hopes for strong, real friendships in which she could allow herself to be vulnerable, but she was also hindered in this as the voice of "getting on with it" told her not to burden others with her problems. As we explored these dynamics, Jessie expressed a desire to reduce the influence that "getting on with it/responsibility" had in her life, defining the alternative as "self-care." As our sessions continued, she would proudly report on times when she had resisted "getting on with it" and

---

44. Teyber and McClure, *Interpersonal Process*, 59.

45. Mary had introduced the subject of spirituality in an earlier session when I had enquired about what had given her strength to cope with the difficulties she was facing.

46. Morgan, *What is Narrative Therapy?*, 24.

chosen "self-care," and we would celebrate and strengthen the development of this storyline in her life.

At other times in my work with Jessie, the "enemies" she faced (depression, anxiety, loneliness, and oppressive discourses) were not only "out on the table" to be made sense of, but also invited to be guests at the table with us. In one session toward the end of our work together, I noticed that the pace of our conversation was slowing as we were exploring some difficult relational situations and feelings for Jessie. We had talked over these issues before, discussed strategies for developing better relationships and holding difficult emotions, but in that moment, it began to feel as if there was nothing else to say—all that was left was to invite it to be present at the table with us. I expressed to Jessie that I felt her sadness at how difficult life was for her and the aloneness she felt as she lived through it. Jessie had never expressed much emotion in session before, but in this moment we shared tears as we sat in silence and felt her aloneness, together. This encounter with one of her "enemies"—painful feelings and loneliness—was made safer for Jessie by my presence with her. Jessie told me afterwards she felt hopeful and content; what could have been a frightening and painful experience became a transformative one. In a later session she referred to that experience as "powerful" and told me that my presence with her in her vulnerability had made her feel loved.

Working with clients who "come to the table" is very satisfying—it enables me to embody the analogy of Psalm 23 in fuller ways and allows me to enjoy the fruit of my work. The experience of grounding my work in this psalm connects with my ideas around what it means to be "in Christ"; that is, to participate in the narrative of Jesus and retell "one's own narrative, [and] hence making sense out of one's own life, by means of the plot of the Jesus narrative."[47] This chapter is an articulation of the sense I make of my identity as a counselor in light of the story of Jesus and Psalm 23. Together, these provide me with a satisfying way to "indwell" the story as I work as a counselor. The results of my "indwelling" of Psalm 23 is varied: many clients do accept the invitation to sit at the table with me, and God, in the presence of their enemies, while others do not accept or even notice such an invitation. Because I would never force another to sit at the table with me, my role becomes simply to continue to prepare the table and wait, in the hope that I am reflecting God's unchanging and gracious invitation to humanity to participate in his life and love.[48]

---

47. Grenz, *Social God*, 329.
48. Volf, *Exclusion and Embrace*, 128.

References

Benner, David G. "The Incarnation as Analogy for Psychotherapy." *Journal of Psychology and Theology* 11 no. 4 (1983) 287–294.
Bond, Tim. *Standards and Ethics for Counseling in Action*. London, UK: SAGE, 2010.
Brueggemann, Walter. *The Message of the Psalms: A Theological Commentary*. Minneapolis, MN: Augsburg Publishing House, 1984.
Carey, Maggie, et al. "The Absent but Implicit: A Map to Support Therapeutic Enquiry." *Family Process* 48 no. 3 (2009) 319–331.
Frost, Julia, et al. "The Loss of Possibility: Scientization of Death and the Special Case of Early Miscarriage." *Sociology of Health and Illness* 29 no. 7 (2007) 100–1022.
Grenz, Stanley J. *The Social God and the Relational Self: A Trinitarian Theology of the Imago Dei*. Louisville, KY: Westminster John Knox, 2001.
Lamborn, Amy Bentley. "Beyond Co-Existence to Mutual Influence: An Interdisciplinary Method for Psychoanalysis and Religion." *Journal of Religious Health* 46 (2007) 516–526.
Mearns, Dave, and Brian Thorne. *Person-Centred Counseling in Action*. London, UK: SAGE, 2007.
Mearns, Dave, and Mick Cooper. *Working at Relational Depth in Counseling and Psychotherapy*. London, UK: SAGE, 2005.
Middleton, Richard J., and Brian J. Walsh. *Truth is Stranger Than It Used to Be: Biblical Faith in a Postmodern Age*. Downers Grove, IL: InterVarsity, 1995.
Morgan, Alice. *What is Narrative Therapy? An Easy-to-Read Introduction*. Adelaide, SA: Dulwich Centre, 2000.
Plantinga, Cornelius. *Engaging God's World: A Christian Vision of Faith, Learning, and Living*. Grand Rapids, MI: William B. Eerdmans, 2002.
Teyber, Edward, and Faith Holmes McClure. *Interpersonal Process in Therapy: An Integrative Model*. Belmont, CA: Brooks/Cole, 2011.
Torrance, James B. *Worship, Community and Triune God of Grace*. Downers Grove, IL: IVP Academic, 1996.
Volf, Miroslav. *Exclusion and Embrace: A Theological Exploration of Identity, Otherness, and Reconciliation*. Nashville, TN: Abingdon Press, 1996.
White, Michael. *Maps of Narrative Practice*. New York, NY: W. W. Norton & Co, 2007.
Winslade, John. "Storying Professional Identity." *International Journal of Narrative Therapy & Community Work* no. 4 (2002) 33–38.

Wosket, Val. "Integration and Eclecticism in Supervision." In *Integrative and Eclectic Counseling and Psychotherapy*, edited by Stephen Palmer and Ray Woolfe, 271–290. London, UK: SAGE, 2000.

Wright, N. T. *Surprised by Hope: Rethinking Heaven, the Resurrection, and the Mission of the Church*. New York, NY: HarperCollins, 2008.

www.ingramcontent.com/pod-product-compliance
Lightning Source LLC
Chambersburg PA
CBHW062018220426
43662CB00010B/1387